Neo-Pragmatism, Communication, and the Culture of Creative Democracy

AF808872

PETER LANG
New York • Washington, D.C./Baltimore • Bern
Frankfurt am Main • Berlin • Brussels • Vienna • Oxford

OMAR SWARTZ
KATIA CAMPBELL
CHRISTINA PESTANA

Neo-Pragmatism, Communication, and the Culture of Creative Democracy

PETER LANG
New York • Washington, D.C./Baltimore • Bern
Frankfurt am Main • Berlin • Brussels • Vienna • Oxford

Library of Congress Cataloging-in-Publication Data

Swartz, Omar.
Neo-pragmatism, communication, and the culture of creative democracy /
Omar Swartz, Katia Campbell, Christina Pestana.
p. cm.
Includes bibliographical references and index.
1. Democracy. 2. Pragmatism. 3. Communication—Political aspects.
I. Campbell, Katia. II. Pestana, Christina. III. Title.
JC423.S9755 306.2—dc22 2009022636
ISBN 978-1-4331-0731-3

Bibliographic information published by **Die Deutsche Bibliothek**.
Die Deutsche Bibliothek lists this publication in the "Deutsche
Nationalbibliografie"; detailed bibliographic data is available
on the Internet at http://dnb.ddb.de/.

The paper in this book meets the guidelines for permanence and durability
of the Committee on Production Guidelines for Book Longevity
of the Council of Library Resources.

© 2009 Peter Lang Publishing, Inc., New York
29 Broadway, 18th floor, New York, NY 10006
www.peterlang.com

All rights reserved.
Reprint or reproduction, even partially, in all forms such as microfilm,
xerography, microfiche, microcard, and offset strictly prohibited.

Printed in the United States of America

For our families and for *all* families.
Tolerance and understanding are *the* important values
upon which a creative democracy can be constructed.

TABLE OF CONTENTS

Foreword BY PHILLIP K. TOMPKINS ... ix
Acknowledgments ... xi
Introduction ... 1

PART I

CHAPTER 1
Democracy and Diversity ... 9
Limitations of a Marketplace Diversity ... 15
Conclusion ... 20

CHAPTER 2
Social Justice and the Critical Imagination ... 24
Rejecting the Entertainment Model of Citizenship ... 29
Creative Democracy and the Importance of the Critical Imagination ... 35
Conclusion ... 41

CHAPTER 3
Communication as Epistemic and the Communicative Imagination ... 43
The Communicative Imagination ... 53
Conclusion ... 57

CHAPTER 4
Exploring Our Theoretical and Methodological Assumptions ... 60
The Critical Paradigm ... 63
Neo-Pragmatism ... 68
Conclusion ... 70

PART II

CHAPTER 5
Perspectivalism and Cosmopolitanism ... 75
Perspectivalism: De-Centering the "Real" ... 80
Conclusion ... 87

CHAPTER 6
The Contribution of Four Philosophers to This Project ... 89
Nietzsche, Cultural Criticism, and the "Good American" ... 89
Emerson and the Unattained Yet Attainable Self ... 96
Dewey's Democracy as a Moral Problem ... 97
Rorty's Anti-Foundationalism ... 101
Conclusion ... 105

CHAPTER 7
Alienation and Power **107**
Power, Alienation, and Communication 108
Conclusion 118

PART III

CHAPTER 8
Contrasting Platonic and Critical Models of Education **123**
Platonic v. Critical Models of Education 124
Critical Education 127
Conclusion 133

CHAPTER 9
Service Learning **135**
Theoretical Bases of Service Learning 136
Social Justice–Oriented Service Learning 138
A Social Justice–Oriented Service Learning Model 140
Conclusion 149

CHAPTER 10
Final Remarks **150**

References 153
Index 169

FOREWORD

Phillip K. Tompkins
University of Colorado, Boulder, Emeritus

When the April 27, 2009 issue of *The New Yorker* arrived at my home, I read with interest a letter to the editor by Allen Harrison of Point Richmond, California. Harrison wrote to disagree with a position taken in a previous issue by George Packer, one of the magazine's staff writers, who had complained that he could not discern the shape of the philosophy at the core of President Barack Obama's policies and actions. Packer puzzled that while some consider Obama to be a pragmatist, he could not agree. "Pragmatism," Packer wrote, "is a description of a temperament, not an explanation of a world view."

Harrison's astute letter to the editor refuted Packer's comment. He pointed out that "from Charles Sanders Pierce and William James through John Dewey and E.A. Singer and down to the present day, pragmatism has been a distinct—and a distinctly American—world view." As I nodded my head in agreement, I thought of a soon-to-be released book of mine—*Who is My Neighbor? Communicating and Organizing to End Homelessness* (Boulder, CO: Paradigm Publishers, 2009). In a flash of insight, I realized that I had not appreciated how much my pragmatic approach in my book had been influenced by a manuscript I read back in 2007, an earlier version of this splendid book by Swartz, Campbell, and Pestana, which I have since reread in its final form.

In writing my book, I had no doubt been influenced by Swartz, Campbell, and Pestana's treatment of the relationships among communication, culture, and neo-pragmatism, by the authors' concern for communication as *the* democratic form of life, and for their treatment of the role of language in constructing notions of truth. Further, I was struck by the authors' treatment of Richard Rorty's powerful meditations on "ironism" and solidarity, which highlights the close connection between pragmatism and democracy that animated my book. Most importantly, in writing about the plight of homeless people, I agreed with Swartz, Pestana, and Campbell's claim that our commitment to democracy requires that we work as a society to diminish human suffering.

The Swartz, Pestana, Campbell book further delights me by continuing a great academic and pragmatic tradition. The first academic discipline in Ancient Greece was Communication, or as they called it, Rhetoric. This was so because the Greeks were pragmatic. They were also experimenting with democracy, however imperfectly, and realized the need to study rhetoric, or communication, so that they could learn to solve problems as a community. As Swartz, Pestana, and Campbell note, we continue to have much to learn from that tradition of that experimentation. For all the above reasons, I hope readers will be open to influence by the ideas of this important work and the intellectual and political traditions in which they were developed.

ACKNOWLEDGMENTS

This book is the result of a collaborative effort between the three authors, conceptualized, organized, and directed by Omar Swartz. The project began in January 2005 when Christiana Pestana, then a masters of science student in the Graduate Interdisciplinary Studies program at the University of Colorado, Denver, enrolled in Professor Swartz's philosophy of communication course, where many of the ideas found in this book first aired. For the next year and a half, the two worked together on Pestana's M.S. thesis of the same title. After Ms. Pestana graduated in December of 2006, Professor Swartz recruited post-doctoral fellow Katia Campbell to help expand and develop the project further. Drs. Swartz and Campbell worked on the project for another year, resulting in the project in its current form. The dominant voice in the text reflects that of Omar Swartz, who alone is responsible for any shortcomings of this work. We would like to thank Professors Lawrence Frey, Phillip K. Tompkins, and Philip C. Wander for their helpful and considerate feedback on earlier drafts of this manuscript. We thank also Deirdre Morgenthaler for her editing skills and help in formatting this book. Parts of this book have appeared in other outlets and are being reprinted with permission:

Swartz, O., Campbell, K., and Pestana, C. [in press] Creative democracy and diversity in the struggle for minority group empowerment and survival. In J. D. Rivera and D. S. Miller (Eds.), *Minority resiliency and the legacy of disaster.* Lewiston, NY: Edwin Mellen Press.

Swartz, O., Campbell, K., and Pestana, C. (2008). Creative democracy and the communicative imagination. *Ethical Space: The International Journal of Communication Ethics, 5,* 43–53.

Pestana, C., and Swartz, O. (2008). Neo-pragmatism, communication, and the culture of creative democracy. In O. Swartz, (Ed.), *Transformative communication studies: Culture, hierarchy, and the human condition* (pp. 91–114). Leicester, UK: Troubador Publishing.

Passages from this book also appear in my 2009 textbook, *Persuasion as a critical activity.* 2nd ed. Dubuque, IO: Kendall/Hunt.

INTRODUCTION

As recounted in Yiddish folklore there exists in Poland a mythical town called Chelm, peopled by fools. For hundreds of years, the denizens of Chelm were, and continue to be, the subject of humorous anecdotes to highlight the absurdities of life, as seen through the eyes of Jews. The good people of Chelm were silly and foolish, but they were seldom irrelevant. Indeed, they transcend the ethnicity that spawned them. One popular story, *The Fools of Chelm and Their History* (Singer, 1973), has particular relevance for our project.

The Fools of Chelm recounts the adventures of Chelm under the leadership of Gronam the First, the venerable master sage and emperor apparent. One day Gronam fretted because, he observed, "Most of our citizens haven't enough bread to eat, they are dressed in rags, and many of them are suffering from coughs and sniffles" (p. 5). Faced with such intractable social problems in the "homeland," Gronam and his council of sages decided that going to war was the best solution for the welfare of their community. With festive flag waving and great patriotic fervor, Gronam decreed war on a neighboring village. The leadership quickly collected and trained the young men of Chelm to march off with clubs and pitchforks to attack the people they were told insulted their honor, threatening their "way of life." After marching in the rain for days and going hungry because no one was left to tend to the crops, this army of self-styled "liberators" ended up in the *wrong* town. This was no problem, however, because all towns not Chelm were considered equally unworthy by Gronam: "The honor of Chelm is in your hands, heroic soldiers!" Gronam shouted to his army. "Show the whole world that Chelmites are not only shrewd but mighty warriors too" (p. 24). Thus reassured and encouraged, the soldiers from Chelm attacked the sleeping village.

The campaign failed miserably and the army of Chelm was defeated. This set into motion a series of additional battles, revolutions, and counterrevolutions, which continued to tax and stress the citizens of Chelm. Gronam, who first recommended war, lost power after the initial defeat and was banished. But after the final military defeat of Chelm's armies, Gronam was invited back as ruler and honored. The story ends with him giving a speech: Despite all—the dead, the wounded, the permanently maimed, the bankruptcy of the treasury—Gronam remained optimistic. Unveiling a new statue of himself, Gronam spoke about Chelm and its influence on the world: "We do not wish to conquer the world," he assured his audience, "but our wisdom is spreading throughout it just the same. The future is bright. The chances are good that someday the whole world will be one great Chelm" (p. 57).[1]

In this book we explore how what we call, along with philosopher John Dewey (1939/1993a), a "creative democracy" can be cultivated and advanced through a heightened awareness of the ways in which communication shapes individuals and society. Being social creatures, we exist because—and through—our efforts to communicate with others. We conceptualize communication as an organic, constructive, and holistic form of human interaction, expressed in our daily struggles and joys of being-in-the-world. Communication, we argue, is existential and constitutive of our life experiences as human beings and knowledge of one-another; it is indicative of the relationship between self and others; we make sense of ourselves and our worlds through communicative action (Shotter, 1993, p. 2). It is through our communicative interaction that we represent others and ourselves. Our language enables us to construct social hierarchies and unequal relationships as well create the means by which we can challenge and subvert such relationships (Burke, 1973; Hauser, 1999; Shiffrin, 1999).

Our goal in this book is to help scholars, activists, and citizens to rethink commonly accepted notions of community in order to imagine new possibilities for social, political, and economic organization—in short, new ways of imagining solidarity and citizenship with others, especially those who languish outside the range of our moral radar. It is through communicative action that we designate who in society is worthy of consideration and whose needs and interests are validated. Those people that exist on the margins of society, or outside the boundaries of community, are often denied fair representation, access, and adequate resources. This process of exclusion is described succinctly by Jere Paul Surber (1994):

> Beginning with a simple turn away from the face of the Other, I may come, "by degrees," simply to ignore the appellations of the Other, later to discredit the Other's discourse, then to deprive the Other of any "right" to discourse, and finally to regard the Other as unworthy of its very existence since, deprived of discourse, "it" can no longer appear to me as an "ethically relevant" Other. (p. 309)

In light of the process described by Surber, we feel that solidarity is important because, in our globalized and technological society, some of the traditional barriers separating humans have fallen and our problems, as well as our opportunities, have become universalized. While the issues impacting us globally are becoming increasingly severe (i.e., global warming, pollution, poverty, militarism), it is apparent that we are also witnessing increased opportunities for positive collective action to counter these problems. We follow the late philosopher Richard Rorty (2006), a pivotal figure in this book,[2] in defining *solidarity* as "accepting reciprocal responsibility to other members of the group for the sake of a common purpose" (p. 61).[3] Solidarity is essential because human beings will live or die as a *species*, not as Christians, Buddhists, Muslims, Jews, janitors, politicians, or venture capitalists. Despite all our pretensions to the contrary, we need each other to achieve common life-preserving and sustainable goals. We believe, in Dewey's (1939/1993b) terms, that democracy "is expressed in the attitudes of human beings and is measured by consequences produced in their lives" (p. 226). Dewey goes on to write that "the cause of democratic freedom is the cause of the fullest possible realization of human potentialities" (p. 229). It is out of such potentiality that we write and articulate our concerns.

Our project is tied intimately with our identities as communication scholars because, as Barbara Biesecker (1992) notes, communication studies "is a discipline animated by a profoundly utopian yearning. By and large, its practitioners operate out of the firm conviction that things can change, be otherwise, different—in fact better—provided that human beings intervene symbolically in a history that is of their own making" (p. 351).[4] Symbolic intervention includes speech and communicative action as well as other nondiscursive symbolic practices and behaviors that enable us to reach out and embrace others in order to co-construct our social worlds. Our public culture and our lives are constructed through the circulation of such discourse and the realities we create with them. Our reality, therefore, can be filled with promise and opportunity—or struggle and strife—depending on the types of discourse we choose to circulate. Philosopher Jean Paul Sartre (1944/1989) was only half correct when he had a character in his play *No Exit* exclaim that there "is no need for red-hot pokers. Hell is—other people!" (p. 45).[5]

Throughout our book, we privilege communication as central for thinking about how we come to know ourselves and our society and maintain that a significant part of such knowledge derives from interaction with other human beings. This interaction includes everything from face-to-face communication to a single individual sitting down and reading a book written by another. Regardless of the medium, once we engage in symbolic co-construction and interpretation, we are inevitably recreating and affirming our interconnectedness with other human beings. It is within this recurrent symbolic practice that we develop both personal and social identities as well as entrenched—to the point of seeming natural and given—ideas about acceptable social stratification and allocation of resources. Symbolic interaction with others is vital because we also assume that our personal knowledge becomes richer and more profound once it is challenged in dialogue with those who might hold alternative perspectives or opinions (Freire, 1970/2000).[6]

As humans, we are creative beings, and our creativity is linked directly to our ability to communicate (Mead, 1914/1982; Schauer, 1982; Shiffrin, 1999; Shotter, 1993). What we understand as politics—the give and take of daily life—is the struggle over previously reified communication and the stasis-of-being that results in a form of existential stagnation. Such reification, as Amardo Rodriguez (2002) notes, "encumbers the evolution of new and different ways of being and understanding the world by promoting rigidity rather than flexibility" (p. 7). This state of reification "blocks the formation of the deep and complex human relations that flow from vibrant meaning creation and interpretive processes" (p. 7). Preventing this stagnation from occurring, we argue, is a fundamental part of a democratic consciousness as well as an important goal of what we are in this book calling the "critical" and "communicative" imaginations.

This book is organized in three sections. Part I (Chapters 1–4) establishes our conceptual, philosophical, and methodological research assumptions. In Chapter 1, we outline the traditional definition of democracy and extend it to include what we are calling "creative democracy," one far more rich and diverse than what we now experience in the United States as "marketplace democracy" or marketplace diversity. In Chapter 2, we go on to emphasize the importance of social justice and the critical imagination for our project and attack the "entertainment mode" of citizenship, one filled with passive, superficial, and, increasingly, overweight individuals. While we reject *weightism*—or the widespread and awful prejudice and discrimination directed toward overweight people with apparent social sanction, we do see a connection between overweight Americans—75% of all Americans will be overweight or obese by the year 2015 according to studies published in the journal *Epidemiologic Reviews* (see Caballero, 2007) and widely reported in the media—and the type of social, ideological, and economic problems we critique in this book. In other words, we view the undeniable trend toward unhealthy lifestyles in this country as symptomatic of the larger disfunctionality systemic to our society.

In Chapter 3, we discuss communication as epistemic as well as the "communicative imagination," an important extension and application of the critical imagination and the citizenship ethos which follows it. Chapter 4 explores the methodologies and philosophical assumptions particular to the reflexive, anti-foundational critical scholarship in the neo-pragmatic tradition within which we situate our book.

Part II (Chapters 5–6) is a journey through the intellectual roots of our vision of the democratic imagination. Chapter 5 consists of a discussion of perspectivism, cosmopolitanism, and the democratic imagination; Chapter 6 explores the contributions of Fredrick Nietzsche, Ralph Waldo Emerson, John Dewey, and Richard Rorty for this vision.

Part III is dedicated to the kind of education necessary for a critical or creative democracy. Chapter 7 contrasts Platonic and critical models of education; Chapter 8 is dedicated to discussing a social justice–oriented service learning model.

In all, what we hope to accomplish with this book is a conceptual framework for understanding what it means to be an engaged citizen. Our goal is to highlight the many possibilities open to us as human beings if we would reorient our relationships with one another and move from isolation and alienation to community and interdependence. Because the ills of our social world are human constructions, we have the ability to reimagine and reinvent a world absent debilitating social stratifications and unjust consolidation of resources.

Notes

1. We thank Philip C. Wander, Presidential Professor of Communication Studies at Loyola Marymount University in Los Angeles for bringing this story to our attention, and for his intellectual inspiration.

2. Sadly, Rorty passed away at the age of 75 on June 8, 2007, while we were in the process of writing this book. His *New York Times* obituary can be found at http://www.nytimes.om/2007/06/11/obituaries/11rorty.html.

3. As ideological critics (in the most general sense), we find the similarities between Rorty's definition of solidarity and James Kavanagh's (1995) notion of ideology striking. As Kavanagh notes, "The distinctive effect of ideology is not theoretical but pragmatic, to enable various social subjects to feel at home, and to act (or not act), within the limits of a given social project" (p. 314).

4. In her essay, Biesecker refers to the field as "rhetoric," but we do not view as important the distinction between rhetoric and communication and use the two terms interchangeably in this book.

5. In the context of the play, a handful of characters are in Hell where they expect to be tortured by demons. No demons arrive, and the accommodations are fairly comfortable. As it turns out, however, no actual demons are necessarily, as the characters in the play torture each other through their conversations. The characters in the play could have just as easily created a more positive experience for themselves.

6. Our fuller discussion of "perspectivism" appears in Chapter 5.

Part One

CHAPTER 1
Democracy and Diversity

The United States is often acknowledged to be both "democratic" and "diverse." The terms "democracy" and "diversity" are frequently bantered about in our society. At first glance, there is nothing wrong with this characterization, as it is correct in many respects. We should not, however, assume that we understand fully what these designations mean, particularly in the context of a progressive society. Although the United States functions as a democratic society, and we do have many different cultural groups represented within our demographics, the common assumption is that we as a society actually *value* and *support* both democracy and diversity, which is not always the case. In our current historical context, the term "democracy" better describes the system of government that we have in place rather than actual practices and lived realities of citizens and politicians. Further, although the term "diversity" best captures the hard data detailing the demographic makeup of the United States, it does not capture the reality of unjust social stratification based on cultural difference, or the systematic methods of exclusion that marginalize the experiences and voices of certain groups of people while privileging others.

In this chapter, we discuss the interconnectedness between democracy and diversity. We begin by first discussing traditional views of democracy and argue that those views ought to be wider and more substantive, particularly when it comes to intellectual, political, and economic inclusion and issues of social justice.[1] In other words, both democracy and diversity must be seen as more than that captured by the "marketplace" metaphor. The public is more than simply a "marketplace of ideas" and governmental and social policies ought to be derived from a much more complex set of processes than through the metaphorical "clash of arguments" in traditional liberal theory. Kaufmann (2004), for example, explored how the "marketplace of ideas" failed in the context of the U.S. invasion of Iraq on March 20, 2003. Since these failures are systemic, we argue, they go beyond the limitations of this one event and serve as a backdrop to the type of critique of existing democracy we make in this book.

Specifically, Kaufmann (2004) noted that, despite the weakness of their arguments and evidence, lies and obvious manipulations, whistle-blowing and overwhelming evidence of corruption, the Bush administration created and maintained for some time popular support for the initial invasion of Iraq. This popularity even seeped over into support for Bush's reelection in 2004 and

Bush's gloating about the "political capital" he earned. Kaufmann identified a number of interrelated factors systemic to liberal theory that accounted for this failure. First, what appears to be the free flow of information is often undermined by "issue manipulation," in which the "median voter logic can often be bypassed by elite manipulation of how issues are framed in debate" (Kaufmann, p. 7). Related to this manipulation is the practice of government secrecy and monopoly on intelligence resources that distorts "the public record by selectively publicizing favorable analyses while suppressing contrary information" (Kaufmann, p. 8). Furthermore, the authority of the presidency does much to circumvent critical thought, as well as graphic exigencies, such as the 9/11 attacks, and how they are manipulated by government elites. As Giroux (2006) noted with regard to President Bush and his lieutenants, "Lying now legitimates itself under the rhetoric of moral certainty, eschewing not only debate but the very possibility of criticism" (p. 65). Finally, and most important for our argument in this book:

> The countervailing institutions on which the marketplace of ideas theory relies to check the ability of those in power to control foreign policy debate—especially the press, independent experts, and opposition parties—failed to do so, and may generally lack the power to fulfill the function that the theory expects of them. (Kaufman, p. 8)

The above condition is central to our book. If these countervailing voices and institutions do not have the power to stand up to imperial pretensions and propaganda, democracy, as people commonly imagine it in this country, is severely compromised. We do not want this to continue; consequently, our book is about this danger and what can be done about it. Citizenship, we argue, goes beyond exercising our right to free speech as we voice our opinions and worldviews; it requires a commitment to others, to creating a society that is fair and equitable, and to standing up against irresponsible power and authority. Similarly, the marketplace metaphor often pays lip-service to diversity but ignores the fundamental elements necessary to truly value diversity. The core of democracy and diversity in the social justice sense we endorse is *inclusion*, "an insistence that a community of integrity cannot exist if some are excluded" (Frey, Pearce, Pollock, Artz, & Murphy, 1996, p. 111).

The term "democracy" comes from the Greek word *demokratia*, a derivative of *demos*, meaning "the people" (or "the common people") and *kratein* "to rule" (Hansen, 1991). Thus, *democracy*, in its simplest connotation, is rule by the people. Democracy, however, is a pliable, multi-nuanced concept that allows for various interpretations and theories (see Lummis, 1996; Terchek & Conte, 2001; Stromberg, 1996). At a minimum, however, democracy springs from the idea that no one individual or no one group has the right to rule the rest at will, that public power flows from the citizens—defined inclusively—and that the citizens may challenge and change public policies and leadership when they believe these do not act on behalf of public opinion, and that they have a right and duty to do so (Terchek & Conte, 2001; Zinn, 1968/2002a). In other words, the state is only a creation of the citizenry to serve the common good, and when the state fails to serve the welfare of the public, it becomes self-serving and loses its authority. This democratic ideal animated the formation of the United States—the notion that people came first, and from an association of the people, government gains authority. As suggested in our Declaration of Independence (and often ignored), citizens have the right to alter or abolish their government when it no longer works to foster life, liberty, and the pursuit of happiness.[2] Along with rights, however, come the responsibility of shaping, monitoring, and critiquing the government; hence, democracy requires a commitment to, and involvement in, tangible, day-to-day civic action.

A political community, or state, can be regarded in different ways; emphasis is placed either on the responsibility and participation of informed citizens who comprise the core of democracy (as the U.S. Declaration of Independence suggests) or on political institutions and processes, such as laws, courts, and elections (Hansen, 1991). In the United States, emphasis is generally placed on the latter (Deetz, 1992). Although valuable in and of themselves, such ruling bodies, procedures, and processes are often assumed *to be* democracy, ignoring more substantive expressions of democracy, such as a socially inclusive, participatory process that entails serious public deliberation for determining the public policies and laws that help society to function.

In U.S. society, democracy, as commonly evoked, often deemphasizes an active role of the citizen; it typically means a system of government in which citizens elect politicians who, in theory, represent the voice of their constituents in political affairs. Otherwise known as "representative democracy," this form of governance is often contrasted with "direct democracy," in which people participate in the political process without an intermediary class of professional politicians—the classic model being Athens during its so-called Golden Age in the fifth century BCE (Hansen, 1991).[3]

Unlike our modern Republic, in which an immense commercial, military, and industrial apparatus makes decisions we are obliged to accept,[4] the citizens of Athens constituted, for themselves, the entire decision-making and implementation processes of governance. Being the embodiment of the state, the Athenian people were proud of what they had constructed and diligent in practicing their statesmanship. Their lives, livelihood, identities, power, and their city's well-being depended on the political and rhetorical decisions they made. That is why they took the study of communication very seriously. Their politics was reflected in their rhetoric and their rhetoric was reflected in their politics. It was within their rhetoric that their politics and community was envisioned and constituted. For example, in his famous funeral oration, Pericles declared:

> Our constitution is called a democracy because power is in the hands not of a minority but of the whole people. When it is a question of settling private disputes, everyone is equal before the law; when it is a question of putting one person before another in positions of public responsibility, what counts is not membership of a particular class, but the actual ability which the man possesses. No one, so long as he has it in him to be of service to the state, is kept in political obscurity because of poverty. (Pericles, 1995, p. 218)

Of course, it is well known that the "community of citizens" in Athenian democracy was confined to males, excluding females and slaves (significant populations that call into question the very significance of the institution). Still, every member of the community, as defined in a limited way, had a voice in the deliberations that shaped public decisions. This opportunity was coupled with a sense of civic responsibility and cultural expectation to be an active agent in politics.[5] To abdicate this responsibility was to be an *idiotes*—literally, an "idiot," a private person unconcerned with the affairs of the community (Hansen, 1991). It is in this sense, not the prior exclusionist and misogynist sense, that we respect their accomplishments and here try to grapple with the pervasive problem of citizen disengagement.

Moving beyond the ancient Greeks, the concept of democracy that we focus on is as a process for human social and political interaction: democracy as a commitment and ideal, one worked toward dialectically and passionately but never fully achieved, rather than as a set of specific laws, institutions, and procedures, "an educative process… a continued process of open and public communication" (Dewey, 1950/1993d, p. 248). Democracy is an attitude that one takes toward life, an appreciation of, and respect for, the fundamental interdependence of all human beings and a recognition that the superficiality of traits and habits separating people, positioning them into hierarchies and arbitrarily bestowing on them conditions of privilege or depravity, is anachronistic and immoral, contributing to what Mills (1963) called the "politics of organized irresponsibility," in which social and political elites "hide the facts of life in order to retain their power" (p. 298).[6]

By *creative democracy*, we mean a society that continues dynamically to evolve in its ability to be inclusive, fair, and just through the active participation of all its citizens, a society without what Marx (1852/1963) called a *lumpenproletariate* (i.e., a dejected underclass or "surplus" population of unusable or dispensable people). Vital components of a creative democracy include decentralized communication (i.e., a suspicion of both government and corporate control of the decisions that affect the lives of millions of people); meaningful constraints of authority and power by systems of checks and balances; agendas established through discussion that are inclusive widely of the population; reciprocity of influence between leaders, social elites, and citizens; flexible and equitable social structures; and encouragement of, and respect for, minority opinion (Pratkanis & Aronson, 2001).

We envision democracy as a community committed, at its core, to rejecting selfishness, greed, nationalism, and a radical atomization as typified in the United States today.[7] For example, on April 1, 2007, the *New York Times* reported that the industrial nations and, in particular, the United States, which overwhelming have created the conditions contributing to global warming, are doing little to mitigate the brunt of the damage in the poorest nations, even as they spend billions to protect their citizens (Revkin, 2007). Such selfishness and greed is symptomatic of an inability or unwillingness to recognize that a democratic orientation must be equitable, inclusive of others, open to an interdependent citizenry, and centered within an ethos that focuses outward onto humanity at large, rather than be seen as a justification for one's own privileges. If nothing else, democracy, as we evoke the concept, has "moral meaning" in Dewey's (1920/1950) terms, at the very least, when the "supreme test of all political and industrial arrangements [becomes] the contribution they make to the all-around growth of every member of society" (p. 147). In other words, as Dewey put it:

> Government, business, art, religion, all social institutions have…a purpose[:]… to set free the capacities of human individuals….The test of their value is the extent to which they educate every individual into the full stature of his possibility. (cited in Rorty, 1998a, p. 33)

Moreover, as Dewey (1939/1993e) noted:

> The ultimate problem of production is the production of human beings. To this end, the production of goods is intermediate and auxiliary. It is by this standard that the present system stands condemned. "Security" is a means, and although an indispensable social means it is not the end. Machinery and technological improvements are means, but again are not the end. Discovery of individual needs and capacities is a means to the end, but only a means. The means have to be implemented by a social-economic system that establishes and uses the means for the production of free human beings associating with one another on terms of equality. Then and then only will these means be an integral part of the end, not frustrated and self-defeating, bringing new evils and generating new problems. (p. 170)

In other words, according to Dewey, "social arraignments are means of creating individuals" (cited in Manicas, 1982, p. 151).

As suggested above, democracy is more than the minimum necessary material conditions needed to support a healthy human individual (a standard by which the United States often fails); democracy *must* be more than that, must go beyond base human material needs to encompass more social intangibles such as happiness, fulfillment, and intellectual growth as embodied in rich self-narratives that have tremendous symbolic and progressive meaning for individuals. We agree with St. John and Shepherd (2004) when they remarked that a

> community whose citizens do not enliven and strengthen it with their physical, discursive, moral, political, and spiritual presence is no community at all; it is a puppeteered collective of unassociated persons whose sense of community has been prepackaged for them by the media, the state, or both. (p. 175)

In contrast, democracy is "creative" to the extent that what we call the "poetry of people"—in the sense evoked by Burke (1984b), Rorty (1989), and Dewey (see Garrison, 1993)—engaged in everyday living, contributes to the collective well-being of everyone, in which people's private visions of the good contribute to, or are compatible with, the larger social good. Democracy is creative when literature (in its most general sense) not law, ideas not power, and hope not faith sustain a community that is continuously redescribing itself—always unsure of its future but aware of its past and, for that reason, committed to and optimistic for the present. Such ambiguity (or "contingency," to use the neo-pragmatic vocabulary we privilege in this book), notes Rodriguez (2002), "makes for new experiences, new understandings, new ways of being, and new kinds of relations with each other by keeping meaning incomplete" (p. 3). Incompleteness, we maintain, is a strong defense against reification and the stasis it encourages. A democratic society, by definition, thus, is incomplete.

Democracy, in sum, is creative when all members of its community have their basic human needs met, as well as a minimum degree of education, such that personal growth replaces survival as a base necessity, enabling everyone to contribute constructively to the larger community. Consequently, if we are to contribute constructively within our democratic system, then, fundamentally, there must be a sense of cultural engagement and the ability of citizens to dissent meaningfully, challenging selfishness, greed, exclusivity, and policies that reflect a general disregard for social inequities. Dissent enables us to participate fully in holding our legislators, as well as private corporations, accountable for crafting policies or practices that stifle creative participation or reify social stratifications that preempt our ability to connect to a larger social good. As noted by Dewey (1935/1999), "The conditions that generate insecurity for the many no longer spring from nature. They are found in institutions and arrangements that are within deliberate human control" (p. 52). Human suffering is largely conquerable, a matter of politics not resources. Under this view, creative democracy, like the experience of communication itself, is an experiment in the human potential, enlarging our ability to imagine and nurture new expressions of our common humanity and to recognize the primacy of our individual selves—a sense of both/and, in the sense that as individuals, we are both *apart* from the world in our unique individualities and, simultaneously, inescapably and essentially *a part* of it. The all-important task of a critical democracy is to reconcile and balance these two tensions. Exemplifying this tension is what we call the limitations of a marketplace diversity.

Limitations of a Marketplace Diversity

Well into the first decade of the twenty-first century, the United States, without a doubt, is dynamic and filled with potential as never before in its history. The diversity of the people who reside in the United States, from every nation of the globe, and the openness of our society to allow nearly any kind of social relationship to form, makes for much social stimulation. With minimum effort, we can interact on friendly terms with people whose origins differ greatly from our own. We can mingle, date, and start families in ways that were unthinkable a generation or two ago. For instance, more couples are living together and not becoming married (from 3.2 million in 1990 to 5.5 million in 2000), and 1 in every 9 households are represented by same-sex partners (Simmons & O'Connell, 2003). Interracial couples now represent over 2 million of the U.S. households, up from 651,000 in 1980 (U.S. Census Bureau, 2007). Although these things were difficult to achieve, and challenging to preserve, few places on this planet are as tolerant of dissenting sexual, social, political, and religious norms as is the United States. This is true notwithstanding the well-publicized and polarizing fight over gay marriage, civil unions, and same-sex parenthood. Such tolerance may rightly be celebrated and should be nurtured; it certainly should not be taken for granted, as we earned it through hard work in fighting the state for our freedom (Zinn, 1980/2005). This is precisely why the fight for gay rights is important and why it is more than just a "gay issue." In a legal sense, society needs a vanguard civil rights issue, for civil rights and human rights build on each other. The more we demand, the more we achieve, and every bit counts. We may never know the beneficiaries of our struggles for justice, fairness, and equality, but beneficiaries do exist. This is moral progress in the law. Silence in the face of hatred and inequality often does, in fact, equal death.[8]

Thus, when we think of American virtue, we think of such tangible experiences as gay coupling and adoption, ability to express irreligiousness or anti-religiousness in public, remnants of our social security benefits and leftovers from the largely extinct New Deal, and the absence of, at least, official persecution of community activism. These possibilities, more so than abstract accolades for freedom, are important for the experience of a democratic life. It is not the nation (or its leaders) we should honor but the diversity of relationships that it allows, the freedom to self-create and form new social knowledge and expressions of inclusion or intimacy, and the ability to lead our leaders on issues of moral vision. It is important to realize, at the start, that these relationships are created from the bottom up—they are seldom top-down initiatives of power. These relationships are generated by popular expressions of outrage when a group of people is persecuted for being different than the mainstream (Irons, 1999). Thus, we the people, not our leaders, deserve recognition for what we have created and for which we are prepared to fight. For millions of Americans, the fight for freedom is not in Iraq—it has been, and remains, here in the United States.

The United States deserves our respect and typifies what we mean by a creative democracy to the extent that it yields to popular demand for inclusion. To the extent that it has, we celebrate. However, much of the openness and acceptance that demarcates our nation is market driven (i.e., commercial), and that should give us pause. Markets are not so sanctimonious as to ensure that people do the right things for the right reasons. In fact, markets are predicated on the belief that people do things for the *wrong* reasons, such as self-interest and profit. Markets assume that people are greedy and that private greed equates to the public good.[9] This view strikes us as utter nonsense, but it is a widely accepted dogma and, therefore, goes by the name of truth. One result of a market-driven diversity is that the diversity reflected in U.S. commercialism, and often imbedded in our interpersonal relationships, tends to be topical and superficial, becoming what Rieff (1998) called "the multiculturalism of the marketplace" (p. 70).[10]

When the richness of diversity is limited to the appeal of commodities, and when we tend to define ourselves in terms of the commodities we consume, diversity is reduced to little more than powerful identification devices to sell products and to create the façade of inclusion and acceptance; in other words, to pander to stereotypes. This view, at best, is a weak notion of diversity, measured by the color of the skin of the person sitting next to us instead of on the potentially liberating character of her or his thoughts. Diversity of thought, we argue, is more important than the diversity of appearance. Below, we provide two examples to illustrate this claim.

The first example occurred in 1991 when Clarence Thomas succeeded Thurgood Marshall on the U.S. Supreme Court.[11] At the time, many conservatives, and perhaps some myopic liberals, applauded the move as preserving "diversity" on the high court. Thomas, a Black man, was awarded what has became known as the Court's "Black" seat vacated by a dying Marshall, who was the first African American appointed to the high bench. However, only in the vaguest meaning of the term was Thomas's appointment about diversity. The diversity in this case was skin deep and driven by the exigency of the political marketplace; Thomas's presence on the high court does nothing to advance diversity on the Court besides gracing group pictures of the Court with his pigmentation. On a much more substantive level, the two justices could not be more dissimilar (Cook, 1994). Marshall was the most liberal of all of our justices, a hero in the struggle for civil rights, and a man who made a day-to-day difference in the lives of tens of millions of people in this country, black, brown, yellow, and white (Williams, 1998). Thomas, on the other hand, is one of the most conservative jurists to sit on the bench, someone who officially repudiates much of the value created by Marshall and the civil rights movement (Merida & Fletcher, 2007). Marshall represents the best and Thomas the worst (at least in post-Franklin Delanor Roosevelt times) face of the Supreme Court.[12]

On announcing his retirement, Marshall was asked by a reporter if it was a good idea for then-President George H. Bush to replace him with another Black person. In response, Marshall stated that it made no difference at all. Knowing Bush's political commitments, and knowing of Thomas's ambitions and track record as an outspoken conservative and opponent of affirmative action, he uttered that "it does not matter if the snake is black or white. It still bites" (cited in Irons, 1999, p. 475). Marshall appreciated what most of us who did not grow up during the civil rights era may not readily appreciate—the fight for civil rights was really the fight for *human* rights. Although the impetus for the struggle was the appalling racism directed against African Americans, thoughtful people realized that, for the struggle to be successful, it had to be about some higher ideal, such as social justice. Social justice, more than anything else, was King's message, one that has largely been repressed because "in the last thirty years we have trapped King in romantic images or frozen his legacy in worship" (Dyson, 2000, p. ix). This idealized and stripped-down representation of King has, as Dyson (2000) argued, allowed us to sanitize his ideas and twist his identity so that "right-wing conservatives can quote King's speeches in order to criticize affirmative action, while schoolchildren grow up learning only about the great pacifist, not the hard-nosed critic of economic injustice" (p. ix).

As a society, we like to think about the civil rights movement for the gains that it brought Black people in this country. To be sure, these remain absolutely and fundamentally important, even as we have lost a social commitment to many of them, particularly in the area of affirmative action (Guerrero, 2002). However, what many leaders at the time understood is that being White or Black was a mere accident (a point much in line with our neo-pragmatism), something an individual had to deal with; the real problem was structural—an institutionalized hatred, greed, and intolerance for difference. Marshall knew, as did Martin Luther King, Jr., that it does not matter if the Supreme Court—or any powerful institution—has women, Jews, or Blacks sitting on it; the Court, as it is situated currently, embodies precious little political or substantive diversity and does not reflect the humanistic values that animate a creative democracy (Kairys, 1993). Although it is imperative that the highest court of the land, and, indeed, all courts, reflect the demographic makeup of the nation, it is *more* important that they break from a largely conservative tradition that has stood in the way of a morally progressive society and that now threatens to turn back the clock on civil rights, reproductive rights, and, indeed, on human rights (Faux, 2004; Northrup, 2004; Saletan, 2006). Politically, the United States has turned right-wing—which is not, and has never been, a good thing—and the judiciary has been for some decades poised to follow. This is not the world that King or Marshall envisioned with their work or the world they envisioned for decades after their death. If we honor them, as we should, we should consider what happened to their vision and use our collective anguish to once again fight for that in which they believed.

Our second example is an even more egregious example of the phenomenon of marketplace diversity, and is highlighted by Alexandra Marshall's (2003) story in *Men's Fashions of the Times*, a popular fashion magazine, on the commodification of Argentinean revolutionary folk hero Che Guevara, who was murdered in 1967 by agents of the United States. Forty years after his death, and almost 20 years after the end of the Cold War, merchandizing of Guevara's image has, to the annoyance of his family, become popular.[13] He appears as a toy action figure and as an image on bikinis, among other things. As Marshall and others point out, this merchandizing of Guevara's image reflects a transformation of what was formally an important socialist icon; it has been divested of its progressive influence, making it safe for circulation in mainstream society. At best, Guevara's image evokes empathy among young people who know little about Central and South American struggles but who wish to express rebellious adolescent discontent. At worst, the poaching of Guevara's image represents a disingenuous profiting from the manipulation of Guevara's heroic image, slandering the hope that he once exemplified, making it more difficult for the next Che Guevara, or for authentic revolt in general, to be taken seriously. The poaching of Che's image is an example of trivialization, as when the status quo absorbs its challengers after neutralizing their message.[14]

Guevara's example suggests that Rieff (1998) is correct when he says that, far from being threatening as it once might have been, cultural diversity seems "to promise new consumers, new profit centers, new pools of talent" and that the "appeal for diversity has in fact led to increased commercialization" (pp. 68, 75). As ethnicities, social groups, or politically disenfranchised people become "targets" to be integrated into the marketplace, the strength of a sub-community ironically becomes the source of that group being co-opted into the status quo and, thereby, denying it a political identity, with the important public policy issues that diversity can raise going undebated. Although groups of people formally experienced as the proletariat, the working-class, second-class citizens, foreigners, and so forth, can "buy" into the American Dream, that is not what the American Dream means or could mean. More poignantly, if that is what the American Dream *does* mean, it is not as moral a standard as many Americans assume. People are more important than the individual or collective strength of their pocketbooks; a market mentality, although useful for some purposes, is fundamentally unable to recognize this point. Dewey (1941/1993f) noted as much when he wrote that the "attempt to identify democracy with economic individualism as the essence of free action has done harm to the reality of democracy and is capable of doing even greater injury than it has already done" (p. 209).[15] Herein lays the root of many paradigmatic U.S. problems, but here, too, is where Americans can find room to change. September 11, 2001 was a wake-up call, and many Americans did *not* get the message that we must work harder to adapt ourselves to the world and not force the world to adapt to us. Under the leadership of President George W. Bush, the inverse, to our detriment, has occurred and still is occurring. Across the board, the two Bush administrations were moral, political, and environmental disasters.

In its ideal expression, the American Dream associates the United States with the principles of compassion, ideology of social responsibility, and the philosophy of hope. The American Dream, in other words, is nothing more than a trope for the practice of political inclusion and, as such, it constitutes the moral language of change. As Rorty (1999b) reminded us:

> The whole point of America was that it was going to be the world's first classless society. It was going to be a place where janitors, executives, professors, nurses, and salesclerks would look each other in the eye, and respect each other as fellow citizens. It was going to be a place where their kids all went to the same schools, and where they got the same treatment from the police and the courts. (p. 33)

As Rorty (1999b) explained, this dream includes a trajectory of moral evolution that started with the Bill of Rights and continued through "the Reconstruction Amendments, the building of the land-grant colleges, female suffrage, the New Deal, *Brown v. Board of Education*, the building of the community colleges, Lyndon Johnson's civil rights legislation, the feminist movement, and the gay rights movement" (p. 16). The values underpinning this trajectory also shape the labor movement and the Green movement. Although continuing "along this trajectory would mean that America might continue to set an example of increasing tolerance and increasing equality," noted Rorty (1999b, p. 16), he correlated this moral development with the widespread U.S. faith in a steadily rising income. Since the 1970s, however, this faith has been eroded, and with it "the political consensus that emerged from the New Deal" (Rorty, 1999b, p. 16). Thus, Americans remain wedded to social elitism, increasingly disdainful of the public good and of civic life, and callously unconcerned with the fate of people outside of their immediate communities. Instead of being a classless society, we are a society in which class is everything—the wealth of parents is a strong predictor of children's chances to survive their teenage years, much less go to college, attain good health care, and avoid long prison terms (Dyson, 2006; hooks, 2000; Kivel, 2004). In a society such as ours, defined in market terms, class identity has replaced racial identity as the mark of privilege.

Conclusion

Our project for creative democracy and the substantive diversity it embodies is inspired and informed by the work of progressive intellectuals and activists—both present and past—and is intended to contribute to this community of dialogue and practice (Dewey, 1927/1954; hooks, 2003; Parenti, 2007; Rodriguez, 2001, 2006; Rorty, 1989, 1999b; Swartz, 1997a, 2005, 2006; West, 2004; Zinn, 1980/2005). *Progressive*, here and throughout this book, refers to a state of mind that values the possibilities of the future over the limited certainties of the past, and which maintains that humans have yet to achieve their potential as a species that recognizes their connection to each other and encourages them to act in ways consistent with this recognition (Wander, 1990). To be progressive means to possess an optimistic, although not necessarily utopian, view of human potential—that we have the capacity to treat each other and the Earth with dignity and respect and recognize that it is in our best interest to do so (Singer, 2002). Thus, we start this book from the position that although U.S. culture has become more socially inclusive and there is greater equality relative to generations past (Zinn, 1980/2005), there is more work to be done if the United States is to be a society that is capable of progressive and ethical world leadership and the cultivation of human potential that we should expect in the twenty-first century.

We believe that there is no reason that we cannot, as a human species, choose to think and live differently than we do currently—in communities marked by mutual suspicion and distrust, where resources are unevenly distributed in obscene ways, and where lifestyles are unsustainable, unhealthy, and frequently oppressive. Of even greater concern to us is the fact that our basic way of living in the United States and, increasingly, throughout the world is fundamentally toxic and suicidal.[16] The material Earth itself repudiates us—one only has to think of the Katrina disaster in 2005 and the destruction of most of New Orleans, as well as global warming more generally.

Aiding us in our critical task is Rorty (2000), who reminded us that our moral growth as a species depends on our transcending tribalism, ethnic provincialism, and religious exclusionism. For Rorty (2000), and we would agree, the "more featherless bipeds you include in your list of who counts, who matters, the people to whom you have obligations, the more morally advanced you are" (p. 110). In fact, we cannot be moral, in Rorty's (2000) view, if we are unwilling to "experiment with various moral identities, various moral communities, and see which of them does the best job of decreasing human suffering" (p. 112).

Similar to Rorty (2000) who wrote that to "those who ask 'What's so desirable about diminished cruelty?' there is, as far as I can see, nothing to be said" (p. 28), we cannot justify our belief, which we articulate more fully in subsequent chapters, that reducing human suffering is the ultimate good other than by saying that is what we believe—that writers such as Nietzsche have convinced us that human beings are nothing more than dominating, egoistic animals with rich, often violent imaginations and powerful wills, and people like Karl Marx, Michel Foucault, and Noam Chomsky, have convinced us that we go through a lot of creative effort to *hurt* each other for greed, pleasure, control, and order, and that people like Martin Luther King, Jr., Nelson Mendela, and Caesar Chavez have convinced us that solidarity among all featherless bipeds is preferable than living in a world of hate, despair, and hopelessness. Nothing justifies our compassion besides the inspiration of our heroes (warts and all) and the visions they bequeathed. It is on the shoulders of these moral giants and many others like them upon which we stand. We also find, as we enter the second decade of the twenty-first century, that the United States is one consequential place that could allow for the type of development we advocate. Humans, and in large part, the subset of humans called "U.S. Citizens" have made the world into what it is today—a diseased and dying place, one of increasing hopelessness for many; therefore, we also have the potential and responsibility to remake it differently. We also have the power to do so in ways that other societies do not. This fact makes our attention and concern all the more imperative.

Notes

1. We recognize that social justice is a vague term; we discuss it in this book in some detail in Chapter 2.

2. The much more conservative and legally binding (as opposed to merely horatory) Constitution replaces "happiness" with "property."

3. BCE stands for "Before the Common Era." It is synonymous with BC (Before Christ) in that it refers to dates before the year 1 as demarcated by the Western calendar; however, it is intended to be a dating system free from a Christian-centric world view. By evoking this phrase, we recognize the world-historical significance of the Christian cosmology in affecting our dating system without reifying and, thus, giving tacit support to such a cosmology.

4. Fitzgerald (2004) argued that the problem is structural, that "too many people in the United States… are dependent on war for their livelihoods" (p. 26). Fear, Fitzgerald wrote, "is still the great lubricant of the wallet" (p. 30). Sadly, "most Americans care more about keeping their jobs than about foreigners losing their lives" (Fitzgerald, p. 31).

5. The Greek statesman Solon (c. 638–558 BCE), known to history as the "law giver," felt that political engagement was necessary for social stability and had passed as one his laws an order prohibiting political apathy. See Dillon and Garland (2000, pp. 87–88).

6. Mills (1916–1962) was an influential sociologist, most famous for enunciating what he called the "sociological imagination," upon which we draw in this book. He is also known for his criticism of elites in this country and his criticism of the structure of U.S. power.

7. A quarter a century ago, Schauer (1982), for example, argued that our society is less a critically debating, sovereign electorate, and more of a society focused on individual interest. This view appears increasingly accurate.

8. The slogan "Silence = Death" was introduced by the AIDS Coalition to Unleash Power (ACT UP) on April 15, 1987, as part of an AIDS awareness campaign. The now ubiquitous message appeared on a poster of a pink triangle (inverted from the ones that the Nazis used to identify gays during the Holocaust) on a black background.

9. Markets are also flouted as being "beneficent," although everybody knows they are *not* supposed to be beneficent. The strong win, the weak lose—helping the "losers" is a waste of resources. The Japanese were very honest in this regard. We recall that after the Los Angeles riots in the summer of 1992, representatives of many nations published short comments in the *L.A. Times*. Each comment explained that U.S. society had too much inequality and argued that this inequality "caused" the riots. Each comment also remarked that the United States should be more "fair" to African Americans and more "just" in the distribution of its wealth. The lone exception was Japan, a country with significant market experience. The Japanese contribution bluntly stated that in a capitalist society there are "winners and losers." Everyone knows this, so why were people surprised when the "losers" rattled the bars of their cage? The Japanese expected this action as an inevitable part of the economic system.

10. The commercialism of diversity represents cultural difference in rather shallow and incomplete ways, which is particularly problematic for the many people in our society who have limited exposure to cultural difference in their lives and who receive most of their exposure through the mass media. These often fragmented views of difference can become imbedded in our interpersonal relationships in various ways. In teaching diversity in our courses, we often hear White students say, "but I have a best friend who is Black [or Jewish, or Latina, etc.]" to either preface why they think they can speak with authority about those particular cultural groups, or to emphasize how much they understand the experiences of members of those groups, or even to position themselves as "culturally aware" as they justify a previously biased or racist statement made about the group. Upon reading their papers or through further discussions, however, it is obvious that their

knowledge and awareness of the experiences of others is still incredibly limited. Because they think that valuing diversity means tolerating differences in perhaps taste, style, or other surface-level things, which is what is mostly represented throughout the popular media, we can see how even their personal relationships become eclipsed by stereotypical and misinformed thinking. Furthermore, in student papers and in some class discussions we have listened as students of various ethnicities articulate that they do have friendships with others who are not in their cultural group, but that they are careful not to bring up any "race" issues because they do not want to upset the friendship. This is not to say, of course, that cross-cultural friendships cannot be authentic, but it is important not to ignore the impact of commercial diversity on interpersonal relationships and interactions.

11. This is not ancient history. Supreme Court justices may sit on the bench for decades, and they continue to affect the nation for generations after they retire.

12. The presidency of Franklin Delano Roosevelt marked a turning point in Supreme Court history. As a Supreme Court steeped in a crude social Dawarianism resisted Roosevelt's "New Deal" legislation under its practice of upholding "economic liberty," Roosevelt forced a constitutional crisis by threatening to pack the Court with his supporters. This move persuaded the reticent Court to change fundamentally its approach to social legislation, allowing for the emergence of the social welfare state and the ascent of political liberalism.

13. Che's family is trying to assert their intellectual property rights of Che's image to prevent this commercialism (Wroclavksy, 2005; also see Llosa, 2005).

14. Throughout world history, cultures borrow and utilize aspects of other cultures for their benefit and appropriation typically occurs both ways between dominant and nondominant groups. The problem, however, is that dominant groups, because of their ability to centralize opportunities, access important resources, and manage the flow of capital, are able to control meaning. Cultural appropriation is inherently political because dominant groups centralize opportunities, access important resources, manage the flow of capital, and, thus, are able to control meaning.

15. Bernstein (1985) discussed this line of thinking in Dewey, noting that "Dewey was sharply critical of a laissez faire ideology, which under the pretense of an appeal to an older liberalism and individualism, 'legitimized' practices that undermined and manipulated communal life" (p. 56). Bernstein concluded that the growing corporate power and the "mentality that it fosters is the most serious threat to the type of communal life that Dewey took to be the lifeblood of a creative democracy" (p. 56).

16. In a report released by the World Health Organization on July 27, 2007 (*Principles for Evaluating Health Risks in Children Associated with Exposure to Chemicals*), four million children ages five and under die annually due to environmental pollution, including air, water, and chemical exposure. Over 30% of disease in children can be attributed to environmental pollution.

CHAPTER 2

Social Justice and the Critical Imagination

As suggested in the previous chapter, an important assumption that we make in this book is that dominant understandings of democracy, diversity, and communication as practiced in the United States—those created and reproduced through conventional and normative politics and disciplinary academic practices—minimize opportunities for individuals to be more aware critically of the forces that shape their lives and to become engaged more conscientiously in creating a society that is inclusive and socially just (Rodriguez, 2001; Swartz, 2005). In response to this overriding condition, we take the need for social justice scholarship as axiomatic and necessary. Scholarship that is ahistorical, acontextual, and abstract runs the risk of being socially irrelevant, even irresponsible, within a creative democratic framework (Mills, 1963). Grounding our scholarship within a social justice frame enables us to understand the historical and constructed nature of our social stratifications, identify those practices that continue to marginalize and degrade essentially the same groups of people over time, and imagine new possibilities for a more equitable future (Koopman, 2006). As well, a proclivity toward social justice buffers us from the often-enticing and easy practice of idealism or utopianism. A social justice focus requires us to be grounded and present within our current social realities with the purpose of preparing us to address adequately those realities that prove dysfunctional, inhumane, and inequitable (Frey & Carragee, 2007b).

There are two major presuppositions underlying our commitment to social justice. First, social justice encompasses the essential value of a critical democracy, specifically highlighting the importance of communication for dissenting or critiquing the government, corporations, or the status quo in general. As Dewey (1939/1993a) noted:

> Merely legal guarantees of the civil liberties of free belief, free expression, free assembly are of little avail if in daily life freedom of communication, the give and take of ideas, facts, experiences, is choked by mutual suspicion, by abuse, by fear and hatred. (p. 243)

A democratic society is healthy only to the extent that it is self-critical, institutionalizing, encouraging, and rewarding rational or sensible counter-normative thinking. We recognize that such thinking is difficult, and an important assumption we make in this book is that contemporary Americans largely ignore or otherwise let atrophy their capacity to be self-critical. As Bender (2006) noted, "At the core of empire as a way of life is precisely [the] incapacity to see oneself as a potential enemy. Confident in their ambition and desire, and sure of their own goodwill, Americans were [or are] strangers to self-reflection" (p. 50).

Dewey (1935/1993c) was sensitive to the need for counter-normative thinking and worried that our society, in particular, was far less committed to it than it imagined itself. He worried that liberty is only tolerated "as long as it does not seem to menace in any way the *status quo* of society. When it does, every effort is put forth to identify the established order with the public good" (Dewey, 1935/1993c, p. 142), effectively shutting down dissent. A pertinent example of this is how much effort the Bush administration put into rhetorically silencing dissent against the Iraq war. In many speeches leading up to the war, as well as during the war, President Bush and other top administration officials made it clear that, from their perspective, there were only two options for Americans or the world to choose. As Bush (2002) himself demanded: "Either you're with us, or you're with the terrorists. Either you're with freedom and justice, or you're on the side of tyranny and oppression" (p. 15). Bush's attorney general at the time of the 9/11 attacks, John Ashcroft, warned on December 6, 2001, before the Senate Judiciary Committee, that dissent helped terrorism:

> To those who scare peace-loving people with phantoms of lost liberty, my message is this: Your tactics only aid terrorists, for they erode our national unity and diminish our resolve. They give ammunition to America's enemies, and pause to America's friends. They encourage people of good will to remain silent in the face of evil. (CNN.com, 2001, p. 2)

These types of statements seek to shut down dissent by characterizing those who disagree with the president or the war as somehow threatening the country. In speeches like this, administration officials identify with the public good by emphasizing how this war and their policies serve to promote justice, freedom, and democracy. Furthermore, administration officials often argue that anyone who disagrees with them or administration policies is against "the homeland," as if this nation, and no others, was synonymous with justice and freedom. One of the strategies of connecting to the public good and discouraging dissent is by intentionally fashioning the United States as an innocent, pure, and just player in this war that was thrust upon it by a vicious and greedy enemy. It was particularly troubling, for instance, when Secretary of Defense Donald Rumsfeld (2003) endorsed the comments of Deputy Undersecretary of Defense Lt. Gen. William Boykin, who characterized the war in religious terms. Like Bush, Boykin reasoned that Islamic extremists hate the United States "because we're a Christian nation, because our foundation and our roots are Judeo-Christian." The enemy, Boykin claimed, "is a guy named Satan" (CNN, 2003, p. 2). When asked by reporters about Boykin's religious connotation of the war, Rumsfeld responded, "There are a lot of things that are said by people that are their views…and that's the way we live. We are free people and that's the wonderful thing about our country, and I think for anyone to run around and think that can be managed or controlled is probably wrong" (2003, p. 7). Because of Boykin's position as Deputy Undersecretary of Defense, he ought have been held accountable for his comments and his views. By not holding him accountable in any way, Rumsfeld implicitly illustrates his support of the belief that the war is simply a struggle between good and evil, with the United States, of course, being on the side of good, and God.

Furthermore, in a speech at the American Legion National Convention in Utah in August of 2006, Rumsfeld methodically criticized the dissenting U.S. voices regarding the Iraq war. He posed a series of questions each aimed to simplify or discount the counter arguments and sentiments regarding the war:

> We need to consider the following questions, I would submit: With the growing lethality and the increasing availability of weapons, can we truly afford to believe that somehow, some way, vicious extremists can be appeased? Can folks really continue to think that free countries can negotiate a separate peace with terrorists? Can we afford the luxury of pretending that the threats today are simply law enforcement problems, like robbing a bank or stealing a car; rather than threats of a fundamentally different nature requiring fundamentally different approaches? And can we really afford to return to the destructive view that America, not the enemy, but America, is the source of the world's troubles? (2006, p. 22)

Rumsfeld's questions were designed to oversimplify the prevailing counter discourse about the Iraq war and to deny completely the legitimacy of these concerns. It is important to consider the international policies and practices and the actions committed by the United States that might bring harm to other nations or that might breed resentment and discontent from those outside our borders. For instance, as Bender (2006) noted, since the Second World War, the United States has become "the most powerful and consistent counterrevolutionary force in the world" (p. 60). However, Rumsfeld (2006) effectively negated the validity of this critique by calling it a "destructive view." Rumsfeld's disdain, and arguably outrageous contempt for those citizens who would like more of a public discussion and more careful deliberation about war, is best summed up when he cautioned that in a long war such as the one in Iraq, "any kind of moral or intellectual confusion about who and what is right or wrong" can weaken the possibility of our success (p. 32).

The above are examples of an observation that philosopher Richard Bernstein (1985) made about Dewey, noting how "Dewey came to believe that the most serious danger for democracy was an internal one—that there was an erosion and distortion of the very conditions required for the flourishing of democracy" (p. 49). In this view, Bush and Bush administration rhetoric hinders democratic thinking. These people—such as George W. Bush, Dick Cheney, John Ashcroft, Donald Rumsfeld, and Condoleezza Rice—are the problem, not the militants we are fighting in Iraq. For Dewey, Bernstein argued, the conditions of democracy involve "the constant challenging task of reconstruction" (p. 54) or criticism over acquiescence to the status quo, a personal commitment to fight for the behalf of justice in human relations. St. John and Shepherd (2004) conveyed well the agency for dissent felt by Dewey:

> To be critical is to discriminate, in the most positive sense of that term. It is to make distinctions between better and worse resources, better and worse conditions, better and worse agendas, and better and worse decisions. Critical thinking is not inert, not passive, and above all not noninterventionist. A good part of the work of communities, then, is found in people speaking and achieving assertively and constructively in the promotion of what they think is best for themselves and their communities. On this logic, not to do what one believes is right is an anticommunal error of omission, a disservice to one's fellow citizens, a ranking of a self-styled apathy over the willingness to act even in the face of potential disagreement or discord. (p. 177)

Related to our first point that a social justice perspective is fundamental to a creative democracy is our ability to see the outlines of such a democracy, to name it and pronounce its potential, and to act on what we have come to know and understand in ways that invite others to join, much as Cindy Sheehan did when she set up camp ("Camp Casey") near President Bush's Crawford residence in the Summer of 2005, temporarily invigorating the antiwar movement (Sheehan, 2006). Of course, the very process of naming is one aspect of acting; what we name we call into being (Swartz, 1999b). However, further action could include anything from engaging in community discussions to broadening awareness to becoming involved within the political arena at the local, state, or federal levels, or even involvement in social protest or civil disobedience. Thus, our second point is that a social justice perspective recognizes and enriches the collective communicative imagination (discussed in Chapter 3), highlighting its political and public dimensions. Coupling a social justice perspective to communication enables marginalized others to discursively form their meanings, representations, and understandings, as well as to challenge those representations circulating in wider publics.

In the communication literature, social justice has been defined as the "engagement with and advocacy for those in our society who are economically, socially, politically, and/or culturally underresourced" (Frey et al., 1996, p. 110; Swartz, 2006). Frey et al.'s article, in which this definition first appeared, is important because it directly and unequivocally makes the case for coordinated social justice research and teaching in communication studies. As they argue, a social justice sensibility has four minimum components: (a) the foregrounding of ethical concerns, (b) the commitment to the structural analyses of ethical problems, (c) the adoption of an activist orientation, and (d) seeing identification with others. By asking scholars and teachers to recognize and engage the grammars or structural inequalities that underpin speech acts that produce or underwrite social injustice, Frey et al. took the unprecedented step of urging communication scholars to bring their skills and resources as disciplinary agents to intervene directly and to rewrite grammars in ways that help the weakest and most marginalized segments of our society. Such "preferential" attention to the weakest among us is not only compatible with our vision for a creative democracy, but is indispensable to it; as Frey et al. noted, "a sensibility toward social justice focuses on the ways that dominant discourses, social structures, patterns of interactions, and the like produce and reproduce injustice" (p. 111).

Social justice, as we use this term, also includes the active and continual process of inquiring, identifying, and challenging the discourses, structures, systems, and norms that institutionalize poverty, inequality, and the dehumanization of others. As scholars, it means "coming to terms with an object in light of [our] values" (Wander & Jenkins, 1972, p. 441). We argue that social justice is something more substantial than electoral politics and the Rule of Law—defined here as an orthodox allegiance to legal norms over, and at the expense of, moral and progressive decision making (see Swartz, 2004a, 2004b)—and that human societies are shaped and transformed largely through communication (Scott, 1967; Shotter, 1993), as well as through scholarship *about* communication (see the essays collected in Frey & Carragee, 2007a), which, as we see it, is a form of *praxis* and a justification for our status as engaged teacher/scholars (Wander & Jenkins, 1972). We, thus, agree with Frey et al. (1996) when they maintain that a "social justice sensibility" means adopting, among other things, an activist orientation, claiming:

> It is not enough merely to demonstrate or bemoan the fact that some people lack the minimal necessities of life, that others are used regularly against their will and against their interest by others for their pleasure or profit, and that some are defined as "outside" the economic, political, or social system because of race, creed, lifestyle, or medical condition, or simply because they are in the way of someone else's project. A social justice sensibility entails a moral imperative to *act* as effectively as we can to do something about structurally sustained inequalities. To continue to pursue justice, it is perhaps necessary that we who act be personally ethical, but that is not sufficient. Our actions must engage and transform social structures. (p. 111; see also Frey, 2006)

Essential to this task of engaging and transforming social structures is the ability to first critically voice our dissent and align our actions accordingly. Following Shiffrin (1999), we define *dissent* as communication "that criticizes existing customs, habits, traditions, institutions, and or authorities" (p. xi) that construct and maintain inequitable social structures. Dissent is fundamentally a creative process because it recognizes that existing ways of conceptualizing or stratifying society are themselves constructions that can and should be re-invented. Dissent is a vehicle through which we challenge the status quo, especially when a particular institution is unjust, discriminatory, or oppressive, and we offer solutions that better meet the needs of both individuals and communities. This perspective requires us to be engaged scholars (Conquergood, 1995) and partisan critics (Swartz, 2005) who embrace the full implications of the ideological turn in communication scholarship (Swartz, 1997a; Wander, 1983).

Within this understanding of criticism, scholarship, and citizenship, individuals—as teachers, students, citizens—are able to create a better society in the United States than the one that exists currently, one less focused on greed, dehumanization, and violence, and more on fairness, equality, and balance with the Earth. Humans may then work toward a society that is socially more inclusive, economically fair, and accepting of intellectual, political, ethnic, and sexual diversity, as well as sensitive to the needs of other species with whom we share this planet. When individuals comprehend the ways in which communication works, they are better able to empower themselves and perceive themselves as change agents for a socially just and creative U.S. society. This view, in part, is what Dewey (1939/1993a) meant when writing that democracy is a way of life, grounded in the possibilities of everyday human beings:

> Belief in the Common Man is a familiar article in the democratic creed. That belief is without basis and significance save as it means faith in the potentialities of human nature as that nature is exhibited in every human being irrespective of race, color, sex, birth and family, of material or cultural wealth. This faith may be enacted in statutes, but it is only on paper unless it is put in force in the attitudes which human beings display to one another in all the incidents and relations of daily life. (p. 242)

For Dewey, and we would concur, democracy demands an agency and commitment to our fellow humans and citizens and, indeed, to the planet and to its nonhuman inhabitants that must be expressed in day-to-day actions, something lived and central to who we are, something that Burke (1984b, p. 71), following philosopher George Santayana, discussed as "piety" to our being—a loyalty to the sources that constitute us. Such piety demands optimism, good will, and a commitment to unending human transformation and possibility.

Rejecting the Entertainment Model of Citizenship

We are cognizant, however, that what we wrote above counters the normative television or entertainment model of citizenship and public life, which encourages passivity and civic disengagement in our society (Postman, 1988/2005). In his widely influential book, Postman argued that Americans have given up public civic engagement in exchange for a steady regimen of mindless, pacifying entertainment. According to Postman, our reliance on television for constructing and communicating culture subverts meaningful dialogue on important civic issues, dumbing down society, and reducing the exigencies of the material world to entertainment; disallowing possibility for serious contemplation on issues that matter.[1]

In the more than 20 years since his book was published the trend announced by Postman (1988/2005) has become more pronounced, as virtual reality and electronic entertainment have grown more sophisticated, pervasive, titillating (including sexist, violent, and anti-intellectual), and escapist. Reality and hyper reality have become intertwined in fundamental ways (Best and Kellner, 1991), further addicting us to material consumption, violence, and terror, with our children growing intellectually and morally crippled, even disfigured by ignorance, obesity, hatred, and fear. We live in an era where violence is portrayed as normal; heroes are manufactured, one-dimensional, and conservative (think Clint Eastwood, Arnold Schwarzenegger, Sylvester Stallone, John Wayne, and Bruce Willis); and the heroic struggles of people fighting for dignity against poverty and state violence are ignored (Parenti, 1993) or repositioned as base irrational terrorism.

These struggles go on tirelessly, but often too quietly in the shadows of the aforementioned pseudo-heroes of Hollywood. The people who fight against state oppression or struggle to bring awareness about issues of social injustice work in myriad ways from consciousness-raising to grassroots activist organizing. Take Paul Kivel (2004), for example, a violence prevention educator and committed social activist. Kivel has structured his life around a mission of educating and preparing people to engage critically in creating a more socially just society. His vision of such a society is one that ensures that "each person is valued regardless of gender, race, cultural background, sexual identity, ability or disability, or access to wealth" and that "such a society would value cooperation over competition, community development over individual achievement, democratic participation over hierarchy and control, and interdependence over either dependence or independence" (p. 227). Kivel attempts to accomplish his mission by engaging in hands-on interactions with fellow citizens through mentoring relationships, seminars, speaking engagements, workshops, and/or professional consulting (in addition to writing books dealing with working toward a more equitable society).

It is likely that there are many people around the nation like Kivel who are working in the shadows to make their corner of the world a better place or attempting to make the entire world a better, safer, and more equitable place to live. However, we rarely get opportunities to learn about their activities and struggles because, more often than not, violent, pacifying, titillating, and/or culturally balkanizing information in our "news" (whether it is television, print, or electronic) trumps any stories of such real and authentic heroic efforts and celebrates, instead, the rather inane activities of athletes who accomplish amazing game-winning feats or celebrities who are at the top of fame and success. This criticism, of course, is not to take away or diminish the accomplishments of our entertainers, whether on the field or in film, but their successes do pale significantly in comparison to the work being done around the country by individuals dedicated to making the United States more fair and less oppressive to marginalized groups. Furthermore, it is disconcerting that celebrities often become the primary role models for young people, especially knowing that they could be exposed to so many other potential role models who are trying to make the world a more just place for them to grow up and live their lives.

Postman (1988/2005) used two benchmarks to argue his point that we are destroying ourselves as a society by succumbing to the seductions of the entertainment industry and the pandering of unscrupulous corporations. The first was George Orwell's dystopian novel *1984* (1948/2003) and the second was Aldous Huxley's equally terrifying (but for different reasons) book *Brave New World* (1932/1998). Along with Postman, we remember the anxiety that was expressed in popular culture during the year 1984 regarding Orwell's predictions.[2] The dreadful year had arrived, with much trepidation in society. When it passed, we released our collective breath when Orwell's hell failed to materialize. Again, we smiled and congratulated ourselves five years later in 1989, when the last remnants of Orwell's fear, at least as it was expressed culturally in the United States, faded for good with the demise of the Soviet Union. However, we often forget that Orwell was describing trends that he saw emergent in *British* society at the time and which are often pronounced in *our* society.

Assuming, for the moment, that we have escaped Orwell's hell—that is, ignoring our tactics in the misnamed war against terrorism (the indeterminate detentions, secret CIA prisons in Europe and Africa, tortures, coerced confessions, invasions and military occupations, and domestic surveillance)—we must remember, as Postman (1988/2005) was correct in pointing out, that Orwell had competitors for the business of outlining our future dystopia. The competitor Postman highlighted is, as already mentioned, Aldous Huxley, whose denizen slaves were genetically manipulated and culturally conditioned to be satisfied with their positioning in the hierarchy; lapses in conditioning were remedied with drugs and sex and not by overt government coercion. However, we have identified another competitor in this genre that Postman did not name—Ray Bradbury, author of the classic novel *Fahrenheit 451* (1953/1996). Under Orwell's (1948/2003) vision, the human will is smothered by external oppression—

Big Brother or the totalizing, omnipotent state—imagine Big Brother and a "boot stamping on a human face—forever" sneers the villainous O'Brien at the hapless Winston. Such a state, in control of language and, consequently, in command of the past, present, and future, squanders humanity to feed itself. As the party slogan bluntly stated, "Who controls the past controls the future: who controls the present controls the past" (Orwell, 1948/2003, p. 119).

Huxley, however, as well as Bradbury (as did Foucault), recognized that the oppressive force of the state is not required to enforce submissiveness and invite totalitarianism. Other threats and other seductions exist to our autonomy, sense of self, and history; there are other ways to squash the human spirit than through fear. In Huxley and Bradbury's worlds, people "come to love their oppression, to adore the technologies that undo their capacities to think" (Postman, 1988/2005, vii). Indeed, in this sense, Bradbury's vision is more in line with Postman's (1988/2005) point—books became illegal in Bradbury's tale because they are frequently contradictory, making people confused and frustrated. Books hurt people's feelings, so people stopped reading on their own, explained Captain Beatty, the embodiment of governmental authority in the novel, there was "no dictum, no declaration, no censorship" (Bradbury, 1953/1996, p. 58). If nothing else, *not* reading made their lives simpler. Later, books were not burned because of an oppressive government but because people wanted the protection of the state—firemen, explains Beatty (p. 59), are "custodians of our peace of mind" from the harm that comes with critical thinking. More than half a century since the novel was originally published, Beatty's apologia to Guy Montag, the disgruntled fireman, is even more resonate:

> Ask yourself, What do we want in this country, above all? People want to be happy, isn't that right? Haven't you heard it all your life? I want to be happy, people say. Well, aren't they? Don't we keep them moving, don't we give them fun? That's all we live for, isn't it? For pleasure, for titillation? And you must admit our culture provides plenty of these. (p. 59)

And so it does. Therefore, fundamental to understanding the need for a creative democracy, with its focus on social justice and inclusive community, is the issue of *alienation*—the condition of profound disconnection between an individual and his or her creativity and agency; a sense of impotence or lack of self-knowledge or concern for others (Freire, 1970/2000; Fromm, 1961/1992; Rodriguez, 2001; Swartz, 2005).[3] In Chapter 7, we explore alienation as a pervasive, unfortunate, and unnecessary human condition in contemporary U.S. society that inhibits individuals from realizing their potential to develop their capacities and contributing to the overall well-being of others. Through the communicative process, we argue, individuals continually develop themselves and their communities (Rodriguez, 2001, 2006; Swartz, 1999a, 2001, 2005). Language is a significant element in the way we shape our understandings of reality; as humans change the way they talk about things, their attitudes, beliefs, and actions also change (Burke, 1984b). Thus, language is an important resource of power for individuals and communities—power that can be used to institutionalize cruelty, poverty, and hatred, or to emphasize human connectedness and facilitate redescription, transformation, and liberation.

In other words, public discourse in democratic political theory is talk about politics—in particular, talk about the political status quo and the possibility for social change. Such discourse may involve approaching legislators with the aim of influencing legislation or talk of political cooperation outside of establishment channels with the aim of making radical changes in the structure of government. The guarantees of minority rights in the U.S. Constitution protect freedom of speech and of assembly to insure that people can come together to articulate their vision of the good, absent interference by the state. The right to freely assemble, clearly articulated within the First Amendment, reflects the imperative nature of people coming together to air grievances, discuss solutions, and/or construct plans of resistance or change (Smith & Hunsaker, 2004). This portion of the First Amendment honors the vitality and possibility of the collective imagination. For instance, the U.S. government has historically been engaged in monitoring, diminishing, or eclipsing activities in the Black public sphere that brought people together to organize against the racist state (Squires, 2001). The purpose of this type of intrusion has always been to preclude organized action that challenges or disrupts the status quo.

For instance, Squires (2001) discussed the attempts of the U.S. government to censor and intimidate the Black press, specifically between the years of 1917 through 1945, explaining that "the state threatened to curtail the fast-growing power of the mass-distributed urban Black newspapers, attempting to stifle or eliminate this new voice of dissent and positive racial identity" (p. 112). The Black press, as other collective community activities in the Black public sphere, represents a key component for Black people to not only discuss the reality of racism but also to develop activist activities designed to combat structural racism and oppression. It has long been evident that the collective acts of deconstructing seemingly natural conceptualizations in addition to creating and imagining new possibilities together have often been the primary catalyst of social change. Specifically, a good example of this principle is *NAACP v. Alabama* (1958), in which the U.S. Supreme Court upheld the right of the esteemed civil rights organization to keep its member rolls secret when the state of Alabama, one of the most intolerant of all the Southern states, was actively harassing, jailing, and beating civil rights workers. Even without these guarantees, democratic theory accords people similar prerogatives that "street democracy"—widespread popular protest, non-compliance with unreasonable state or corporate authority, and mass civil disobedience—protects (see Zinn, 1968/2002). We define further *street democracy* as mass mobilization and direct action by the people with the least ability to affect normative power through ordered means established by power so reified that it becomes unwilling to change. As Zinn (1968/2002a) explained:

> Democracy is not just a counting up of votes; it is a counting up of actions. Without those on bottom acting out their desires for justice, as the government acts out its needs, and those with power and privilege act out theirs, the scales of democracy will be off. That is why civil disobedience is not just to be tolerated; if we are to have a truly democratic society, it is a *necessity*. (p. 23)

Seen in this light, it is not the Constitution that matters; rather, what matters is that part of ourselves that has allowed our heroic ancestors to stand up for social justice in the face of legally reified exclusionary practices. We owe to them, not to the state, the law of the state, or to normative politicians, our moral and social progress (Irons, 1999; Rorty, 1999b, p. 257).

This courageous dimension of an individual's self we call the *critical imagination*. The critical imagination is about meaning, understanding, and figuring out the place of the human in the world. It is the progressive antithesis of the social manipulation of society by economic and political elites. It involves creating *our* place in response to theirs, *our* space for constructing a fair and just world out of the poverty and degradation that arrogant power has created and forced on us. In this way, the critical imagination is particularly important to *counterpublics*, those people in society who have come together at a certain time in history, around a certain event or events, and who identify with one another based on shared experiences of exclusion or oppression from a wider, dominant public that also asserts itself at particular moments in history. For Asen (2002) counterpublics referred to "those publics that form through mutual recognition of exclusions in wider publics, set themselves against exclusionary wider publics, and resolve to overcome these exclusions" (p. 358). Counter-publics, therefore, often entail a group of people sharing a collective identity and consolidating either physically or rhetorically around a particular event or issue. Counterpublics matter and the ways in which they matter are significant.[4]

In sum, the critical imagination concerns the myriad things that matter to us as people in our fight against hunger, poverty, ignorance, and disease. It enables us to not only resist but also to transform existing social structures that are unjust. The critical imagination allows us to represent ourselves within the overall public sphere and do so in such a way that encourages others to respect our needs. The critical imagination, in other words, is an important tool for enacting social justice.

Creative Democracy and the Importance of the Critical Imagination

As suggested above, the critical imagination is concerned with questions of *praxis* and power, issues that we engage with constantly without giving them much thought, thus giving up control of our destinies. Whether we are cognizant of the fact or not, our day-to-day politics and behaviors are determined by how we contemplate or fail to contemplate opportunities of power and *praxis*. This is why control over the media by corporate interests is consequential and why it is detrimental for society to avoid asking hard questions of media ownership and public reporting by deferring to the First Amendment of the Constitution, which reifies the power of the corporate media (Allen, 2005). It is not enough that our heavily consolidated media overwhelmingly support capitalistic values (Kellner, 2003), but that those values pervade to the detrimental eclipse of other values, such as critical thinking, fair representation, inclusivity, and civic engagement. As Kellner (2003, p. 9) noted, "Media spectacles demonstrate who has power and who is powerless, who is allowed to exercise force and violence, and who is not" to such an extent that we begin to imagine ourselves as powerless. Furthermore, media "dramatize and legitimate the power of the forces that be and show the powerless that they must stay in their places or be oppressed" (Kellner, p. 9). It is because of media conglomeration that it is incredibly difficult to see any other possibility, especially considering that we can and often do experience an entire day reading, watching, listening to, and engaging with a seemingly endless variety of media choices without ever leaving the same "parent" company, whose so-called "bottom line" serves to maintain the status quo of stratification, mental numbness, and blind consumption.

Although these media conglomerates seem like massive power behemoths over which we have little to no control, the opposite is actually true. At one very fundamental level, we can simply opt out—turn off our televisions and seek out alternative sources of news and entertainment.[5] This is what we do, and we are better people for it—freer in our thoughts and self-identifications, less manipulatable, and happier. When we mention this to our students, they seem aghast. It is unthinkable for many of them to live this way. Other options, however exist. We can, for instance, exercise our agency on a day-to-day basis simply by paying attention to what we are consuming in terms of media and being aware of the types of viewpoints and voices we are exposed to, as well as being aware of all the possible voices that are silenced due to media ownership, and, furthermore, seeking out independent news sources and information (see Barsamian, 2001). As communication scholars, we see ourselves as valuable resources for our students in helping to make them not just media savvy, but media rebels. In this way we are not-so-subtly subversive of the established order—we provide students with the tools and encouragements they need to rethink their own minds. We would not call this "paternalistic," as might be suggested; rather, it is our job to shake things up, to model (and thus to subject ourselves to the same intellectual demands) and encourage other ways of being human for our students—this is how we conceive education in the humanities.

At still another level, it is important for us to recognize the opportunities that we *do* have as citizens to come together and collectively voice our discontent. For instance, the Federal Communications Commission (FCC) will often hold public meetings and hearings on the issue of media ownership for the purpose of providing an opportunity for the public to speak about media ownership and representation issues (fcc.gov). Of course, these opportunities are not necessarily well advertised or broadly presented but by becoming more aware of them (usually by joining particular web sites or activist causes that monitor these institutions, such as Moveon.Org, freepress.net, and StopBigMedia.com), we can exercise more control over the type of media and information we receive. Our collective voices of discontent, in fact, do affect decisions made by the FCC. Consider in 2003 the public outrage (what McChesney, 2004, called the "uprising of 2003") over the attempt by Michael Powell, then chairman of the FCC, to change ownership rules that would promote further media conglomeration, when "millions of Americans registered their opposition to the relaxation of long-stranding media ownerships rules" (McChesney, 2004, p. 254). Specifically, over 3 million people contacted members of the U.S. Congress and the FCC to speak out against these rules, which ultimately forced the FCC to reevaluate ownership regulations (Stop Big Media, 2006). Furthermore, this collective discontent and dissent led to the creation of a campaign and website to limit media ownership (www.StopBigMedia.com).[6]

We can only *be* different if we can *think* differently, and we can only think differently if we have information about alternative views that are precluded by the omnipresence of the mainstream press and their pressure for conformity (McChesney, 2004). By preferentially embracing street democracy and citizen advocacy over constitutional democracy and its privileging of private property and the needs of the wealthy over human needs, the critical imagination embodies the quest for alternative views at the same time that it battles orthodoxy and the corrupting values of the status quo.

The struggle for dissent and counter-discourse to amplify a voice is to struggle against *public* or *discursive amnesia*, the collective forgetting, underemphasizing, or decontextualizing of events and history that call into question the apparent beneficent qualities of our current self-concepts and national identifications (Lee & Wander, 1998). This concept helps to explain how few individuals or nations view themselves unfavorably: We all like what we see when we look in the mirror; few of us are self-proclaimed psychopaths who relish violent self-images of ourselves. Nation-states, however, which are comprised of individuals, are responsible for immense cruelties, whose practitioners find ways to keep their idealistic self-images intact. This is the function of what Lee and Wander (1998) called *discursive amnesia*, "specific acts of collective forgetting that perpetuate privilege and interest in a particular economic and political context"; through it "a group identifies itself not only through what it publicly or officially recalls but also through what it systematically forgets" (pp. 152, 154). It is the exclusion of the Other and the history of its suffering that unites us. Hence, they are the most difficult issues to discuss, the ones that we do not even think about, the ones that we ignore conveniently to keep the illusion of our moral identities intact, a type of "motivated forgetting" (Lee & Wander, p. 153). Our community boundaries remain solid because those who are in a position to question them are annihilated, either physically or conceptually, and the language of their critique vanishes.

The progressive lessons of the past, the struggles against power and for social justice, are subjugated by the power of the present that defines the "good" in its own terms, by excluding the humanity of others. When power acts in such fashion, it, in fact, says that all featherless bipeds are *not* equal—"some animals are more equal than others," read the revised law proclaimed in Orwell's *Animal Farm* (1945/2003, p. 80)—that the better community is *our* community.[7] To be an intellectual, we argue, particularly to be a critical intellectual, is to not allow oneself the good feeling that comes from imagining that we are on the side of truth and justice, to not mistake one's wealth and privilege as divine acknowledgment for being morally good or on the "right" side of history, and to speak plainly in condemnation when a representative of some dominant power demands that we honor it by pronouncing it True (Swartz, 2005). To "speak truth to power," in the non-essentialist sense that we are evoking the phrase, is to point out to power that its existence is not about truth and that what matters most is how the powerful treats the most vulnerable. Nietzsche (1954/1976) exemplified this sentiment beautifully when he wrote that "when power becomes gracious and descends into the visible—such descent I call beauty. And there is nobody from whom I want beauty as much as from you who are powerful: let your kindness be your final self-conquest. Of all evil I deem you capable: therefore I want the good from you" (p. 230).[8]

This is the only truth that we care about as critical scholars, the only truth that matters: The existence of suffering and the political/social/religious/and ideological mechanisms that not only demand suffering but, rather, relish in it, "the fascism in us all, in our heads and in our everyday behavior, the fascism that causes us to love power, to desire the very thing that dominates and exploits us" (Foucault, 1983, p. xiii).

Because "we," whoever "we" are, invest in our communities an inherent moral quality (which, in fact, is not moral), the progressive experiences of generations of activists, as well as victims, thereby, are ignored in policy debates, during political deliberation, by corporate media in their so-called "watchdog" function, and in school textbooks and in other educational environments that neuter the critical imagination and direct it into the service of the nation-state (Loewen, 2000, 2005). Public amnesia is present when challenges to established ways of talking about or understanding the world are voided by existing institutional and social arrangements that anchor the epistemological and ideological foundations of wealth and power.

To fight public amnesia, champions of a critical imagination point out that human beings are enriched tremendously with the ability to vocalize and, thus, to actualize their worlds. Such thinkers take seriously the human capacity for liberation and insist on what Baker (1995, p. 7) called a "critical memory" that judges severely, censures righteously, and renders hard ethical evaluations of a past it never defines as "well-passed." The essence of critical memory's work is the cumulative, collective maintenance of a record that draws into relationship significant instants of time past and the always-uprooted homelessness of now.

People engaged in critical memory actively interrogate episodes in U.S. history and relate them to both the present and the future state of affairs. Zinn (2002b) said it best when he wrote that without a critical understanding of history:

> It's as if we were born yesterday, in which case any person in authority can speak to us with impunity—can deceive us in a hundred ways. Having no history, we cannot subject their deceptions to the scrutiny of experience, cannot judge their words by the truth of similar words uttered to us in the past. (p. 30)

With a critical memory, however, things are different; we learn that there is no reality so reified, no system of thought so impenetrable, no political regime so entrenched that it cannot be overcome by the human will to freedom, the will to overcome one's self and the limitations of one's society. This phoenix-like will is the quintessential act of liberation. Contrary to many skeptics on both the left and the right, liberation is not a failed project, although its scope is more nuanced and less static than theorized previously (see Chapter 7). Simply, liberation involves the humanistic act of breaking down normative beliefs and values that deprive us of our potential to grow as individuals and as a society. If nothing else, liberation involves defeating the fear, arrogance, and greed cultivated by conservative forces resisting the transformation of human morality to include proactively the needs of the poor and dispossessed of the world. In this sense, liberation equates with social justice.

As we problematize our world through the critical imagination and engage in the progressive revisioning of ourselves, we engage in society at the level at which it is constructed and deny the permanence of that construction. In the face of permanence, we advocate change, a way of taking back the world to reorient and humanize our priorities. As illustrated by an important insight from Lu Xun (1985), a pivotal figure in modern Chinese literature, this critical power is part of our libratory *telos* as inspired and thinking human beings who engage seriously with the power of our humanity.[9]

Xun (1985) wrote in the beginning decades of the twentieth century, a period of time in which Chinese society was in utter disarray. The imperial dynasties that had ruled China for many thousands of years had come to an end, the National Republic that replaced the rule of the emperor was criminally corrupt and tyrannical, and China had been invaded by marauding Japan, and, before that, by many of the European countries, including the United States (Murphy, 2006). In short, China had come to the point in its history in which its existence as a civilization was seriously imperiled. Considering the immense importance of Chinese culture in human affairs, and the sheer number of people on Earth who call themselves Chinese, the impending dissolution of China was no small event. It was out of this crisis—perhaps the largest in magnitude of the twentieth century—that the communists eventually came to power in 1949 promising, and largely delivering, independence and national pride (Snow, 1938/1994), but not democracy.

This context is important because Xun (1985) said something very wise that greatly informs our discussion of hope and the power of a critical imagination and, indirectly, of democracy: That we often take for granted our world. We treat our world as if it were permanent, unchanging, and stable, the result of a divine plan or intelligent design. When we do, we forget that the world was created, constructed, and put together in a particular way by humans. It is communication, or discourse, that puts together the world, but we do not see this clearly because our world is often constructed before we are born, and it takes some catastrophic event to unsettle our sense of reality enough for us to see how it is impermanent, how much at risk are each of us to the twists and turns of contingency. Such an event happened in China, once a world-consequential civilization, and enabled Xun (1985) to comprehend a fundamental point. He looked at the death and chaos around him and wrote:

> Hope cannot be said to exist, nor can it be said not to exist. It is just like roads across the earth. For actually the earth had no roads to begin with, but when many men pass one way, a road is made. (p. 101)

Hope, in other words, is not a *thing*, such as a God or a government. Such things are "idols," externalizations of an inner human agency. Instead of seeing hope in this way, as most of us do, as a truth, Xun saw it as a *practice*. We manifest hope through our actions. Hope, therefore, can never be lost as long as humans retain their freedom to act; it is through our actions that hope or despair come into the world.

This pragmatic idea is implicit in the critical imagination; it is given its firmest expression by philosopher Michel Foucault. Foucault's work evidences some of the best historical or empirical documentations to support the power of a rhetorical understanding of human agency. In his many histories—he called them "archaeologies" or "genealogies"—Foucault demonstrated the link between rhetoric, knowledge, and power (see McKerrow, 1989), illustrating how the progression of human intellectual history involves a series of raptures and breaks in thought, of discontinuities, rather than continuities (Foucault, 1972). In other words, we are not simply progressing (to the extent that we *are* progressing) as a culture because we are building on more and more rational or "true" types of discourse (e.g., capitalism, American values, conservatism, Religion, Rule of Law, and God). On the contrary, we have *always* been rational. What Foucault showed us, as Nietzsche did before him, is that the rules of the game, the norms of rationality, frequently change. Practically, this means that the way that we talk changes, and each change creates a whole new moral and psychological universe (Kuhn, 1962/1996).

Once we change, we lose our social and moral connections to the past. The artifacts remain, but their meaning is lost, like the ancient Chinese encyclopedia that Foucault (1970) famously discussed in the preface to his book, *The Order of Things*. What is left is the subject of archeology in the modernist sense—the bones, fossils, and myths, but not the life. To understand the critical imagination, then, is to understand the breath that animates a particular community in a specific historical context under a certain set of contingencies. As critics in an era of a global "war on terror," the community we study is our own, the historical context is the present, and the stakes monumental.

In our contemporary environment, formal education is an important site of communication in the U.S. social and cultural landscape (see Chapters 8 and 9). However, this space is less "open" than one would hope for in a society, such as ours, that considers itself democratic (Giroux & Giroux, 2004). We contend that the lack of open social and cultural space in U.S. society for *edifying communication*—defined as communication that is intellectually transformative and inspires moral development—and self-creative processes to occur is a major factor contributing to the alienation of much of our citizens. Yet, the potential exists for changing this condition and we owe it to ourselves to do so.

Conclusion

Throughout this chapter, we argued the necessity of rethinking our current approach to education and public discourse, outlining the need for critical memory and critical imagination. We recognize the exigent circumstances of our failing democracy and the resulting inequitable social stratifications that continue to subvert, degrade, and marginalize particular groups of people. We privilege the need to situate scholarship, education, and democratic theory within a social justice framework. By privileging social justice, we acknowledge that the basic element of a functioning democracy is an affirmation of the humanity in all of us, regardless of social categories, and that each of us possesses the agency to reinvent ourselves, our relationships to others, and our environment. Exercising critical imagination requires humans to understand the constructed nature of our society and the processes by which we create our social world through communicative action. Once we can identify those communicative practices that preclude equal civic participation, stifle critical thinking, and dull our abilities to recognize our repression, we can work to recreate a society that is more inclusive and equitable.

Notes

1. In writing this, we may be oversimplifying the effects of television. Television itself neither is helpful or harmful, one may argue; it is the extent to which it is controlled by certain forces that produces the result. Might we conceivably have a social justice–oriented form of entertainment? Our short reply is "of course," better or worse programming exists. We point to critic and novelist Ariel Dorfman (1983) who describes working for the media (including television) in Chile under the progressive government of Salvador Alende in the early 1970s and the liberating effects it had on the population. Still, in the larger picture, we stand by the implications of Postman's critique and maintain that television, in contrast with print-based entertainment, is a roadblock to critical thought. It does not matter who controls the media, or if so-called "educational programming" exists, if people are spending their time watching television or movies instead of being engaged actively in other productive cultural expressions they are, in an important sense, dehumanized and subject to manipulation.

2. By *popular culture*, we mean those cultural institutions that can be readily accessed by the majority of the population, such as newspapers, television, news programs, and political speeches (Straubhaar & LaRose, 2002).

3. With what we can imagine as a sigh, Rorty (1998b) remarked, "We shall turn off our TV sets when they tell us about the misery of strangers" (p. 15).

4. The 1960s is a paradigmatic example. Not only did the Black public sphere emerge powerfully at that time in resistance and challenge to dominant White social hierarchy and racist oppression but other social issues instigated collective engagement and ultimately

had an impact on the wider public. When King joined the Memphis, Tennessee sanitation workers in 1968, who were both poor and Black, and publicized the plight of poverty, in addition to race, it helped to create public awareness of the complexities of race *and* class. As Dyson (2001) explained, "King's Poor People's Campaign was a hard sell, perhaps because it forced those who were used to thinking about race to think also about class, while forcing those who puzzled over economic inequality to think about race. King sought to forge a coalition of the truly disadvantaged by bridging the many gaps between poor whites, blacks, and Latinos" (p. 79). Because of King and many other civil rights activists representing a broader counterpublic, we have more of an awareness of the intersections and overlaps that characterize marginalized groups in terms of race, class, gender, and other important characteristics.

5. In writing this, we are aware of the rapid decline of U.S. newspapers and alternative literatures, the result of competition from online sources, which may not have the resources, ethic, or integrity of the print-based traditional muckraking news agencies or subscribe to its traditional "watch-dog" function.

6. See Coopman (2007) for a case study regarding the creation of low-power FM as another example of collective grassroots influence on the FCC and media conglomeration.

7. Orwell's *Animal Farm* is a much-celebrated novella in which an animal revolution against human farmers is an allegorical depiction of the corruption and failure of the Bolshevik revolution in Russia under the leadership of Joseph Stalin. After defeating the human farmers, the animals establish a commune whose cardinal principle was that "all animals are equal" and work to build their utopia. By the book's end, however, the pigs, which represent the Bolshevik class under Stalin, become indistinguishable from humans and surpass them in their cruelty toward the rest of the creatures on the farm.

8. For a discussion of compassion in Nietzsche's writing and its importance for the creative imagination, see Frazer (2006).

9. Xun, the first person to translate Nietzsche into Chinese, was a writer who has been compared favorably to Nietzsche (see Cheung, 2001).

CHAPTER 3

Communication as Epistemic and the Communicative Imagination

Fundamental to the work of the theorists and philosophers discussed in this book is the notion that democracy is much more than a political system or the right to vote. Democracy is a process of deliberation, inquiry, and experimentation that takes place in, and emerges from, localized communities and the needs of its individual members (Freire, 1970/2000). Creative democracy, as we describe it, ultimately is constituted in the attitudes and character of individuals and the activities of communities to which they belong, not in the political or economic machinery of a society. Democratic society, particularly if it understood in terms of creative democracy, implies that communication is an important aspect in the life of all citizens. We define a *citizen* as an individual who is aware that she or he is connected to others through a larger community, has opportunities to participate actively in shaping that community, and understands that communal engagement is a primary way of developing individual and collective human potential. Such a perspective of citizenship entails understanding that we all are implicated in the same future, and, therefore, we all bear responsibility for its creation and ethos.

In a creative democracy, individuals are most effective as citizens when they see democracy as a personal responsibility and as a way of life, comprehending the ways in which communication is critical in claiming one's power to direct individual and social change. Citizens, in this sense, relate to others from all walks of life, thereby enhancing their ability to engage in political and social solidarity. Taking this claim one step further, individuals are only effective citizens to the degree that they are able to engage in acts of communication that are necessary to live a fully human life (Freire, 1970/2000; Frey et al., 1996; Rodriguez, 2001). Humans need to be able to speak and act in the world; suppression of these needs stifles their ability to engage fully in developing themselves and the communities to which they belong. Rodriguez (2001) underscored the importance of communication in human life when he stated, "Only human beings possess a natural existential striving to bring meaning to bear on the world. Through communication, human beings are humanized. Communication is the constitutive attribute of being human" (p. 10).

Unfortunately, language usually is viewed as merely a mechanism for transmitting, relaying, and expressing messages and meanings—this, in fact, remains the dominant view in communication textbooks (see Rodriguez, 2006). Such a perspective, rooted in a Western tradition stretching back to Plato, is based on the assumption that "Truth" or other transcendent goals exist outside of human experience but may be accessed by a select group of people who possess special capacities, be it Reason, Divine Wisdom, or some other faculty. From this ontological perspective, language is limited in value. According to Rodriguez and others (see Rorty, 1979; Scott, 1967; Swartz, 1997a), the discourse of Truth is believed to be neutral, free of subjectivity, and unfettered by human perceptions. One of the consequences of this philosophical position is that only those who have access to this Truth, this "neutral" language (such as experts, guardians of knowledge, and other "naturally" privileged groups of people) should have the authority to shape society.

This perspective of language gives rise to the *guardianship theory* of public rule against which Dewey (1929/2005) and others stand: the assumption that average people inherently are too irrational to engage responsibly in self-government and, therefore, governance must necessarily be concentrated in the hands of those who possess political wisdom, such as those who "know" what is good, right, and just (Talisse, 2004). In other words, viewing communication as transmission naturalizes or reifies human-constructed meanings and creates an intellectual environment in which ideas and perspectives are mistaken for Truth (Swartz, 1997a, 2005). Under this view, democratic participation is inhibited and dissent in such circumstances is seen as irrational, irresponsible, or even immoral.[1]

Dewey (1939/1993g), on the other hand, wisely stated—and we cannot emphasize this enough—that "democratic ends require democratic methods for their realization" (p. 205); in other words, people must be involved in the decisions that affect their life. He believed that inquiry, deliberation, consultation, persuasion, negotiation, and cooperation must be exercised in all arenas of social interaction, such as in the workplace and in schools, and should not be reserved for a special group of people, such as experts or political leaders. He argued that public involvement in deliberation must extend to all social relationships and aspects of culture, including economics, politics, education, art, and religion (Caspary, 2000). Yet, as Mills (1958), a fierce critic of elitism in the United States, cautioned:

> We cannot today merely assume that in the last resort men must always be governed by their own consent. For among the means of power which now prevail is the power to manage and to manipulate the consent of men. (p. 29)

Furthermore, Mills noted that "if men do not make history, they tend increasingly to become the utensils of history-makers as well as the mere objects of history" (1958, p. 31). Such objectification is the nemesis of the engaged critical scholar.

Assuming communication to be *merely* a *mode* of information/knowledge transmission, the vast majority of people are likely to acquiesce to the claim that knowledge is the realm of experts, priests, and philosophers, and that as "average" citizens, they do not have knowledge or the "authority" to speak. Consider President George W. Bush's defense of his leadership decisions, even before the mounting public criticism of his second term in office. In his first term of office, before the invasion of Iraq, Bush said:

> I'm the commander. See, I don't have to explain why I say things. That's the interesting thing about being the president. Maybe somebody needs to explain to me why they say something, but I don't feel like I owe anybody an explanation. (cited in Murphy, 2003, p. 617)

Later, as public opinion turned against support of Bush and the war on Iraq, the president became increasingly dismissive of the public (up until, at least, the 2006 elections, in which the Republican Party suffered a major defeat, the result, in part, of Bush's low popularity ratings).

Dwindling poll numbers aside, Bush's arrogance seems particularly unwarranted in the face of military debacles and the increasingly clear culpability of Bush administration insiders for leading the nation into war under false and manipulative pretenses (Scheer, Scheer, & Chaudhry, 2003).[2] This attitude is illustrated in the comments that Bush (2006a) made on his decision to retain Secretary of Defense Donald Rumsfeld amid public discontent about the handling of the war on Iraq by civilians and retired military generals.

> I hear the [critics'] voices, and I read the front page, and I know the speculation. But I'm the decider, and I decide what is best. And what's best is for Don Rumsfeld to remain as the Secretary of Defense. (p. 62)[3]

In such a guardianship theory of democracy, protest is little more than a formality intended to be an escape valve for social unrest when citizens become too discontented. Bush (2006b) admitted as much in a speech he gave to students at John Hopkins University when he stated:

> I take protest seriously… . I think this is the great thing about a democracy. There needs to be an outlet. If people feel like their government is not listening to them or doesn't agree with them, there ought to be an outlet for their discontent. (p. 53)

That public protest is regarded as merely an activity for the release of pent-up emotions indicates that, for Bush, *public discourse is not taken seriously as a fundamental aspect of democracy*. This dismissal of opportunities for substantive public discourse is problematic when a society, such as ours, describes itself as "democratic," with democracy understood not merely as voting but as a selfless position one takes toward the world. Such a relationship to communication alienates individuals from their experiences of the world, discourages them from questioning that which authorities and experts tell them, and inhibits them from viewing themselves as change agents for a more inclusive and just society. What results is a public of consenting spectators and a small ruling class that makes decisions for, or simply ignores, the vast majority, even as the members of that ruling class do not themselves suffer the consequences of these decisions (Mills, 1963). This view of language limits opportunities for individual and social transformation because it treats knowledge and the authority to speak truth as a privileged, specialized domain that falls within the purview of elitist groups.

A perspective of communication more useful for transformative purposes is one that understands language as the way in which humans create their understanding of reality. In this view, known as the "epistemic" or "constitutive" perspective of communication, the creative edifying aspect of language is emphasized. It is through language that we establish and normalize social hierarchy and "how indifference to violence against those on the bottom is rationalized and normalized" (MacKinnon, 1993, p. 31). Language that cultivates our human relationships and perceptions of superiority and inferiority are present throughout various areas of our society.

Legal scholar Catherine MacKinnon argued that this constituted dimension to language was exemplified in pornography and argued that, far from being harmless "speech" or "entertainment," pornography is a constitutive act of power, forming and defining unhealthy relationships between men and women, with reverberations throughout all of society. She gave the example of "White only" signs that hung for decades in many places of business in the segregated South. The posting of that type of sign is often considered to be a discriminatory act of segregation that is committed through speech (MacKinnon). Those signs not only discriminated and enforced segregation but they also played a vital and pervasive role in maintaining a social hierarchy that privileged Whites and consistently denied Blacks basic citizenship rights.

Similarly, MacKinnon argued that pornographic images carry with them the weight of centuries of female oppression. These images espouse a theme of abuse and degradation of women that permeates the psyche of consumers and constitutes a social reality for women. MacKinnon's perspective inspired the city government of Indianapolis to define *pornography* as a practice that discriminates against women. In the language of the statute, "pornography is central in creating and maintaining sex as a basis of discrimination. Pornography is a systematic practice of exploitation and subordination based on sex which differentially harms women. The bigotry and contempt it produces, with the acts of aggression it fosters, harm women's opportunities for equality and rights [of all kinds]" (Indianapolis Code § 16-1(a)(2)).[4] The acts that are committed, photographed, filmed, and repeated in pornography make acceptable that which is unacceptable and "normal" that which is selfish and dehumanizing. As MacKinnon (1993) explained:

> Pornography brings its conditions of production to the consumer: sexual dominance . . . . [It] makes the world a pornographic place through its making and use, establishing what women are said to exist as, are seen as, are treated as, constructing the social reality of what a woman is and can be in terms of what can be done to her, and what a man is in terms of doing it. (p. 25)

Because pornography is so abundant and available in our society, coupled with the fact that, in general, people accept it unquestioningly, it becomes a way of life, a normative, even ritualistic experience. The result, according to MacKinnon, is that the abuse of women is overlooked and ignored: "Before, each woman who said she was abused looked incredible or exceptional; now, the abuse appears deadeningly commonplace" (p. 9).[5]

Examples of language as constituting a culture that accepts and justifies maltreatment of those on the lower end of the social ladder are far too prevalent. Consider the orchestrated vilification of the gay, lesbian, bisexual, and transgender (GLBT) community by the fundamentalist Christian right (think of the rhetoric of Jerry Falwell, Pat Robinson, and James Dobson). Language, in this case, is the fundamental agent, or constitutive force, in the discriminatory justifications of these rhetors. Language has constituted a way of thinking that compels us to individually and collectively recreate an unjust social hierarchy. Those at the bottom, therefore, become unprotected from discrimination, oppression, disenfranchisement, and violence. These abuses come not only in the form of individual interactions but also in how we vote, what types of political and social organizations we join, how we hire, and so forth. As MacKinnon (1993) explained, social "inequality is substantially created and enforced—that is, *done*—through words and images. Social hierarchy cannot and does not exist without being embodied in meanings and expressed in communications" (p. 13).

Understanding language as constitutive enables us to see democracy as fundamentally fluid and incomplete—a mixture of contradictions, aspirations, failures, and hopes. Because current systems of inequality and greed have been constructed, they can be deconstructed and reimagined. Recognizing this fluidity and its historical dimensions is the function of higher education, an institution that nourishes our project. The point of what Rorty (2006) called "non-vocational" higher education is "to make people more aware, through the study of alternatives to present institutions and ways of thinking, of the possibility that the future might be made better than the present" (p. 98; for an extended discussion, see Rorty, 1999b).

All human knowledge is interpretive; humans "know" through their thought processes and the language used to describe these (Rorty, 1979, 1999b; Schiappa, 2003; Scott, 1967). Furthermore, new understandings of the world and ourselves (that is, what we "know") are mediated by our existing knowledge. James (1907/1965) spoke of the way truths are formed when he said that what we call truths simply are ideas made into knowledge through a process of verifying and testing against other ideas that we hold to be true. Ideas that diverge too greatly from normative understandings of reality and that cannot be reconciled with what currently is known are considered irrational, illogical, or absurd. As evidence, experience and new ways of talking about things emerge that, together, challenge normative beliefs; dissonance and disruption of taken-for-granted truths occur, allowing new truths to gradually form. Communication, understood in this manner, is a way of knowing (Scott, 1967).[6]

Literary critic Kenneth Burke (1966) contributed greatly to the epistemic view of language, emphasizing the creative aspect of language through his "dramatist" perspective that explained communication as a symbolic act, i.e., language as symbolic action. According to Burke, use of any terminology involves selection, whether deliberate or spontaneous. When a term is used to name something, this naming selects, directs, and deflects among different perspectives (1966, 1969, 1984b). Simply by saying something is one thing, we imply it is not another; we highlight certain aspects, and, in doing so, we imply that other aspects are unimportant to consider. Burke (1966) referred to this characteristic of language as "terministic screens" (p. 45). Partial and selective assignment of meaning to a situation or object always is related to assumptions and existing meanings held by the individual or group doing the defining. These assumptions and existing meanings, as well as the language choices used in the definition, cast a particular view on the situation or object. This process is much like the way a photographer or documentary filmmaker uses background, light, and the camera lens to direct the viewer to see the subject in a particular way. In both instances, the framing of the issue or object leads the viewer to understand the subject in a particular fashion. In practice, representation is political because it inevitably involves interactions of power. Those members of society who are part of the dominant group often have the ability to represent not only themselves but also other people. These meanings are constructed and circulated within society, especially through popular media, and often disadvantage those groups that do not have similar types of access to represent themselves. Furthermore, most people do not examine critically the normative vocabularies that define them and their world, and, consequently, people often accept at face value the terms they encounter.

The way terministic screens operate can be understood through examining the various terminologies used to describe impoverished countries. Take, for example, the vague term "developing country," which implies progress and change, but not just any progress—progress away from "backwardness" and toward the model of "modern," "developed" countries, with similar economies, industries, technologies, and other characteristics that exist in the image of the United States. Another term used to describe very poor countries is "the South," referring to the Southern Hemisphere, bringing attention to the geographical location of poor countries and appearing to evoke neutrality in terms of politics, history, and culture. Such positioning directs attention to a North-South divide that exists generally between wealthy and poor countries (a label that is not entirely accurate, as there are many exceptions), as though geography itself is the cause of poverty and history (i.e., human agency) plays no role. This framing ignores the fact that at various periods in history, civilizations in the "South," such as the Maya, Aztecs, Egyptians, Chinese, and others, were highly advanced in their respective periods of human development and wealthy in many ways, including access to, and masterful use of, natural resources. A third term for these countries might be "former European colonies," which brings into focus the relationship between poor states and a history of having been colonized brutally (Beaud, 2001). Shiva (1997) pointed out the way that language is used to frame and name by describing how the colonizers' "freedom was built on the slavery and subjugation of the people with original rights to the land," yet "this violent takeover was rendered 'natural' by defining the colonized people as nature, thus denying them their humanity and freedom" (p. 3). As this perspective illustrates, viewing communication as merely a means of information transmission distracts from the power of language to *shape* understandings of reality (see Black, 1970).

Communication is a creative act that generates certain attitudinal, intellectual, emotional, and/or behavioral responses (Burke, 1966; Schiappa, 2003). Different definitions invoke different attitudes and imply that certain types of actions and responses are appropriate and that others are inappropriate (Burke, 1966; Schiappa, 2003). In this way, the language we use literally shapes our social world and future. The U.S. response to the attacks of 9/11 provides a current example to examine the consequential nature of language. In the days immediately following 9/11, President Bush made a number of speeches that defined the situation surrounding the event. On September 11, 2001, Bush (2001b) said that the attack on the World Trade Center was an attack on "our way of life, our very freedom" (¶ 1) and "an act of "evil" (¶ 9). He claimed that "America was targeted for attack because we're the brightest beacon for freedom and opportunity in the world. And no one will keep that light from shining" (¶ 4). In defining the situation in these ways, Bush created a simplistic, dualistic drama in which the United States is the heroic freedom fighter for all that is "just" and "right" in a battle of Good against Evil.

By appealing to emotions, particularly fear and pride, and using *ideographs*—symbols representing a community's ideology (McGee, 1980), such as "freedom" and "evil," that conjure up strong value connotations in U.S. culture and yet are sufficiently vague to allow for various interpretations—Bush named the crisis (or defined the 9/11 "rhetorical situation"; see Bitzer, 1968), establishing a framework from which certain actions would follow.[7] Following this speech, Bush utilized the public commitment for defending the ideals of "freedom" and "democracy" to begin a process of erosion of freedom and democracy in the United States (e.g., the Patriot Act), and to justify the unjustifiable military invasion and continuing occupation of Iraq, among other things. All of these actions occurred without evidence connecting Iraq with the terrorist actions of 9/11, weapons of mass destruction, and with little to no authentic public debate or criticism in primary public or widely accessible spaces for communication, such as secondary schools, universities, the U.S. Congress, television, and mainstream newspapers.[8]

As of mid-June 2009, the actions that were set into motion with the framing and defining of the 9/11 situation have cost the lives of more than 4,315 U.S. men and women in Iraq (with another 31,354 wounded, in many cases seriously), an estimated 92,368 – 100,843 Iraqi civilians dead, and over half a trillion in taxpayer dollars (inclusive of all costs associated with the war)—money that could have been used, among other things, to ensure that all children in the United States (and perhaps throughout much of the rest of the world) received education, health care, and proper nutrition.[9] Instead of spending its resources responsibly and constructively, the United States (under the auspices of a so-called battle against "terrorism") has embarked on a war against a people that had nothing to do with the September 11th attacks and everything to do with our imperial and selfish ambitions. For example, in his overview of the history of "regime change" in U.S. foreign policy, journalist Stephen Kinzer (2006) noted that each time this country has invaded a foreign nation and overthrown its government, "it cloaked its intervention in the rhetoric of national security and liberation" (p. 3). Kinzer also noted that, in most cases, the United States "acted mainly for economic reasons—specifically, to establish, promote, and defend the right of Americans to do business around the world without interference" (p. 3).[10]

This discussion leads us to examine the term "terrorism" itself. In recent years, "terrorism" has become a paradigmatic example of the dangers of reductionism stemming from the offering of simplistic explanations for complex social and political problems (problems, incidentally, that were left over from our unreflective victory in the Cold War against the former Soviet Union). Yet, as Fish (2002) noted, international terrorism

> cannot be the name of what we are up against. Strictly speaking, terrorism is the name of a style of warfare, and those who employ it are not committed to it but to the cause in whose service they adopt terrorism's tactics. It is that cause, and the passions informing it, that confronts us. (p. 30)

By labeling the problem simply as "terrorism," the history and the larger context surrounding the tragedy of 9/11 is conveniently ignored, made invisible and absent from the public's view. Fish went on to state that, contrary to President Bush and to what many U.S. citizens believe, we have not "seen the face of Evil"; rather, he noted, "we have seen the face of an enemy who comes at us fully equipped with grievances, goals, and strategies" (p. 29). By using language that reduces the "enemy to the abstraction of 'Evil,' we conjure up a shape-shifting demon, a wild-card moral anarchist beyond our comprehension and therefore beyond the reach of any counter-strategies we might devise" (Fish, p. 29). Writing in the direct aftermath of the 9/11 attacks, Sontag (2003) was much blunter than Fish in highlighting (and condemning) the reductionism of Bush and other administration officials:

> The disconnect between last Tuesday's monstrous dose of reality and the self-righteous drivel and outright deceptions being peddled by public figures and TV commentators is startling, depressing. The voices licensed to follow the event seem to have joined together in a campaign to infantilize the public. Where is the acknowledgment that this was not a "cowardly" attack on "civilization" or "liberty" or "humanity" or "the free world" but an attack on the world's self-proclaimed super-power, undertaken as a consequence of specific American alliances and actions? How many citizens are aware of the ongoing American bombing of Iraq? And if the word "cowardly" is to be used, it might be more aptly applied to those who kill from beyond the range of retaliation, high in the sky, than to those willing to die themselves in order to kill others. In the matter of courage (a morally neutral virtue): whatever may be said of the perpetrators of Tuesday's slaughter, they were not cowards. (p. 215)

Sontag went on to argue:

> Those in public office have let us know that they consider their task to be a manipulative one: confidence-building and grief management. Politics, the politics of a democracy—which entails disagreement, which promotes candor—has been replaced by psychotherapy. Let's by all means grieve together. But let's not be stupid together. A few shreds of historical awareness might help us understand what has just happened, and what may continue to happen. "Our country is strong," we are told

> again and again. I for one don't find this entirely consoling. Who doubts that America is strong? But that's not all America has to be. (p. 216)

As both Fish and Sontag pointed out, the actions that followed from the way that this situation was framed and continues to be framed by the president and others arguably has had some success in fueling the grievances of those who see the United States as an enemy worth resisting, not in making the United States or the world safer or more secure. In fact, the head of the U.S. military in Iraq, General David Petraeus, in his September 10, 2007 report about the war admitted that he did not know if the war in Iraq was making the U.S. any safer (CNN, 2007, p. 13).

As shown by Bush's rhetoric on his fight against "terrorism," humans can engage in communication in ways that create separation, fear, mistrust, and hatred, and this use of communication can and should be resisted. However, communication also can be used to foster understanding of human connectedness and identification (Rodriguez, 2001), and this use of communication should be cultivated and nurtured. We argue, along with many others (Frey et al., 1996; Rodriguez, 2001; Rorty, 1989; Swartz, 1997a, 2005), that we have no better project than to use communication for humanistic and social justice purposes; with proper attention, communication can be liberatory, not misleading or deceitful in the sense that Fish and Sontag mention above. Although post-Foucault, we should be cautious when employing the term "liberation," it still is a useful concept. As Rodriguez (2001) defined it, *liberation* means "becoming fully human through the forging of deep and meaningful relations," and through these relationships, "continuous evolution of new ways of being" (p. 2). Liberation can be thought of as building community and as moving beyond dogmatic thinking that restricts us from fully experiencing our potential.

An inspiring example of communication as liberation is the remarkable personal transformation of C. P. Ellis, an uneducated, onetime Ku Klux Klan leader who became a preeminent civil rights and labor activist (Davidson, 1996; Terkel, 1980). Ellis was born into poverty within a racist Southern culture that held faith in the virtues of being a God-fearing, law-abiding citizen and working hard for a better life. He married at 17 years of age and soon had a family of four to support. Ellis worked two jobs, as much overtime as he could, was an honest citizen, and yet was unable to provide a better life for his children than he had. No matter how hard he worked, his family subsisted on the edge of a perpetual poverty—a condition that relegated his children to the status of "poor White trash." Alienated, embarrassed, and angry, Ellis was drawn to the Ku Klux Klan, as was his father, because of the community and sense of power and belonging that membership in that organization offered. The Klan's targeting of Blacks as the problem for poor Whites provided a scapegoat for the injustice that he was experiencing, providing him with psychological comfort. As Ellis explained:

> All my life, I had work, never a day without work, worked all the overtime I could get and still could not survive financially. I began to say there's something wrong with this country. I worked my butt off and just never seemed to break even.... I really began to get bitter. I didn't know who to blame. I tried to find somebody. I began to blame it on black people.... I was led into a large meeting room, and this was the time of my life! It was thrilling. Here's a guy who's worked all his life and struggled all his life to be something, and here's the moment to be something.... It disturbs me when people who do not really know what it's all about are so very critical of individual Klansmen. The majority of 'em are low-income whites, people who really don't have a part in something. (cited in Terkel, 1980, pp. 201–203)

As a member of the Klan, Ellis was elected by the city of Durham, North Carolina, to serve on a citizen committee to address emerging issues related to school desegregation. He was soon asked to co-chair the school committee with a Black civil rights activist named Ann Atwater—a proposition that he nearly was unwilling to do because of his hatred for Black people. However, through his tumultuous work relationship with Ann and their many yelling matches, arguments, and, later on, discussions and conversations, Ellis began to realize that Atwater and other Black people were experiencing the same problems as he and other poor Whites faced. He saw that their differences were less significant than he had assumed previously and that they both wanted the same thing: a better life for themselves and their families. He began to see that the problems that he and others were facing were systemic, a result of institutionalized and protected privilege for a small powerful group of people rather than the fault of Blacks who shared the experience of disenfranchisement with him. As Ellis explained:

> I met a black person and talked with him, eyeball to eyeball, and met a Jewish person and talked to him, eyeball to eyeball. I found out they're people just like me. They cried, they cussed, they prayed, they had desires. Just like myself.... I'd look at a black person walkin' down the street, and the guy'd have ragged shoes or his clothes would be worn. That began to do somethin' to me inside. (cited in Terkel, 1980, p. 205)

Ellis and Atwater became close friends, and Ellis became a dedicated civil rights activist and a labor organizer. The communication between Ellis and Atwater, thus, allowed them to create new realizations together that they shared many of the same struggles and hopes, and is illustrative of the potential for communication to provide liberatory, transformative experiences for people, allowing them to transcend their previously "fixed" understandings of reality and their acceptance of ideas as "given" truths.

The Communicative Imagination

As discussed previously, communication is the primary process through which humans create their collective and individual realities and identities (Deetz, 1992; Engen, 2000; Rorty, 1989; Swartz, 1997a, 1999, 2005). It is through communication that meanings are developed, norms established, social practices justified, imaginations expanded or constrained, and opportunities for empowerment and self-development born.

Possibilities for a more participatory democracy and greater social change would occur if more people developed and enacted their communicative imagination. The *communicative imagination*, a concept articulated by Engen (2000) and further elaborated by Swartz (2005, 2006), is an orientation by which individuals possess a heightened state of awareness of the influences of communication on their life. As discussed previously, humans communicate through systems of verbal and nonverbal symbols, and the overall picture of what is considered to be "reality" is comprised of these symbol systems. Burke's (1966, p. 16) description of human beings as the "symbol-using, symbol-making, and symbol-misusing animal" aptly pointed out that humans cannot separate themselves from the symbolic; we live within a symbolic world created by us. Like breathing, symbols are such an integral part of human experience that individuals forget that symbols exist, and they forget that symbols, and the meanings they take from them, are human creations (Nietzsche's, 1954/1976, "coins," as discussed below in Chapter 5). In so doing, humans take for granted the symbols that they create, mistaking their presence for something "real" outside of human culture. The communicative imagination, however, attunes individuals to the role of the symbolic in everyday life:

> Individuals with well developed communicative imaginations possess a *state of mind* making them especially attuned to both the significance and complexities of the meaning production process in general and human social interaction in particular. They examine their interactions in dyads, groups, and organizations and come to terms with the way they influence others and others influence them. They look at their symbolic environment and realize, just as did William Carlos Williams, that "the closer you look, the more one picture turns into two and three and four and more." (Engen, p. 42)

Individuals with strong communicative imaginations, in other words, have developed faculties of awareness that enable them to "see" symbols as discrete human creations and to perceive relationships among symbols that, together, comprise a "picture" of reality.

An analogy that may serve as illustrative here is found in art. Although an individual with an untrained eye may stand before an oil painting of a landscape and see the portrayal of a 14th-century feudal village, a trained artist would perceive specific forms, how the forms relate to each other, and how each brushstroke of paint purposefully is placed to create what the viewer experiences as a village. The painter's choices of brush, medium, color, and placement create this visual experience, and an individual who is perceptive to these choices would be able to view the painting not only as a village but as a set of distinct creative decisions on the part of the artist. Similarly, a communicative imagination allows one to see symbols as discrete human creations—communicative acts that give form to the cultural, political, and social landscapes of human communities.

A communicative imagination, however, goes beyond a general awareness of the symbolic to competence in using symbols to build human relations. It requires movement from individual to collective imagination, which Asen (2002) argued "takes shape through discursive engagement among interlocutors in context of varying structure, scope, and formality" (p. 349). This discursive aspect of imagination operates as both a background and an active process; rather than functioning as transmission, it acts as a constitutive force. As Asen explained:

> As background process, the collective imagination constitutes a constellation of shared assumptions, values, perceptions, and beliefs for matters identified explicitly as topics of discussion.... Active engagement of the collective imagination occurs in situations where advocates explicitly call upon their audiences to rethink relations to one another. At these moments, participants in public discussions explicitly reflect on the rights, responsibilities, and obligations granted, entitled, and owed to one another. (p. 348)

Discursively using a collective imagination strengthens our connection to others and allows us to envision and articulate ideologies that reflect common social goods. When we are involved collectively in this creative process, we begin to see others as being more similar to ourselves than different and their interests and well-being inherently coupled with our own. For instance, Engen (2000) incorporated into his construct Nussbaum's (1997) *narrative imagination*—the ability to imagine the experiences and perspectives of others different from oneself, and to suspend one's worldview and judgment to open oneself to the experience of another. Such an ability allows individuals to increase their capacity to see others as human and as not so different from themselves. This ability also paves the way for the development of *moral intelligence*, another aspect of the communicative imagination, that Engen and Nussbaum described as a quality possessed by human beings who recognize their connections to others and understand the power of language to reify or reject human connectedness. Moral intelligence is not only comprised of this intellectual understanding but also incorporates acts of compassion and respect for others through the careful and considerate use of communication.

Legal scholar James Boyd White (2006) provided a recent example of how moral intelligence can be understood through communication. The central motif in White's book is drawn from philosopher/activist Simone Weil's (1977) notion of the *empire of force*, the personification of tyranny internalized in people's self-identities that Weil conceptualized during her antifascist/anticapitalist struggles in France early in the twentieth century, and in her literary study of Homer's *Iliad*. Human beings, Weil claimed, have a moral obligation to humanity, writ large, to recognize and to resist such force. As White explained, this force involves

> the ideology, the way of imaging the world and oneself and others within it—that is always present in war and required by it, but present also in our lives whenever people deny the humanity of others whom they destroy, manipulate, or exploit. (p. 2)

For White (2006), the empire of force consists of "humanity-erasing languages—ways of imagining and thinking and speaking and achieving—that exist in our minds, that shape our sense of the world" (p. 7). This force is not grounded merely in materiality—such as in the guns and boots of soldiers—but in speech, emotions, psychology, and ideology. What is important is not the physical or external forces that make demands of us but the inner ones, the "forces at work within the mind and imagination" (p. 5). In this way, the

> empire of force has presence and power in the minds of each of its agents and servants and supporters—in each of us who does not oppose it, who does not understand it and know how *not* [italics added] to respect it. (p. 5)

The empire of force, in other words, is a "habit of mind" that the communicative imagination—our increased sensitivity to see how language constructs and often limits our moral identifications and our lived connections with other humans—can do much to change.

White (2006) elaborated, somewhat reductionistically, that all speech is either "living" or "dead"; that is, speech either serves the empire of force or helps us to resist such force. White (p. 11) defined *living speech* as having an "extraordinary value," with a sense of presence and immediacy absent in ordinary, functional speech. Living speech is sincere and "deeply meant," which can help us to "resist the work of the empire of force in our lives" (p. 11). Living speech is significant, White claimed, because it "makes a real claim upon one's attention and promises to reward it" (p. 14). Living speech is "worthy of real attention; speech upon which both individual and shared life can be built" (p. 16). This type of speech, and no other, White argued, is capable of "expressing the workings of the individual mind and imagination" (p. 17). Being able to identify this type of speech in our practices is important, for that is how we each learn to resist the forces of moral degradation. This skill is particularly consequential for judges, justices, and other cultural figures who have the power to enact and give cultural force to such speech in their public expressions, helping the rest of us to live richer, more imaginative and empathetic lives.

Opposing such living speech and the possibilities such speech enables is "dead" speech, speech that is mechanical and bureaucratic; manipulative speech that does not express a person's thoughts or feelings but, rather, short-circuits them—paradigm cases being commercial advertising, propaganda, and much that passes for political discourse in our society. This heavy, mind-numbing speech is exemplified in "slogans, sentimentalities, falsities, and denials, of trivializations and dehumanizations" (White, 2006, p. 8). Such speech, White argued, is fundamentally destructive of personality, contributing to a void or emptiness in our imaginative and ethical identities, and corrupting community life. White's overall goal, worthy and inspiring for those committed to a creative democracy, is to help us figure out ways to use language to recognize the humanity of other people and to enter into conversation with them.[11] As such, our collective goal is to find creative ways for encouraging people—social and political opinion leaders (or other "strong poets," to borrow a phrase popularized by Bloom, 1973, and by Rorty, 1989),[12] to direct the resources of language toward creating a more inclusive and edifying society. Pragmatic suggestions in this area constitute some of the best scholarship the communication discipline has to offer (for examples, see the essays in Frey & Carragee, 2007a).

Conclusion

In this chapter, we outlined key components to establishing a creative democracy with a focus on the communicative imagination. It is through the communicative imagination that citizens can actively engage with one another by examining communicative practices that create systems of unequal social stratification and reinvent a more just social world. By exercising the collective communicative imagination, we argue, people can begin to overcome feelings of alienation and isolation and move toward social connection and community. In sum, a healthy communication imagination helps us to recognize that words have the power to reify hierarchy, cause harm, and normalize social stratification. Alternatively, words can heal, create bridges of understanding, and be resources for empowerment. By realizing that we are each inherently interconnected with others and that the foundation of our democracy depends on us working as a collective, we can reimagine a society that affirms the humanity of each citizen and promotes the growth of both individuals and the greater community.

Notes

1. In writing this, we are not arguing that communication should not be viewed at all from an intentional, information-sharing perspective but that it needs to be complemented by

another perspectives. It is not a matter of either/or; either an information-based *or* a constitutive-based perspective; rather, it is a matter of understanding the wide range of ways in which communication functions philosophically and critically in human society.

2. Toward the end of his time in office, the weight of Bush's multiple lies and unwillingness to respect even fundamental legal norms and constitutional principles has led to record-low approval rates and a growing, mainstream movement to have Bush and Vice President Dick Cheney impeached. This, of course, never happened, and Bush left office at the end of his second term with a whimper.

3. Rumsfeld was dismissed from his position only after the disastrous midterm elections, a convenient scapegoat for a larger political malaise infecting the White House.

4. Interestingly, in *American Booksellers v. Hudnut* (1985), the United States Court of Appeals for the Seventh Circuit basically agreed with MacKinnon's argument. While striking down on orthodox First Amendment jurisprudence the city of Indianapolis's ordinance, Judge Easterbrook wrote that there "is much to this perspective" (p. 26). He noted that "depictions of subordination tend to perpetuate subordination. The subordinate status of women in turn leads to affront and lower pay at work, insult and injury at home, battery and rape on the streets" (p. 27).

5. We are not arguing for the type of censorship that characterized the discourse about sex and sexual relations for centuries, and we are not trying to close down discourse about sex. We are certainly not arguing from a religious/fundamentalist world view, nor is MacKinnon. Rather, we recognize that pornography is power and it is prevalent, and we are very much concerned in this book with the type of worlds we create with the power of communication. Part of the reason that Judge Easterbrook gave for striking down the Indianapolis anti-pornography ordinance was that it punished a disapproved view of women—misogyny—no matter how minor the sexual expression, and allowed all types of graphic sexual material that did not portray women in a subjected manner. Such content discrimination is anathema under well-established First Amendment doctrine (see *R.A.V v. City of Saint Paul* (1992)). Presumably, pro-pornography feminists would also be concerned about the misogynistic content of most mainstream pornography and would advocate for a form of pornography that was responsive to female sexuality and equality with males. We also want to acknowledge that MacKinnon's is not the only view on pornography and power, although from a communication perspective, it strikes us as highly persuasive. For a contrast between the MacKinnon/Dworkin camp and their opposing pro-pornography camp of feminism, see Allen (2001).

6. Although an important area of study, this chapter does not address nonverbal communication but is focused, instead, on the use of language, as language is a primary way in which democracy is produced and reproduced.

7. Meanwhile, other crises go unattended. For example, Herbert (2007) noted that since the September 11 attacks, nearly 100,000 people have lost their life to murder in the United States. As Herbert observed, "No heightening of consciousness has accompanied this slaughter, which had nothing to do with terrorism. The news media and most politicians have hardly bothered to notice" (p. 5).

8. The *New York Times*, for example, admitted compliancy (or "flawed journalism") in Bush Administration deceptions (Okrent, 2004).

9. Sources for these factual claims came from *www.antiwar.com/casualties*, which provides a running count on deaths and casualties of U.S. Americans in the war in Iraq; *www.iraqbodycount.net*, which lists the number of civilian deaths related to the war in Iraq; and *http://nationalpriorities.org/*, which indicates the cost of war by state, county, and local communities.

10. In his new book, former Fed Chairman Alan Greenspan (2007, p. 463) acknowledged that Bush's decision to invade Iraq involved oil: "I'm saddened that it is politically inconvenient to acknowledge what everyone knows: The Iraq war is largely about oil." While Greenspan backpedaled on his written statement concerning oil as the motivation for invading Iraq, he did make it clear in his book and in his public statements regarding it that removing Saddam Hussein from power was important for the global economy.

11. That said, we are disappointed by White's reliance on these kind of dualisms—such as "dead" versus "living" speech—which seem to reduce complex arguments down to either/ors, which is too dilectical or dichotomous (as opposed to dialectical) for most critical scholars.

12. As Longford (2001) explained, "Throughout history some have felt the urgency of the task of self-creation more acutely than others. Such individuals—romantic poets, philosophers, scientific geniuses, and political revolutionaries—are compelled to create whole new vocabularies, metaphors, and forms of life by the urge to disaffiliate from inherited and convention ways of seeing, saying and doing things" (p. 578). These are the people that Rorty christened "strong poets."

CHAPTER 4

Exploring Our Theoretical and Methodological Assumptions

We conclude the first part of this book by engaging in a brief meta-methodological and meta-theoretical discussion of the assumptions and perspectives informing our project. *Methodology*, in the sense that we evoke it here, refers to a framework and justification for our approach to scholarship rather than a specific set of research techniques (Swartz, 1997a). It is, first and foremost, an argument style, a "rhetorical discourse" (Hollihan, 1994, p. 233), an intellectual commitment and ethos. This approach to scholarship is appropriate because we do not intend this book to be a scientifically "objective" or neutral study that uncovers and simply presents facts devoid of our moral engagement with the issues we address. Following Frey et al. (1996), who argued that if scholars are going to focus on social justice, they need to draw on a different set of virtues than dispassionate objectivity, we affirm that there is an appropriate place for values and emotions in the research process. To disregard emotions is to deny an important aspect of humanity that can be used as a powerful resource and starting point for mobilizing and directing progressive scholarship and social change. As Allen, Orbe, and Olivas (1999, p. 404) noted, the norms that dominate academic writing and scholarship require one to create a distanced "expert voice" by suppressing the way in which the scholar's convictions and emotions inform their research. They challenged this notion and argued for a dialogic scholarship, one that utilizes self-reflexivity as a part of creating knowledge.

"Objective" scholarship—that is, scholarship that seeks to create a separation between the self and that which is studied—is not useful for all human inquiry. In our project, moreover, it is not desirable, for, in some sense, it is a surrogate for the reproduction of the alienation that exists in hierarchical society against which we and others stand (Rodriguez, 2001; Swartz, 1997 & 2005).[1]

Examples of how objectivity fosters hierarchy easily can be found, with the infamous Tuskegee syphilis study being one such paradigmatic case (Gray, 2002). That study, which began in 1932, was a 40-year research project conducted by the U.S. Public Health Service to trace the progression of syphilis in African American men. The research targeted a study group of African American men with the disease and a control group of men who were not infected. As many as 100 men in the study group died from syphilis-related diseases and others suffered from blindness, insanity, and heart disease as a result of the researchers not only withholding clear information about their disease status and treatment from them but also discouraging and even preventing them from seeking outside treatment for syphilis, despite the fact that the health consequences were known and satisfactory treatment was available. Autopsies conducted on these men were the final data-collection activity of the study (Solomon, 1985).

In 1972, a reporter named Jean Heller published the details of the study and public outcry sparked an investigation that determined that the study would not even have met the standards for research ethics accepted in 1932, which were less stringent than they later became. This study was conceptualized, implemented, and continued over the course of *4 decades,* including the publishing of 13 progress reports—one of which detailed the dire health consequences incurred by the patients—in major medical journals, and yet only two objections to the study were documented during that time. This "moral astigmatism" (Jones, cited in Solomon, 1985 p. 234) was made possible by the normative communication mode of the objectivist paradigm—a mode that obscures questions of value and ethics and excludes "non-scientific" perspectives. By employing the communication conventions of objective science, socially, economically, and politically marginalized African American men were redefined as merely sites for the gleaning of scientific knowledge and a "scene" for the "dynamic agent"—the disease—to unfold. As Solomon (1985) explained:

> The consequence is dehumanization and a process of division (as opposed to identification) between patients and the scientific community.... Although the doctors were withholding treatment which could alleviate the suffering of victims, they redefined their activities as the observing of the consequences of the disease "uninfluenced" by treatment.... Knowledge becomes an absolute value.... (pp. 242–243)

In other words, through the careful use of such neutral "objective" language, the infected patients were intentionally targeted and dehumanized, and the dire ethical and moral dimensions and consequences of this project were rendered invisible or irrelevant to readers and medical research staff. As Solomon concluded:

> The reports encouraged readers to dissociate themselves from the subjects by highlighting the differences between the two groups and by dehumanizing the men involved. Rhetorically, the generic conventions of scientific writing not only encouraged neglect of ethical questions but also played an important role in the study's continuation. (p. 234)

As illustrated above, and as historian Howard Zinn (1990) pointed out, there is a wide misconception of the meaning of "objectivity." Objectivity is something that is generally regarded highly because it is assumed to be a neutral position, free from moral bias and effects. However, as Zinn made clear, this misconception inhibits us from seeing the potential consequences of objectivism as well as the value of engaged scholarship:

> The myth of "objectivity" in teaching and scholarship is based on a common confusion. If to be objective is to be scrupulously careful about reporting accurately what one sees, then of course this is laudable. But accuracy is only a prerequisite. That a metalsmith uses reliable measuring instruments is a condition for doing good work, but does not answer the crucial question: will he now forge a sword or a plowshare with his instruments? That the metalsmith has determined in advance that he prefers a plowshare does not require him to distort his measurements. That the scholar has decided he prefers peace to war does not make him distort his facts. (p. 10)

For Zinn (1990), moral objectivity is something altogether different than a commitment to practical and effective methods. The fact that we want bridges to stand, planes to fly, and medicine to heal should not prevent us from being passionate people committed to worthy social goals. In this light, we agree with Mills (1963) when he argued that objectivity "need not be an academic cult of the narrowed attention; it may be more ample and include meaning as well as 'fact.' What many consider to be 'objective' is only an unimaginative use of already plotted routines of research" (p. 299). We, thus, argue that scholarship best serves social justice ends when the scholar engages her or his ethical concerns and related emotions as a starting point for the research. In other words, a social justice view of scholarship engages questions of morality from the start of the process of inquiry—and views itself as an inherently moral activity. As Frey et al. (1996) noted:

> Research is never a politically neutral act. The decision to study this group rather than some other, to frame the research question this way rather than another, and to report the findings to this group or in that journal rather than in some other forum privileges certain values, institutions, and practices. (p. 114)[2]

We have constructed this book within the critical paradigm (Kersten, 1986) and rely heavily on use of the neo-pragmatist tradition of Richard Rorty, both of which are discussed in detail in the two remaining sections of this chapter. A *paradigm* is a broad area of disciplinary scholarship comprised of several related communities that share common assumptions, language, and practices (Kuhn, 1962/1996; Anderson, 1996). These assumptions, language, and practices function as markers of identity/identification for scholarship communities and distinguish one community of scholarship from others, establishing the criteria on which the research is to be evaluated (Kersten, 1986). Scholarship from a neo-pragmatist perspective, for example, must be evaluated by how well it measures up to the standards that its community has developed, and on those grounds may be accepted, rejected, or revised. Individuals have a tendency to impose their criteria for determining what is true on alternative paradigms, but doing so engenders distorted understandings of the knowledge that those paradigms produce and hinders transformative learning opportunities.

The Critical Paradigm

The *critical paradigm* refers to a form of scholarship that, broadly speaking, distinguishes itself from traditional, supposedly "objective," value-free modes of scholarship that promote exactitude and certainty. Communities of inquiry in the critical paradigm include variations of Marxism, critical theory, feminist theory, poststructuralism, and postmodernism, among others. Although differences exist across the various streams of critical scholarship with respect to their ontological and epistemological assumptions (discussed below), two common assumptions held by these traditions are that critical scholarship maintains an aim of progressive social change and rejects the separation of science or criticism from social and moral responsibility (Anderson, 1996). In other words, fundamental to all critical scholarship is the notion of *praxis*.

In its most general sense, *praxis* is "reflection and action upon the world in order to change it" (Freire, 1970/2000, p. 36). More specifically, the concept of *praxis* originates in the Greek word *prasso*, which means "doing" or "acting," and the Aristotelian idea that thought and action together comprise the ethical and political life, as opposed to pure logic and theory, which become separated from practical life (Schrag, 1999). *Praxis*-oriented scholarship raises the importance of practice to that of knowledge and emphasizes the dialectical relationship between thought and action. A balance between ideas/theory and action is constantly negotiated in critical scholarship. Although ideas and theory have the potential to help us see and think beyond the constraints and limitations imposed by social, political, and material conditions of everyday life, they best achieve significance when they are transformed into action in the social realm (Swartz, 1996b). For example, ideas and principles such as "freedom" and "equality" mean little if they are not translated into substantive practices in everyday life (Rorty, 1999b; Swartz, 2005). Scholarship, in itself, has little value for improving human communities if it cannot be made into practical wisdom (*phronesis*) for living. The Aristotelian concept of *phronesis* involves deliberation of the concrete problem at hand and strives toward what is the "good" in a given situation. In deliberating on the concrete problem, general theories are utilized as a starting point from which a situation can be viewed, but they are modified according to the situation. Finally, *phronesis* requires that action must be taken through a decision that works toward that which has been determined to be the "good" in the situation (Arnett, 1990). A commitment to *praxis* and *phronesis* rejects the Cartesian hierarchy that privileges the mind over the body, the ideal over the practical, and faith over hope, and, instead, views scholarship as a potentially important activity in improving human life.

The moral dimension of knowledge is another important assumption in the critical paradigm. By this we mean that critical scholars recognize that scholarship has political and social implications and consequences (see, e.g., Anderson, 1996; Kersten, 1986; Swartz, 1997a) regardless of whether it is intended. For example, the argument put forth by Richard Herrnstein and Charles Murray in their book, *The Bell Curve* (1994), links the so-called "Human Intelligence Quotient" (IQ) to social and economic differences among racial groups in the United States. According to these authors, IQ has a large heritable factor and is essentially immutable, and that African Americans, as a *racial group*, as opposed to a socioeconomic *class*, have a lower IQ than Whites, a tenuous and offensive claim. As Gould (1994) accurately noted, this research supports and extends the political argument of a repugnant and discredited social Darwinism—namely, that class and other socioeconomic differences are merely the outward manifestation of natural and immutable inferiority and superiority of groups of people. The theory of social Darwinism is based on the assumption that where equality of opportunity exists, those who are raised in the higher socioeconomic classes are naturally (genetically) superior (e.g., more brilliant, talented, and constitutionally stronger), whereas those who remain in the lower classes are naturally inferior, incompetent, and unworthy. The implications of Herrnstein and Murray's work include the naturalization of racial inferiority and a permanent relegation of African Americans to a marginal status, justifying institutionalized hierarchy and exonerating society as a whole from taking responsibility for social issues such as racism and poverty (see the essays in Fraser, 1995).

The long tradition of communicatively relegating African Americans to the margins and justifying heinous treatment of that group as a whole continues to have very real, material effects. Consider the tragic aftermath of Hurricane Katrina in 2005 on the New Orleans residents who were mostly Black and poor. Even though the role that race played in the response to Katrina has been hotly contested by politicians, commentators, and everyday people, it is hard to ignore the fact that the United States has an extensive history of vilifying, despising, and ignoring the Black community—a sentiment that was publicly aired by rap/hip-hop artist Kanye West when he remarked, "George Bush doesn't care about Black people" during a live hurricane relief concert aired on NBC (cited in de Moraes, 2005). Although that one-line comment was the most talked about in popular media at the time (see, e.g., msnbc.com, cnn.com, and news.yahoo.com), what was ignored, in general, were the other things West said within the context about treatment of African Americans in the United States. As West explained:

> I hate the way they portray us in the media. You see a black family, it says, "They're looting." You see a white family, it says, "They're looking for food." And, you know, it's been five days [waiting for federal help] because most of the people are black . . . with the way America is set up to help the poor, the black people, the less well-off, as slow as possible. (cited in de Moraes, 2005, p. 9)

West's commentaries were off-the-cuff and obviously delivered in a high-pressure situation with Michael Myers, who was co-commentating with him, standing beside him in visible shock at West's impromptu remarks, but the full impact of what West was articulating is not lost on us. West was clear to point out how the media and the public respond to Black and poor people very differently than they do to Whites by remarking on the Associated Press photographs of Blacks (during the mayhem after the disaster) carrying bags of food with a caption describing their actions as "looting," whereas the actions of Whites in very similar images carrying bags of food were described as "finding" (Christensen, 2006). West further pointed out that there are many people who would ordinarily be able to help with the rescue effort but could not due to fighting a selected war overseas in Iraq, and furthermore, that authorities gave permission to police officers in New Orleans to shoot people at will (de Moraes, 2005). Kanye West's comments are quite shocking because these types of statements are rarely made to a rather broad, diverse, and listening public, not to mention the White public. However, these sentiments have long been held by Black people and articulated within Black communities (see, e.g., Dyson, 2006; hooks, 2000; Smiley, 2006). Senator Barak Obama made it clear that although the actions after Katrina may not necessarily have been *intentionally* racist, the racist impact, nevertheless, was felt by many: "I see no evidence of active malice, but I see a continuation of passive indifference on the part of our government towards the least of these" (cited in Dyson, 2006, p. 20). Racial narratives, "objective" racist scholarship, racial discourse, and pervasive passive indifference pervade the way people think about racial groups, the way they interact, and the way they are governed. Dyson (2006) emphasized the constructed nature of our collective racial thinking:

> Our conscious decisions are drawn from the reservoir of beliefs, attitudes, and dispositions that form our group's collective racial unconscious. When we gear up for response to a particular event, when we dissect or process a specific item of information, we pull from these resources, which have shaped our understanding of what can and should be done. The collective racial unconscious, and the rhythms, relations, and rules of race, together constitute the framework for making decisions, even those that apparently have nothing to do with race.... It should be clear that although one may not have racial intent, one's actions may nonetheless have racial consequence. (p. 20)

Any scholarship has the potential to help create a collective racial unconscious in addition to constructing problematic conceptions of gender, class, sexuality, and so forth. That is why it is of particular importance that we be aware of the moral significance of the experiments, studies, and theories that form the foundation of our scholarship. Critical scholars, in contrast to scholars working in the traditional mode, recognize that scholarship has serious and potentially harmful implications and, as such, they make explicit the social and politically overt aims of their work.

To place our work in the critical paradigm and state explicitly our philosophical assumptions, we identify the distinction among the types of critical scholarship. We include a description of the major distinctions of critical scholarship because we believe, for our project, that the differences are important. By distinguishing a "reflexive critical" from "foundationalist critical" scholarship, we underscore that the intention of this project is not to create a new "program" for social change but to put forth an argument for thinking things differently based on our convictions as scholars, citizens, and individuals, to ward against what Aronson (1999) called "the privatization of hope" (p. 480).[3]

Broadly speaking, critical scholarship can be split into foundationalist and reflexive approaches, respectively (these distinctions were adopted from Anderson & Baym, 2004). A primary distinction between the two approaches to critical theory is that, generally speaking, *foundationalist critical theory* (including Marxism, critical theory in the Frankfurt School tradition, and second-wave feminism) assumes it is possible to discover authentic descriptions of social reality that are free from ideology, descriptions that can be found through social-scientific methods and the use of reason (Anderson, 1996). Although a central concern of critical theory is emancipation of humans from domination by alienating social, political, and economic systems, foundationalist critical theory grounds this project in a search for non-ideological, non-distorted meaning. This approach, simply illustrated, is found in the Marxian call for workers to escape from "false consciousness" and to recognize their "true interests." This is the idea that if humans, particularly the "working class," could free their minds from capitalist ideology, the Truth would make itself evident and workers would be inclined to work together to be liberated from oppression once and for all.

Although useful pragmatically for mobilizing marginalized people against repressive systems, faith in absolute, totalizing Truth has its limitations (Foucault, 1984a). One of these limitations is that, in Burke's (1935/1984a) terms, this "tragic-frame" approach to social change obscures the negative consequences of their solutions. The tragic frame is one of Burke's dramatist perspectives in addressing social change. In situations of social conflict, the tragic frame represents a lack of hope in a redemption of the "enemy," and approaches social change as only being able to occur through a "death." In other words, social transformation is only viewed as possible by ritualistically killing the enemy. What often results in a practical sense is a cycle of scapegoating, usurping, and overthrow of the reigning ideology—only to be replaced by another—continuing *ad infinitum*. As Foucault (1984b) observed, the

> claim to escape from the system of contemporary reality so as to produce the overall program of another society, of another way of thinking, another culture, another vision of the world, has led only to the return of the most dangerous traditions. (p. 46)

Although we would qualify Foucault's comment, and believe he would as well if he had not been speaking in an interview, with the word "mostly" or "often," instead of "only," his point is well taken, although easily missed by Foucault's detractors. Thus, when Foucault (1977) stated infamously in an interview that "to imagine another system is to extend our participation in the present system" (p. 230), we recognize that what he meant is that an *uncritical* or *unreflective* reliance on past models is the problem, as he explained in the part of the interview that is often ignored, when he discusses how the revolutionary Bolshevik government in Russia reconstituted itself along czarist lines. In other words, we should be extremely cautious and tentative (which is, to say, pragmatic) in formulating strategies of resistance and redescription.

Thus, although the quest for certainty and ideologically-free Truth is appealing for many reasons, it has limitations for creating new and transformative forms that further the progressive goal of liberation from institutionalized domination and hierarchy, one of the main goals of critical theory. As Burke (1966) pointed out, humans are "the symbol-using, symbol-making, symbol-misusing animal, inventor of the negative (or moralized by the negative), separated from [their] natural condition by instruments of [their] own making" (p. 16). As creative, symbol-using/making/misusing beings, humans exist in a constant state of interpreting and creating their understanding and experience of the world through symbols and instruments that they themselves develop (Swartz, 1996a). This condition poses a challenge to the assumption that non-ideological meanings can be discovered, a key tenet of foundationalist critical theory.

Reflexive critical scholarship, the approach that we prefer, encompasses perspectives embodied in postmodernism, poststructuralism, and pragmatism, among others. Common to these perspectives is the idea that what humans take to be "Truth" is actually a set of meanings that are themselves created by humans; as such, we cannot access ideologically-free understandings of reality. Therefore, the subjective/objective binary—the idea that social reality can be understood apart from our subjective interpretation—is not desired among reflexive scholars. To employ such a binary would undermine the assumption of reflexive critical scholarship that knowledge is created not discovered, taken, not given (in Dewey's, 1929/2005, sense), and, thereby, distance ourselves from our creative power of *phronises* and *praxis*.

Neo-Pragmatism

As suggested earlier, this book also draws on the neo-pragmatist tradition. *Neo-pragmatism*, the branch of philosophy that Rorty (1979) is credited with bringing into academic discourse since the early 1980s, complements the reflexive critical approach and is utilized in this book as an additional lens through which our research issues are engaged. Neo-pragmatism's origins are found in *pragmatism,* a U.S. anti-foundationalist philosophical tradition, originating in the late nineteenth century through the writings of Charles Peirce, William James, John Dewey and others (see McDermott, 1989; West, 1989). For our purposes, neo-pragmatism is distinguished from pragmatism in that it highlights the role that language plays in the construction of truth. Although not without controversy in his portrayal of pragmatism (see Brodsky, 1982, Englund, 2000; Margolis, 2002; Johnson, 2000; Wilshire, 1997), Richard Rorty is the philosopher who is most well known for this variation of pragmatism.[4]

Pragmatism assumes that truth is made, not "discovered"; it is the upshot of argument, persuasion, and consensus within a community. William James (1907/1965) laid out a basic assumption of pragmatism when he stated that the "truth of an idea is not a stagnant property inherent in it" (p. 97). For James, "Truth happens to an idea. It becomes, is made true by events. Its verity is in fact an event, a process: the process namely of its verifying itself, its veri-*fication*. Its validity is the process of its valid-*ation*" (p. 97). In Rorty's (2007) terms, "Attributions of reality or truth are . . . beliefs that have won their spurs, paid their way, proved themselves useful, and therefore been incorporated into accepted social practices" (p. 7). For Rorty (2006), "The word *true* is a compliment we pay to beliefs that are serving to guide action better than their competitors, rather than a term signifying accurate representation of reality" (p. 95).

Pragmatism rejects the foundationalist project of knowledge as representation because it attempts to formulate an "ultimate context of thought" (Rorty, 1979) that exists above the terrain of human experience and historical contingency. Pragmatism sees this attempt as not being useful for human inquiry and is more concerned with consequences that various forms of knowledge produce and the ways in which alternative truths may help human communities to solve the problems that arise rather than trying (impossibly) to identify timeless, transcendent absolute universal principles. Rorty (1999b) distinguished the difference between foundationalist philosophy and pragmatism by stating that pragmatists think there is no point in asking whether a belief accurately represents reality; rather, the right question to ask for pragmatists is for "what purposes would it be useful to hold that belief?" (p. xxiv). The implication of this approach is that it brings philosophy out of the proverbial ivory tower and into everyday life of costs, benefits, and consequences. As West (1993) noted, "The pragmatist tradition is widely associated with a distrust of theory that curtails its ability to fully grasp the operations of power within the personal, social and historical contexts of human activities" (p. 137).

Rorty (1979) took the pragmatist notion of dissolving the boundary between "certified knowledge" and "mere belief" a step further by framing all knowledge in terms of vocabularies and "descriptions." He distinguished between scientific or philosophical knowledge and other types of knowledge by referring to them as "privileged" versus "alternative" descriptions. In doing so, he reduced the differences between philosophy and poetry or literature to that of style, habit, or prejudice. Rorty (1989) argued that the habit of identifying an ultimate vocabulary to encompass all possible vocabularies is much less useful for human progress than understanding what vocabularies are more or less useful for certain projects and understanding the vocabularies of others to increase human cooperation and solidarity. Thus, whereas foundationalist philosophy searches for certainty and transcendent truths, neo-pragmatist philosophy is concerned with the kinds of descriptions that enable humans to reduce needless suffering and humiliation. According to Rorty (1999b):

> What matters for us pragmatists is devising ways of diminishing human suffering and increasing human equality, increasing the ability of all human children to start life with an equal chance of happiness.... It is a goal worth dying for, but it does not require backup from supernatural forces. (p. xxix)

Such goals as the above for philosophical inquiry are a hopeful alternative to the limitations of foundationalist scholarship; employing intellectual power to solve real-world problems because it seems the right thing to do with the knowledge and understanding we have currently is a useful approach. A key limitation of foundationalism and "objectivism" is that they obstruct possibilities for moving forward in addressing social injustices (Wander, 1990). Concern about gaining consensus on what counts as pain, suffering and injustice distracts us from making change in the direction of social justice (Frey et al., 1996, Swartz, 1997a, 2005). This preoccupation with commensurability is captured by Goodheart's (1997) criticism against Rorty's pragmatist approach to social change. According to Goodheart, Rorty's campaign against cruelty, though laudable, is "vacuous." Goodheart complained that Rorty's project proscribes "against pursuing the so-called metaphysical questions about justice and right action that would enable us to determine what constitutes cruelty" (p. 234). From our perspective, this concern makes little sense. It does not necessarily follow that to stop doing things as a society that inflict suffering on people (such as collectively allowing our children to go hungry as we use resources to wage so-called "preemptive wars" against other countries, such as Iraq), we must first engage in a traditional philosophical project of determining what is "cruelty." The quest for certainty and commensurability appears absurd in statements such as this, especially when placed against the striking imbalance between the willingness to fund wars at the same time that extreme and devastating poverty is prevalent and growing worldwide. It seems ridiculous that we should be distracted by defining cruelty when we know that to ensure a basic level of health, education, water, and sanitation for the world's poor would require an extra \$47 billion a year in aid, yet the annual global military spending is approximately \$1 trillion (Oxfam, 2006). The reflexive critical mode of scholarship, informed by a neo-pragmatist perspective, thus, provides an approach to scholarship that is useful for developing a more just society and working toward progressive goals that value addressing the existential conditions of human beings.

Conclusion

In this chapter, we argued that the reflexive critical mode of scholarship is a useful frame by which to approach the exigent social problems that exist today. The reflexive critical mode of scholarship allows us to be cognitively flexible in imagining solutions to current inequitable social structures, as opposed to the foundationalist approach, which often focuses more on the search for a limited truth and proscribed certainty. We reject this sense of the objective approach to scholarship because it precludes us from exploring all of the creative possibilities that exist when approaching social problems. As noted by Englund (2000), the

> main characteristic of neo-pragmatism [is its] concern for communication as a democratic form of life, that is the development of communicative and deliberative capabilities for democracy. The idea of deliberative democracy as an educational process, where individuals bring different perspectives to an on-going communication. (p. 306)

By applying theories, research, and conclusions to real-world contexts based on our political and social commitments, we are able to more fully engage the real problems that face us as a society and, specifically, we are able to address issues of social justice and social inequality.

Notes

1. This hierarchy includes, unfortunately, the academy, and we are fully cognizant of our unorthodoxy, even by the standards of critical scholarship. Our experience has been, unfortunately, that obsessive and closed-minded professionalism often works to shut down dissenting and counter-normative scholarship. bell hooks (1991), for example, described

how students around the country are not able to include her work in official contexts because that work is deemed by professors as not being "scholarly enough" (p. 9). By any standard, hooks is an exemplary critical scholar. If hooks does not "count," then who does? Do we not want more people like her writing?

2. We want to stress that we are in no way rejecting a post-positivistic, post-scientistic conception of research that seeks to establish causal relationships between variables. This is important in-and-of-itself and has lead to remarkable scientific breakthroughs. Nor do we suggest that having the "correct" attitude or emotional commitment is sufficient for constructive social justice work. We are not arguing against methods per se, as methods are only tools. We are simply arguing that for our research, and for critical research in general, other methods or approaches may be more appropriate for the claims and arguments that we make. We aim to supplement—not supplant—traditional as well as much critical scholarship.

3. For Aronson, hope becomes privatized when grand, collectivist, and secular hopes for social progress are lost, and what remains are "only partial and limited social projects and an infinity of individual ones" (p. 480). Aronson wrote that "what distinguishes the newly privatized hope is precisely the mutation of what had previously been regarded as public themes into private ones" (p. 480). Now private, localized hope may be all that we can really have, and there is nothing necessarily wrong with that. Still, the trend toward privatization is frightening. For example, an article in *The New York Times* (Uchitelle, 2007) reported that today's "titans often see themselves as pillars" of a new age of prosperity, "one in which their successes and philanthropy have made government less important than it once was" (p. 3).

4. We acknowledge that Rorty is an extremely controversial figure. Few people who read him remain unmoved, one way or the other. Margolis (2002) went as far as to call the differences between Dewey and Rorty's versions of pragmatism "irreconcilable" (p. 119). Perhaps the kindest description that we have been able to find regarding Rorty's relationship to classical pragmatism comes from Blake (2007), who wrote that Rorty "has picked up the dusty old windowpane called pragmatism he found in the attic above the philosophy building and laid it down hard on his desk, cracking what was once a single piece of glass into a spider's web of delicate shards" (p. 98).

Part Two

CHAPTER 5

Perspectivalism and Cosmopolitanism

In Part I of this book, we established our conceptual, philosophical, and methodological research assumptions. We defined democracy as traditionally understood and extended it to include what we call creative democracy, one far more rich and diverse than what we now experience in the United States as marketplace democracy or marketplace diversity. We emphasized the importance of social justice for our project and attacked the "entertainment mode" of citizenship, contrasting it with a critical imagination. We discussed communication as epistemic, as well as the communicative imagination, an important extension and application of the critical imagination and the citizenship ethos which follows it. We ended Part I by exploring the methodologies and philosophical assumptions particular to the reflexive, anti-foundational critical scholarship in the neo-pragmatic tradition.

Foremost among our philosophical and critical assumptions is belief in the potential of human beings to make and to remake their worlds in light of important humanistic values—such as political inclusion, substantive equality, a commitment to reducing suffering, and a hostility to excessive privilege and aristocracy—to resist despair through the power of communication and redescription. Moreover, we argued, it is essential as conscientious, progressive citizens to work toward a social condition where a critical democracy could become possible, where *all* human beings matter—have an intrinsic or "immanent" value as humans—and where everyone has the tools and resources to flourish intellectually and creatively in her or his fashion; a place where interdependence is recognized and honored, and compassion is expressed passionately and unconditionally throughout society. In the words of Cornel West (2002), we "have to cut through all forms of provincialism, parochialism, and tribalism—this is the perennial struggle of being a progressive" (p. 13).

Contrary to how West's sentiment might appear, our vision for the future is not utopian or wishful thinking in the negative sense of an unwillingness to engage the world and human nature as it *is*. We neither believe in human nature nor in the inevitability of the current state of the world; nothing has to be as we find it currently. Rather, what we offer is a tacit recognition that humans, and humans alone, are responsible for our problems as a species—in particular, our cultural ones, and that recognizing this reality, and deciding to do something about it, constitutes a tremendous power, a power that we already have as people but are encouraged by systemic education and the media to ignore. Our argument is utopian only in the sense that humans need a goal and will strong enough to pursue it (Nietzsche, 1954/1976), and we join with others such as Cornel West in acknowledging this condition.

More practically, Rorty's (2006) defense against the charge of utopianism is compelling. Rorty (2006) asserted that the "only way we can criticize current social rules is by reference to utopian notions which proceed by taking elements in the tradition and showing how unfulfilled they are" (p. 25). Likewise, Zinn (2002b) remarked that to "be hopeful in bad times is not just foolishly romantic. It is based on the fact that human history is a history not only of cruelty, but also of compassion, sacrifice, courage, kindness" (p. 32). Zinn reminded us that small "acts, when multiplied by millions of people, can transform the world" (p. 32). Recognizing the power that comes from Nietzsche, Rorty, and Zinn's sentiments is the first step in rethinking the future, to remake it consciously in the image we construct, and to honor our collective global dreams for a secure, healthy, and sustainable life free from hatred and despair. Although there are other goals we could posit for human beings, such as outworn racist, sexist, nationalist, or class-based ones, as have been formulated in the past with tragic results, we agree with Rorty (1999b) when he asserted that "hope for social justice is . . . the only basis for a worthwhile human life" (p. 204). If we are in any sense religious, it would be in this temporal, but no less inspiring humanistic sense. Humanity is our faith. In Dewey's (1917/1993h) words, "Faith in the power of intelligence to imagine a future which is the projection of the desirable in the present, and to invent the instrumentalities of its realization, is our salvation" (p. 9).

As scholars situated in the humanities, we see it as our *raison d'être* to search out and help nurture worthwhile human lifestyles and cultural/political arrangements.[1] Traditionally, religion in its various forms has served with some success this goal, but largely, we think, with undesirable side effects. Left political movements, to which we are much more sympathetic, have also faltered in this goal, perpetuating many of the evils they attempted to eradicate. Nevertheless, as Rorty (1999b) noted, "The Marxists were absolutely right about one thing: the soul of history *is* economic" (p. 227). What Rorty meant by this is simple: resources matter. As Hadler (1999) noted:

> Longevity correlates less with the wealth of the nation than with the magnitude of the discrepancy in the wealth of its citizens. People who are less well off in countries that are more stratified fare less well, even if they are better off than the poor in countries that are less stratified. (p. 617)

Hadler added, "But the poor always die younger than those who are better off" (p. 617).

Rorty was no Marxist, and he was fashionably anticommunist; nevertheless, as he (1999b) lamented:

> [T]he last few decades have witnessed the increasing inability to believe that some day we shall ever have a classless global society: one in which there are no vast differences between the opportunities open to children in one nation and in another, or between those open to children in one section of a city and those in another section of the same city. (p. 230)

"Classless," in the sense in which Rorty used the term, means little more than traditional Americanism in its idealized form, in which everyone has an opportunity to be part of the same civic community, one committed to the well-being of all; a society in which the rulers and the ruled were pretty much the same people; a society without institutionalized privilege; and one in which no one suffers from preventable pain. Rorty (1999a) said it best when he wrote:

> Our children need to learn, early on, to see the inequalities between their own fortunes and those of other children as neither the Will of God nor the necessary price for economic efficiency, but as an evitable tragedy. They should start thinking, as early as possible, about how the world might be changed so as to ensure that no one goes hungry while others have a surfeit. (p. 218)

In this chapter, we explore further traditional and creative meanings of democracy and citizenship and argue that we do not have to accept narrow—or what we call "thin"—descriptions of democracy. Instead, we should insist that democracy can, and should, involve a cultivation of individual capacities, personal and communal well-being, and human solidarity. A thick description of democracy and citizenship helps us to imagine if not a "classless" society, one that is more radically egalitarian than what exists currently. Toward that end, our view of democracy as "creative" rejects militarism, imperialism, and corporatism—three cornerstones of U.S. might and the three major threats to U.S. democracy—and insists on the cultivation of human moral intelligence[2] and "thick" substantive meanings of democratic social interaction within both the United States and in our dealings with people throughout the rest of the world. We sketch the need to view democracy in terms wider than how it has been conceived of previously in this country.

We reject on equity grounds formalistic notions of democracy (as described in Swartz, 2004a, 2004b) and view excessive hierarchy as dysfunctional to the health of a creative, inclusive society. We argue that democracy, in the sense we celebrate it here, involves a sustained commitment to integrity and freedom of individuals to maximize their talents, form their self-identities, and work in conjunction with others to construct and reconstruct their lives. Although voting and procedural accountability are undoubtedly important, in themselves, they are not adequate for insuring the type of progressive society that we envision. We look at existing democracies, especially our own, and see much that is lacking (Sklar, 2003).

The terms "thin" and "thick" come from anthropologist Clifford Geertz's (1973) classic description of observation in the context of anthropology. Geertz distinguished *thick descriptions* from thin ones in that the former are comprised of deep readings (i.e., "stratified hierarch[ies] of meaningful structures," p. 6) of symbols to understand as wide as possible their meanings. The goal is to add additional, richer layers of understandings by moving beyond the limitations of assuming that one understands because one has a collection of facts. Thick descriptions help to contextualize those facts—the classic example being Geertz's distinction between "twitches," "winks," and their variations.[3]

In contrast, *thin descriptions* are interpretations of symbols at a superficial level, the level at which they are prescribed by authority and presented to others for uncritical acceptance. In evoking this distinction, we maintain that knowledge of democracy, in the sense that we evoke the term, constitutes a personal living through, a celebration of, a movement beyond a particular instance or form (i.e., the normal or assumed practices of our constitutional system) to explore context and reconceptualize the way in which a cultural expression is manifest and made meaningful through the experiences of a community. In this way, we begin to immerse ourselves within the tensions experienced by people in this country rather than assume the existence of a community. Community, in this sense, is conceptualized as an act, not an end product. We do not assume that a community simply exists outside of or above any contextual event or situational context; rather, we are interested in the ways in which community is formed in response to specific cultural, political, and social circumstances.[4] Rorty's (1996b) comments, although more than 10 years old, are even more true today:

> The existence of a moral community which can plausibly and without qualification identify itself as "we, the people of the United States" is still a project rather than an actuality. In a few respects, my country is closer to accomplishing this project now than it has been ever been, thanks to the Civil Rights Revolution of the 1960s and to the continuing pressure exerted by feminists. In most respects, however, it is losing ground. For the gap between rich and poor Americans is widening steadily, and the latter are increasingly bereft of hope for their childrens' future. (p. 11)

A more specific example of viewing community as incomplete and reacting to social/historical conditions can be found in Baker (1995). In his description of the Black, Southern community, Baker argued that it is

> possible to acknowledge that racial segregation in the United States both necessitated and gave birth to a remarkable black southern public sphere . . . in its codes of class, patriotism, respectability, dissent, consensus, tolerance, justice and ethics, the

> black public sphere offered a sometimes radical critique of the dominant white society with which it coexisted. (p. 23)

In this case, the Black community was manifest in response to the tensions of living within a racist culture; it did not necessarily coherently exist outside of the felt tensions of being Other within an incredibly unjust society. This condition holds true for many other communities, or publics, other than the Black community; tension, context, and responsiveness all enable individuals to collectively join with one another and communities to take shape. Dewey frequently emphasized the importance of "associated living" and "habits of interaction" and a fundamental interdependence among communities. Through the different expressions of associated living, people create and maintain publics. These publics exist under "conditions of flux" (Brouwer & Squires, 2003, p. 210). Viewing community as an act of continuous manifesting, diminishing, and reshaping allows us to avoid a fixed and complete notion of community that would further limit the understanding of the importance of community as a transformative and redescriptive force.

Our plan for Part II of this book is as follows. We first offer a corrective vision for the Greek concept of the *idiots* or idiot, a phenomenon dangerously present in the United States today. Specifically, in Chapter 6, we discuss the ideas of Friedrich Nietzsche, Ralph Waldo Emerson, John Dewey, and Richard Rorty, four immensely inspiring and edifying writers. We argue that their work continues to provide a rich source of ideas for challenging thin descriptions of democracy, creating new descriptions by which we can change and grow as a society. Their ideas are especially relevant intellectually for moving us beyond a thin interpretation of democracy as primarily a system of political governance, elections, and laws to one in which democracy is better understood as a way of life, an ethos one takes with regard to self and others. Their work offers rich intellectual material for invigorating a conception of a more empowered, creative, and socially conscious citizenship. In discussing each of these figures, our intent is both to offer a motif by which this construct we create—the critical, historicist, progressive individual—can be imagined and cultivated for engaging in the democratic process we describe, and to offer a culturally richer and more meaningful understanding of democracy than the one that exists currently in the United States.

Before discussing each of these thinkers in terms of their contributions to our project, we first, however, in this chapter, clear the philosophical ground for the type of constructive growth that we seek to nurture. By de-centering or resituating notions of the "real" in a rhetorical perspectivalism, we use our communicative imaginations to highlight the rhetorical and communicative constructions of our everyday lives and, thereby, contextualize our epistemological world within a radical, historicist anti-essentialism. We apply what we have learned here to Chapter 7 to unpack the interconnections between power, alienation, and communication.

Perspectivalism: De-Centering the "Real"

As the neo-pragmatist, postmodern, communicative orientation of our creative democracy suggests, notions of the "real"—the material and social world we take for granted—must be historicized and decentered to move beyond self-imposed limitations of the possible. In other words, all constructs are simply that—constructs—and they must be situated morally—for example, in Nietzsche's and Foucault's genealogies (Foucault, 1984a) and questioned. They should not be blindly accepted in any realist sense—but rather, situated in what, following Nietzsche, Hatab (1995) called "an open field of interpretations" (p. 146). Such contextualization allows us to engage critically with our life-world, the backdrop of our existential horizons, and our being-with-others in the possibilities of the moment (Habermas, 1985). Historicized and contextualized, the democratic principles of equality, liberty, and justice for all are not givens but, instead, are ideas—and they must be contended for among competing visions in the ideological environment in which we exist. As Dewey (1939/1993a) argued, we need to shift our thinking such that instead of thinking of our "dispositions and habits as accommodated to certain institutions we have to learn to think of the latter as expressions, projections and extensions of habitually dominant personal attitudes" (p. 241). Instead of thinking of democracy as something we take part in at particular moments in time, such as when we vote, we ought to think of the ways in which we enact democracy on a daily basis—that is, how behaviors and interactions might be influenced by an overall democratic sensibility. As Dewey (1939/1993a) explained, "Democracy is a *personal* way of individual life; that is, it signifies the possession and continual use of certain attitudes, forming personal character, and determining desire and purpose in all the relations of life" (p. 241).

When ideas of equality, liberty, and social justice become habitually assumed, they permeate all aspects of life and become interconnected with our interactions and behavior rather than being something separate from our everyday behavior that we only "practice" during key moments. Phrases such as "an exercise in democracy," "practicing democracy," or "our democratic duty" become irrelevant when a democratic sensibility is an element of our character. In other words:

> Democracy as a personal, individual, way of life involves nothing fundamentally new. But when applied it puts a new practical meaning in old ideas. Put into effect it signifies that powerful present enemies of democracy can be successfully met only

> by the creation of personal attitudes in individual human beings; that we must get over our tendency to think that its defense can be found in any external means whatever, whether military or civil, if they are separated from individual attitudes so deep-seated as to constitute personal character. (Dewey, 1939/1993a, pp. 241–242)

As Dewey's passage makes clear, "society" is the manifestation of who we are as individuals, collectively and interdependently—with few exceptions, we also are connected with others through our actions. The self and society are inextricably woven—without others, the self has no meaning, is unable to develop; without individuals, there is no society. Merely being alive in the world today means we have an impact on the lives of others without even being aware of it (e.g., through our occupation or our consumptive habits).[5] To change the way we do things as a society, we must change the way we do things as individuals. If we are to break free from the limitations of our current thinking, which supports social injustice and hierarchy, and move beyond the limitations of the status quo, we must begin to talk, think, and act differently as did C. P. Ellis, the former leader of the Ku Klux Klan we discussed in Chapter 3. In an amazing transformation later in his life, Ellis rejected his racist past and became a respected and influential civil rights and labor activist. What we learn from Ellis, and from other people who have had the courage to change and grow along with their language and self-descriptions, is that transformation happens when we are willing to "step into another's shoes" and view reality from different points of view—that is, to demonstrate perspectivalism. Perspectivalism requires a suspension of the belief systems we have come to accept and an ability to understand in a concrete, emotional, and cognitive manner the lives and values of others (Alexander, 1995). This is the communicative imagination in action: the ability to understand the ways in which the narratives and explanations for social issues are perspectival and to use communication for community building—sort of a Tower of Babel in reverse.

Consider, for example, our provocative claim that constructs such as gender, race, religion, and national origin are not *givens*, for they are not found in nature in ways that we suspect commonly. These categories, therefore, are not structurally grounded in reality or the eternal. They are not immutable. They are not gifts or designs from a deity, nor do they embody in-and-of-themselves any hierarchy of value—they are not to be confused as constituting the "essence" of people. Like playing cards, they have meaning only in terms of a particular game—other than that, cards are merely paper, plastic, and ink. The pleasure we get from playing cards comes not from the cards but from the meanings we attach to them. Otherwise stated, the cards are no different from the "coins" that Nietzsche (1954/1976) famously described to illustrate what he meant by the contingency of truth. Coins hold value only to the extent that their value is recognized by us; eventually, the pictures on the coins rub off through years of handling and matter to humans only as metal. As Nietzsche explained:

> What, then is truth? A mobile army of metaphors, metonyms, and anthropmorphisms—in short, a sum of human relations, which have been enhanced, transposed, and embellished poetically and rhetorically, and which after long use seem firm, canonical, and obligatory to a people: truths are illusions about which one has forgotten that this is what they are; metaphors which are worn out and without sensuous power; coins which have lost their pictures and now matter only as metal, no longer as coins. (p. 47)

To be "truthful," Nietzsche concluded, "means using the customary metaphors… the obligation to lie according to a fixed convention" (p. 47).

When people commonly talk about Truth, what they typically mean is that there is something that is timeless, ahistorical, and non-contingent that can be known and understood as such by rational human beings. Something is not Truth if it is true today and false tomorrow. It is not Truth if one person believes in X and another rational person does not. Truth, as it is frequently asserted, is "self-evident." In the end, there can be no confusion. Part of the power of Truth is its ability to dispel illusion, as light chases the shadows from the crevices. According to this theory of Truth, every human being, if she or he can "polish" her or his mind effectively, can learn to reflect back the Truth of the ages—an idea famously critiqued by Rorty (1979). If Truth does not meet these needs and criteria, it is not Truth but something else.[6]

Obviously, readers may not agree with our line of reasoning, and there is no reason why, other than our ability of persuasion, they should. As philosopher Bertrand Russell (1928/1993) wisely pointed out, "We must be skeptical even of our skepticism" (p. 109). We must not, as critics, create even the appearance of a crude postmodern nihilism, the type of world that Nietzsche himself rejected (see Kaufmann, 1974). Still, the question that is important for all people to confront is: Do we live in a world in which the primary responsibility for constructing it, taking care of it, nurturing it, and changing it is ourselves, or do we allow standards of meanings to be placed outside of ourselves to rule over us?

The above question, in a nutshell, concerns the sense in which truth becomes understood from the neo-pragmatic framework that we endorse. Constructs such as gender, race and the like only have importance in small, localized, and idiosyncratic ways—they are, first and foremost, expressions of style, games we play to get what we want, idealizations of "movies" that we project in our mind. Some games we are forced to play by other people's racism or sexism, as when people label others, expect things from them, or act on them, but this is an example of power in its traditional sense and means only that among the contingencies of the world, there exist bullies and mean people, people who seek to deprive others of their self-descriptions. Recognizing the presence of such people is not to belittle the importance that these perspectives have for individuals and groups of people who take pride in a reified racial or sexual form (e.g., the "Chicano," "Black," or "Gay" pride movements); rather, it is to recognize that they have significance *only* to the extent that an individual experiences it as such (and we may also be our worst bullies, having internalized society's biases and hatreds).[7] This desire to universalize our joys or our pain, noted Nietzsche (1954/1976), is an after-effect of our prior beliefs in eternal forms, a desire to invest our lives with transcendental or metaphysical meaning. This is an example of what Rorty (2006) described as "Nietzsche's quasi pragmatism" (p. 19). More specifically, Rorty (1999b) viewed the post-Nietzschean tradition and the pragmatist tradition as linked in moving aside both Plato and Kant; that is, the belief "that there are unconditional transcultural moral obligations, obligations rooted in an unchanging, ahistorical human nature" (p. xvi). No matter how comforting to humans such purposes may be, it removes an important agency from them. To attribute to them any greater significance is to argue for, and to accept, our limitations and to impose those limitations on our children.

Restated, categories such as race, gender, religion, and national origin are superficial in the strongest sense of the term, created and maintained for the political and social economies they service (for a persuasive argument, see Haney-López, 1998). The fact that these terms exist means that they remain important in that economy. Terms that lose their cultural importance—such as "miscegenation," "racial pride," "blood lines," "illegitimacy," "wedlock," and "divine right of kings"—drop out of circulation, thankfully, becoming the curiosities of social historians. In other words, the constructs that we think we find in nature are *takens*, concepts that humans have molded from the raw material of nature for their use; hence, they are conveniences for getting the human things we want done (Dewey, 1929/2005).

We learn from Nietzsche (1901/1968) that facts do not exist but only interpretations based on our needs, that all observations are theory laden and anthropomorphic, and that what we often call truth is error in relationship to error. As Nietzsche noted, "The world in which we are concerned is false, i.e., is not a fact but a fable and approximation on the basis of a meager sum of observations; it is 'in flux,' as something in a state of becoming, as a falsehood always changing but never getting near the truth" (p. 330). In other words, our understandings of the world are human through-and-through, forcing others, when we can, to conform to our prejudices. Education, therefore, in the sense that we discuss it here and throughout this book, should not be aimed at codifying these distinctions, as that would be a lie—an error in relationships to error—an attempt to box in and assign an essence to things, which, by our experience, change in relationship to us.

In less philosophical terms, such error in relationship with error has traditionally been known as the "banking model of education" (Freire, 1970/2000), in which experts capture truth and transmit it through supposedly clear and unfettered channels of communication to intellectually prepared and ideologically screened students who are prepared to accept it, as chicks, wide mouthed, accept nourishment from their parents. Instead, education should be seen for what it is, a radical act—it is the way by which we interpret the interpreter who, in turn, interprets us through the dialogic process (we discuss this in more detail in Chapters 8 and 9).

This is the dialogical approach to education we have been discussing, education as deinstitutionalization and resistance to reification—education as freedom. In this way, we resist placing into our children our values so that the future may justify ourselves (for the most part, the banking model of education is wholly egotistical in that the educators teach to justify themselves rather than for the goal of their students surpassing them). Rejecting this view is disturbing to many people who want the future to be no different from the past and, thus, fear a dialogical and progressive education. As McDermott (1989) explained:

> For some, to see ourselves as transients rather than as participants in some fixed scheme, is chilling, even depressing. Yet, for a wider vantage point, such an attitude is liberating for it places the meaning of our lives in our own hands. If we see ourselves as creators rather than as followers, our experience takes on a texture of possibility too often closed off to those of us whose eyes are fixed on an eternal meaning. The pragmatic approach is clearly temporalistic and finite, thereby placing enormous emphasis on the moral gravity of all of our activities. (p. 255)

It is important, we argue, that we learn to realize how our beliefs in "real" constructs, such as race and sex, control and often limit our experience of the world; we tend to see the world as women or men, Black or White, or Jew or gentile. For many people, these things matter and, hence, they are content. That does not mean, however, that *we* should be content with being boxed in by the limitations of others.[8]

Each identification we have in the world, be it religious, political, social, racial, or gendered, brings with it a wealth of perspectives, as well as many limitations. The key is to realize, as Burke (1966) explained, that any one way of seeing blinds us from seeing something else; each coloring of the world, each identification, accentuates one aspect of reality, and blurs, or obscures, another. Furthermore, there is no place where we can stand, or where we can teach our children to stand, that will give us the larger or more complete picture of the way things "really" are. The best we can do is to equip ourselves to see the world through different lenses, to experience the world from other points of view, and to encourage our children to do the same.

To help readers understand how this coloring of experience works, think for a moment about how a photograph or television works. When we contemplate a snapshot or watch television, we must be careful to not be led into thinking that the image before us represents or has captured a piece of the world as it is. The pictures on television or in newspapers are nothing but perspectives; they are small ideologically mediated slices of the world that direct our thinking in conceptual and limiting terms. Since we cannot appreciate the total "essence" of the world, and because such an essence does not exist, it is useful and practical to have certain perspectives accentuated. Thus, we must never forget that the picture is not the "thing," just like we must never forget that any particular religious, political, or racial perspective is not the "correct" description of human nature. Rather, each perspective is simply one interpretation, one snapshot of a larger phenomenon called the human experience that cannot be accurately represented.[9]

A further barrier to engaging in transformative communication, thought, and, thus, human development is adherence to dogmas and reliance on transcendent authorities for moral decision making. For example, saturating our communication with absolutist terms such as "truth," "inevitability," and "right" hinders opportunities for working together toward change, growth, and connectedness, which benefits and respects the diversity of human life. As Dewey (1935/1993b) pointed out, such commitment "is always the fruit of dogma; intelligence does not pretend to know save as a result of experimentation, the opposite of preconceived dogma" (p. 147). In other words, varying perspectives, belief systems and worldviews are critical to the diversity needed for creative resolutions to problems. Dogmatic thinking and systems of thought that proclaim to be the "only right way" strip democracy of its strength and potential to cultivate a society in which freedom of ideas and diverse ways of life can coexist and contribute to the enrichment of the collective. Such diversity is not merely something to be tolerated; diversity has inherent value because human potential "is dependent upon cultural diversity for its realization; human beings blossom only in the context of other humans" (Swartz, 2005, p. 123). Fundamentalism and foundationalist notions of Truth hinder transformative communication, suppress diversity, and deny the capacity of human beings to develop; they also foster the idea that hierarchy is necessary and that we cannot trust people to collectively solve problems. As noted by Rodriguez (2001):

> It is difficult for most of us to fathom nonhierarchical human relations. For without hierarchy, religion threatens us with damnation, government threatens us with anarchy, society threatens us with lawlessness, capital threatens us with underdevelopment, and education threatens us with regression to animality…constant to all the arguments is a deep distrust of human beings. Hierarchy supposedly controls our evil and destructive ways and makes for better human beings. (p. 17)

As Rodriguez pointed out, hierarchy is often believed to be necessary, for humans cannot be trusted to learn how to make decisions that promote their well-being. Without authority, tradition, and "law and order," human beings would not thrive. This belief, however, is an impoverished view of humans and is antithetical to the democratic ideal that trusts the human potential for creating a better future. Dewey (1939/1993g, p. 205) noted that "democratic ends demand democratic methods for their realization," and that much of this trust grounding such methods is lacking. As Dewey further argued:

> In homes and in schools, the places where the essentials of character are supposed to be formed, the usual procedure is settlement of issues, intellectual and moral, by appeal to the "authority" of parent, teacher, or textbook. Dispositions formed under such conditions are so inconsistent with the democratic method that in a crises they may be aroused to act in positively anti-democratic ways for anti-democratic ends; just as resort to coercive force and suppression of civil liberties are readily palliated in normally democratic communities when the cry is raised that "law and order" are threatened. (p. 229)

A more useful way of working toward the democratic society that we describe is a commitment to a community-centered, participatory, deliberative democratic process. Taken from Dewey's theory of deliberative democracy, such a process utilizes the rich, active, local environment of the community to shape norms and social practices. Communal inquiry, dialogue, and experimentation with resolutions to problems in local communities offer ways to contribute to knowledge for social development, taking into account the needs and visions of diverse groups represented in specific communities. A central trope in this process is creative democracy as *cosmopolitanism*.

Nussbaum's (1994) notion of cosmopolitanism best describes, we think, the summative goal of the four thinkers we discuss in Chapter 6. Such profound cosmopolitanism, what Nussbaum (p. 15) described as an escape "from the comfort of local truths, from the warm nestling feeling of patriotism, from the absorbing drama of pride in oneself and one's own," demands that we understand the individual in light of our power for self-reflection and redescription. Cosmopolitanism recognizes that all of our inherited characteristics are accidents of time and chance. Thus, as Nussbaum noted:

> We should not allow differences of nationality or class or ethnic membership or even gender to erect barriers between us and our fellow human beings. We should recognize humanity wherever it occurs, and give its fundamental ingredients, reason and moral capacity, our first allegiance and respect. (p. 7)

Nussbaum continued by writing, "we should give our first allegiance to no mere form of government, no temporal power, but to the moral community made up by the humanity of all human beings" (p. 7).

To be such a citizen, however, does not, noted Nussbaum (1994), mean that we have to give up our local idiosyncratic quirks, as they remain quite important to us as individuals. All politics are, as the slogan states correctly, local. In fact, all the progressive intellectuals discussed in the next chapter see this as the particular strength of humans as a species. Rather, Nussbaum suggested that we think of ourselves as in the middle of ever larger circles:

> The first one is drawn around the self; the next takes in one's immediate family; then follows the extended family; then, in order, one's neighbors or local group, one's fellow city-dwellers, one's fellow countrymen—and we can easily add to this list groupings based on ethnic, linguistic, historical, professional, gender and sexual identities. Outside all these circles is the largest one, that of humanity as a whole. (p. 9)

We are each, therefore, already connected to a larger whole. This largest circle represents that which is common to all humans. It transcends the local and is something to which we can all speak.

Conclusion

In our effort to work to achieve the cosmopolitanism that Nussbaum (1994) wrote about, in what follows, we use the ideas of four critical intellectuals discussed in the next chapter, selected for their culturally useful and inspirational perspectives on communication, irony, and belief in the human potential, to develop an alternative and culturally richer description of democracy (i.e., "creative democracy") as an idea and as a normative aspiration rather than merely a political system. Using ideas offered by Nietzsche, Emerson, Dewey, and Rorty, we highlight the value of a postmodern democratic cosmopolitanism, one in which the "real" will have been decentered and replaced by a perspectival agon (Hatab, 1995). Such cosmopolitanism stresses self-reliance, knowledge as a communal, perspectival process rather than as access to ahistorical truth, and how "ironism," the ability to see the limitations, as well as the strengths of our beliefs, can help us to develop a sense of solidarity with our fellow human beings.

Notes

1. In Rorty's (1999b) terms, we see it as our job to "instill doubts in the students about the students' own self-images and about the society to which they belong" (p. 127). We aim to be the teachers Rorty (1999b) celebrated "who help insure that the moral consciousness of each new generation is slightly different from that of the previous generation" (p. 127).

2. Brouwer and Squires (2003) wrote that "Dewey argued that intelligence was not an individual possession but something that had to be integrated into the social matrix, hence his call for us to think of 'social intelligence' rather than individual intelligence" (p. 208).

3. By engaging a "thick description" of an event, a critic, according to Geertz, can delineate the difference between an "involuntary twitch" such as a "blink" (i.e., a physiological response to a foreign irritant such as bright light or sand) and a camaraderie "wink" between two "conspirators."

4. See Underwood & Frey's (2007) on communication and community in which they discussed the difference between a transmission-based and constitutive view of the relationship between these things.

5. Writing for the United Nations, Kent (2002) argued that world hunger can be attributed, in part, to international trade (see also Mousseau & Mittal, 2006, who discussed how food-deficit nations focus their agricultural production on non-food commodities for export, such as tobacco and coffee).

6. We are not here or elsewhere talking about truth in its small, obvious sense. Clearly, there exist practical standards for determining true statements from false ones. The sentence, "The keys are on the table" is either true or false depending on where the keys are in relationship to the table. That the Earth circles the sun, the moon controls the tides, or that the human gestation period is approximately 9 months, are all correct statements. However, that is not the type of truth that we are talking about here. These types of "truths" do not have any moral or epistemological significance (see Rorty, 1998c).

7. Frye (1983) pointed out that "many of the restrictions and limitations we live with are more or less internalized and self-monitored, and are part of our adaptations to the requirements and expectations imposed by the needs and tastes and tyrannies of others" (p. 14).

8. It is these chains, as much as any other, that we want to smash. Like Foucault's work in general, we write to eviscerate the selves that others have forced us to be, to no longer slave under the representations of others.

9. This point can be made in another way, as originally illustrated by Burke (1966). Take any object, such as a vase. Photograph that object with different colored filters. Do not move the camera and do not change the lighting. If we do these things, each picture will be different; the pictures will vary not only in color but also in tone and texture. Each filter will accentuate a certain part of the vase and deflect our attention from another part. Moreover, the relationship between the vase and the background will change, depending on the color of the filter. The vase does not only exist in time and space but also in terms of our perceptions. It is "real" only to the extent, and in such a way, that we perceive it to be. In a similar fashion, our identifications of such constructs as gender, race, and national origin affect the way we and our children see and interact with the world.

CHAPTER 6

The Contribution of Four Philosophers to This Project

In this chapter, we ground our notion of creative democracy in the writings of Friedrich Nietzsche, Ralph Waldo Emerson, John Dewey, and Richard Rorty. Creative democracy, as we see it, maintains that democracy is a state of mind, a commitment to promoting social justice and inclusion, and a cultural way of being that places the potentiality and humanity of people above blind allegiance to religious dogma, Rule of Law, patriotism, the U.S. Constitution, or other stifling meta-narratives (see Swartz, 2004a; 2004b). Democracy is more than a political system; it is an attitude, a state of mind that orients people to be committed to the idea that there is always more that we can do to be more inclusive and creative, and that human beings are reservoirs of potential that have not been fully tapped into. This view of democracy believes that our best days as a species have yet to arrive. This alternative vision of democracy provides the backdrop against which the primary topics of this book unfold; these are the ways in which we can engage communication in such a way that we empower ourselves and others to recognize and work against systemic alienation and become agents for social justice.

All four of the thinkers we discuss in this chapter—Nietzsche, Emerson, Dewey, and Rorty—start from the assumption, discussed in the previous chapter, that the "real" is a fiction, and in their different ways, they set out to decenter that fiction. All of them maintain that what counts as truth is the socially appropriate manipulation of rhetorical tropes and figures, and that the use of such tropes and figures is morally, socially, and politically consequential, demanding our great attention as intellectualizing beings. In other words, all four thinkers argue, very strenuously, for a revitalized human agency as the source and resource of knowledge and community life. What follows from their collective ideas is something like what we have been calling, using Dewey's (1939/1993a) term, a "creative democracy."

Nietzsche, Cultural Criticism, and the "Good American"

At first glance, including Nietzsche in this group of democratic theorists appears to be mistaken, as he is not normally thought of as a democratic thinker or as politically progressive in the traditional left-right-wing topology.[1] In the most literal sense, Nietzsche is *not* a democrat and he is politically a reactionary. He wrote frequently and fervently to denounce the democracies of his day and belittle the democratic ethos unleashed by the French Revolution (which we, as progressive democrats, endorse). He frequently condemned socialism, anarchism, and other so-called "leveling" movements, and was a tireless apologist for aristocracy and cultural elitism. This is *not* the Nietzsche that we find heuristic, just as we reject the allegedly misogynist Nietzsche, and the Nietzsche who was twisted by proto-Nazis at the end of his life, and by Nazis after his death, into supporting fascist and anti-Semitic ideology. There is, however, much more to Nietzsche than this baggage, however substantial and erroneous it may be (Kaufmann, 1974). Although Nietzsche was undeniably intolerant politically of democracy, he was, spiritually, in our opinion, among the most edifying and democratic of thinkers—the most attuned to the illusions and limitations of alienation and reification—whose cultural criticism provides us with much inspiration for the social and political tasks of this book.

Although we reject Nietzsche's politics as aristocratic, elitist, and hostile to the democratic values we champion, we laud, as do other scholars (e.g., Brown, 2000; Hatab, 1995), his ability and willingness to challenge openly his society to improve itself, thus inspiring future generations of critics to engage energetically and sharply with their society. Like no other thinker of whom we are aware, Nietzsche frees us from ourselves as pigeonholed and static individuals wrapped in our warm comforts, and he frees us from the cocooning effects of dogmatic belief and the dependence on authority and tradition. Nietzsche believed in the creative, curative power of the human spirit, and the limitless possibilities of the human potential, and he recognized the reticence of the status quo to allow for change. He waged an intellectual war against this reticence to revitalize what he discerned was a decline in the sustainability of the human race—the decline of the human spirit. No less than the esteemed radical Emma Goldman, a feminist anarchist (someone whom Nietzsche presumably would have found repugnant), found Nietzsche to be inspiring. Referring to Nietzsche in her autobiography, Goldman (1931/1970) wrote, "The magic of his language, the beauty of his vision, carried me to undreamed-of heights" (p. 172). A few lines later, Goldman added:

> I had to do my reading at the expense of much-needed sleep; but what was physical strain in view of my raptures over Nietzsche? The fire of his soul, the rhythm of his song, made life richer, fuller, and more wonderful for me. (p. 172)

Goldman (1917/1969) lectured on Nietzsche and considered him a "giant mind" (p. 44) and went so far as to declare that "Nietzsche was not a social theorist, but a poet, a rebel, and innovator. His aristocracy was neither of birth nor of purse; it was the spirit. In that respect Nietzsche was an anarchist and all true Anarchists were aristocrats" (1931/1970, p. 194).[2]

Goldman's sentiment reflects the Nietzsche we embrace, the thinker most associated with the idea that the collapse of "cognitive, moral, and metaphysical warrants" will disrupt confidence in traditional hierarchical systems (Hatab, 1995, p. 11). Nietzsche reminded us that critical, partisan, and passionate engagements in the things that matter subjectively *are what matters*, not the platitudes and herd thinking pervasive in many democratic societies. Hatab, author of a provocative book on the democratic potentials of Nietzschean thought, cited approvingly, as do we, the French philosopher and political activist Claude Lefort (1988), who argued that "democracy is instituted and sustained by the *dissolution of the markers of certainty*. It inaugurates a history in which people experience a fundamental indeterminacy as to the basis of power, law and knowledge" (p. 19).

Nietzsche, who was born in 1844, lived in a deeply troubled era, a time when the seeds of future world wars and mass social upheaval were being sowed. Nietzsche (1908/1967b) discerned many of these evils and attempted to warn his society, which remained oblivious, about them:

> For when truth enters into a fight with the lies of millennia, we shall have upheavals, a convulsion of earthquakes, a moving of mountains and valleys, the likes of which has never been dreamed of. The concept of politics will have merged entirely with a war of spirits; all power structures of the old society will have been exploded—all of them are based on lies: there will be wars the like of which have never yet been seen on earth. (p. 327)

Nietzsche wrote not as a German but as a self-identified "good European," a person above petty provincialism (in effect, what Rorty, 2000, would call a "featherless biped"). For example, in a letter to his mother, Nietzsche wrote, "For even if I should be a bad German—in any case *I am a very good European*" (cited in Kaufmann, 1974, p. 44). Elsewhere, Nietzsche (1878/1996) wrote that one "should not be afraid to proclaim oneself simply a good European and actively to work for the amalgamation of nations" (p. 175). In this statement, Nietzsche expressed his "untimely" commitment to a diverse range of progressive projects and positions, such as to Voltaire, the Enlightenment, racial intermarriage, and intellectual integrity in the face of religion and the state hegemony.

Although we, and presumably others, find Nietzsche's sentiment inspiring, this was an uncommon and unpopular notion at the time that Nietzsche wrote, when the modern nation-states of Europe were taking form, buttressed by the vilest forms of nationalism and colonialism. Two world wars and almost a hundred years were needed for the importance of Nietzsche's sentiment to take hold on the Continent (as of March 2007, the European Union celebrated its fiftieth anniversary). In this respect, Europe is to be applauded, even as the Europeans have much work to do. Although the nation states of the European Union (EU) still exist, they have given up much of their sovereignty in the interest of a wider pan-European solidarity and political vision, and we wish them well on their project. In fact, we agree fully with Rorty (2003) when he cited the development of the EU approvingly, seeing it, among other things, as a hopeful counterbalance to U.S. hegemony. As Rorty (2003) argued, "The European Union is the only likely sponsor of an alternative to Washington's project of a permanent *pax Americana*" (p. 24).

Across the Atlantic, however, in the United States, the cosmopolitanism of which Nietzsche spoke still has not taken hold, despite the increased heterogeneity of our society. In fact, quite the opposite has occurred. Since September 11, 2001, much talk has centered on what it means to be a "good American" and to define this creature in some essential way as *different* from the rest of the world: Americans, we are told, are somehow better, wiser, and more beneficent than people from other nations, and that we are blessed with God's gratitude (see, e.g., Judis, 2005). The message, above all else, is that we are deserving of our privileges and just in our effort to guard them; that U.S. self-interest overrides any other concern that the rest of the world might have. In a speech preparing the U.S. population for war with Iraq, President George W. Bush (2002) focused our attention on the "threat" to America and his commitment to confront it:

> On September the 11th, 2001, America felt its vulnerability—even to threats that gather on the other side of the earth. We resolved then, and we are resolved today, to confront every threat, from any source, that could bring sudden terror and suffering to America. (p. 4)

Although there has been some focus on the threat of terrorism worldwide, Bush often highlights the threat to the United States and disregards how our policies abroad negatively affect other nations, even those that he considers allies. In the same speech, Bush (2002) went on to defend his position of asking Congress to approve military force in dealing with Saddam Hussein:

> I have asked Congress to authorize the use of America's military, if it proves necessary, to enforce U.N. Security Council demands. Approving this resolution does not mean that military action is imminent or unavoidable. The resolution will tell the United Nations, and all nations, that America speaks with one voice and is determined to make the demands of the civilized world mean something. (p. 44)

It is clear in this speech that President Bush was overriding the concerns expressed by many in the United Nations about engaging in war with Iraq. Bush positioned the United States as the moral authority to make demands of other nations. What we do, by definition, is *just* and the actions of others will be determined by any arbitrary standard that *we* set. Equally problematic, Americans, it seems, do not have many problems with this view. Although we quibble over particular policies, few of us want to give up the illusion that God or Providence has some special plans for us as a nation; we are addicted to the power that comes from this belief and from the privileges it bestows (Andreas, 2004).

Of course, being a "good American" comes with responsibility. We have an obligation to increase our rate of consumption, recite daily the Pledge of Allegiance, attend church (or at least believe in God), support the military, and, above all else, during the dark days of the two twenty-first-century Bush administrations, to express a self-righteous indignation toward skeptics of executive policy (Ghosh, 2002; O'Leary & Platt, 2001). We have a responsibility to do what we are told and not question authority or the privileges of the wealthy. Most importantly, we are discouraged from dissenting; if we do so, we must dissent in a way that does not make our leaders uncomfortable. In the run-up to the U.S. invasion of Iraq, former advisor to President John F. Kennedy, the historian Arthur Schlesinger, Jr. (2003), observed that today "the feeling seems to be spreading that the imminence of war must suspend debate, that patriotic Americans must follow their leader, that challenging the presidential judgment is a form of *lese-majeste* [treason against a sovereign]" (p. 1). Another commentator (Moskos, 2002) advocated mandatory military service as the price of citizenship that can be exacted, in part, by linking federal college aid to military or quasi-military service.

This quietism, consumption, and nationalism, although challenged frequently as the war in Iraq grows increasingly unpopular (and only because we are "losing"—Americans do not complain when we successfully subjugate an opponent),[3] are undesirable trends in our national psyche, as these and related phenomena—commercialism, patriotism, and militarism—are, we argue, the *causes* of our troubles as Americans, not solutions. They are the evils against which we critical citizens struggle. Our hope in this struggle is directed toward the lessening of their influence; against their darkness we seek to shed the light of social justice and the goal of a future free of pollution and fear. From the point of view of our humanism, it is unacceptable that Dewey's (1950/1993d) comment sounds remarkably contemporary: "Living as we now do in what is almost a chronic state of crises, there is danger that fear and the sense of insecurity become the predominant motivation of our activities" (p. 247). Dewey wrote this statement four years *after* the end of the Second World War, a time in which the world should have been most hopeful. Dewey went on to write that when "we allow ourselves to be fear-ridden and permit it to dictate how we act, it is because we have lost faith in our fellowmen—and that is the unforgivable sin against the sprit of democracy" (p. 248).

In light of the progressive and internationalist climate developing in present-day Europe, the ugly nationalist attitudes calcifying in U.S. political discourse are presumptuous and backward, as Nietzsche considered these traits in Germany in the late nineteenth century with its imperial and cultural pretensions. Nietzsche discerned correctly that nationalist identifications lead to a general malaise throughout the larger human community. Such malaise, thought Nietzsche, stunts human development. Nietzsche (1954/1976) saw the human species as constantly changing, as the animal with the potential for self-overcoming, as "a bridge, not an end"—as a becoming that must be freed from the weight of superstition and venerated tradition.

Nation-states, however, treat their subjects as if an end has been achieved, that the best of all possible worlds has been created, and that critical thought just gets in the way. Each nation-state proclaims that its norms and laws are the only thing standing between civilization and chaos. For instance, in reference to the "war on terror," President George W. Bush (2001) claimed that the "only alternative to victory is a nightmare world, where every city is a potential killing field" (p. 36). Yes, we students of the twentieth century know about killing fields and what horrors are planted there, and we are familiar with the harvest and the harvesters, with the images of ourselves (Karnow, 1983/1997; Vickery, 1984). In the life of our nation, we have tasted blood and felt the crimes we have committed against humanity—and continue to commit. Bush does not need to lecture us on this point; rather, he needs to come clean. In his 2007 Proclamation of National Sanctity of Human Life Day, Bush opined that the day serves "as a reminder that we must value human life in all forms, not just those considered healthy, wanted, or convenient. Together, we can work toward a day when the dignity and humanity of every person is respected" (p. 4). Such hypocrisy is sickening. What Bush denies is that he has no investment in this economy of murder and mayhem, and no responsibility for the death and chaos he, and the nation he purports to serve, has sowed. His statements about the "sanctity of life" and the "culture of life" are disingenuous at best, given his continued attack of the working poor and the middle class, exuberant engagement in rogue warfare, and shameful negligence of the victims of Hurricane Katrina. Clearly, Bush does exactly what he reminds us not to do—he ranks life. The lives of those who are not White, upper class, heterosexual, and Christian are inconvenient for Bush and people who do not fit into his preferred categories, therefore, are systemically underserved and underresourced.[4]

Many Americans and others throughout the world today fear the United States more than they fear the threat from al-Qaeda, and see the terrorist threat as a reaction to the irresponsible and largely unaccountable extension of U.S. hegemony around the globe. For instance, in a comprehensive poll of international opinion conducted by the Pew Global Attitudes Project ("Global Unease with Major World Powers," 2007) released in June 27, 2007, majorities in 47 nations believe that the United States ignores their interest in its foreign policy and that the United States contributes to the widening gap between wealthy and impoverished nations. The report also found that the world views the United States as the primary party responsible for environmental degradations. What is particularly interesting in relationship to our argument in this book is the study's determination that majorities "in 43 of 47 countries surveyed—including 63% in the United States—say that the United States promotes democracy mostly where it serves its interests, rather than promoting it wherever it can" ("Global Unease with Major World Powers," p. 5).

Perhaps nothing is so inevitable about so-called "terrorism" that a less selfish foreign policy could help to eliminate. There is nothing so inevitable about war that could not be cured by less divisive worldviews and a strong sense of fraternity and solidarity among people. In short, the assumption that "what's good for America is good for the world" is an untenable premise on which to ground U.S. foreign policy, as it creates enemies and perpetuates the same sickly culture that will be a legacy to our grandchildren. Americans have at least as much to learn from the rest of the world as it has to learn from us, and perhaps more. The colossal arrogance of Americans is a disservice to both world culture and world peace.[5]

Similar to Nietzsche in his day, we are living in a time in which the seeds of future world war or global catastrophe may be brazenly nurtured. At some point, the "war on terror" may morph into a third world war; it may already have, as such wars do not have to be declared to have their effect. With irony, we recall Nietzsche's (1954/1976) announcement, "the greatest events—they are not our loudest but our stillest hours. Not around the inventors of new noise, but around the inventors of new values does the world revolve; it revolves *inaudibly*" (p. 243). Our nationalist identifications prevent us from perceiving this danger, of being aware of our many destructive psychoses, and our practice of democracy and democratic institutions are too feeble to stop it. We are not alone in discerning these evils; others, both inside and outside of academia, struggle to articulate dissent and bring democratic values to hold power accountable. With a chorus of similar voices—voices that may soon come in from the margins—we "good humans," we antipodes of patriots and nationalists, may be more successful than was Nietzsche in helping others to realize the grave consequences our present habits portend for the future.

Emerson and the Unattained Yet Attainable Self

Ralph Waldo Emerson, the nineteenth-century poet, writer, speaker, and cultural critic was an influential figure in Nietzsche's thought (Kaufmann, 1974), as well as in shaping a narrative of the U.S. democratic citizen, which had a wide impact on the cultural and political landscape during his time. Emerson's concern with democracy emphasized the intellectual capacities and strengths of character of citizens needed, according to him, to comprise a democratic society, rather than the political structure or mechanisms for democracy. He argued that a genuinely democratic community is not exclusively constituted by the operations of the political system but, more importantly, by individuals who think for themselves; challenge taken-for-granted values, knowledge, and norms; and seek to actualize their creative and productive potential (Garvey, 2000; West, 1989).

Emerson was especially known for his praise of the self-reliant individual. The emphasis on "self-reliance" may appear initially as a paradigmatically male-centered, "pull yourself up by the bootstraps" U.S. attitude that places a small value on care-taking among people. However, self-reliance is more usefully understood as Emerson's celebration of the creative and inventive potential of human beings. He saw humans as having an abundance of talents, capacities, abilities and potentials, and he was compelled by the transformative potential in human history—the idea that humans can do better than they have done in the past. Personal stagnation, intellectual or otherwise, and the absence of creative innovation in people's lives, for him, were tragic limitations (West, 1989), and Emerson (1841/1983) encouraged individuals to strive for what he called the "unattained yet attainable self." Emerson encouraged individuals to be concerned more with developing themselves than with following the norms of society, for "nothing," he claimed, "is at last sacred but the integrity of your own mind…. I am ashamed to think how easily we capitulate to badges and names, to large societies and dead institutions" (p. 148).

We interpret Emerson's view of self-reliance as a celebration of the human being, in that humans are reservoirs of creativity with the potential to change the course of our individual and communal futures. We are, however, often prevented from developing this potential by the intellectual, political, economic, and social limitations that we place on ourselves and others. The striving to actualize this creative potential urges individuals to examine critically those limitations and engage in thought and communication that challenges them. Emerson's emphasis on the strong, empowered individual may appear contradictory to the notion of an egalitarian, socially just and inclusive democracy we have been sketching. However, this reading would not take fully into account his perspective. Although Emerson (19841/2003) expressed disdain of dependence on others for intellectual and material sustenance, he also rebuked those who accumulate wealth and power through others and do not contribute to the common wealth—the well-being of society. Emerson argued that every person must have a "just chance for his bread," and that "amelioration in our laws of property" should "proceed from the concession of the rich, not from the grasping of the poor" (p. 145).

Emerson was suspicious of the state and, to some degree, the political process of the time. He was an outspoken critic of the United States for a number of reasons—most notably, for its policies and practices that suppressed individual freedoms, such as slavery and the genocidal repression of Native Americans (West, 2004). Such injustices were correctly seen by him as crimes against humanity, and he believed that strong individuals were needed, as they are now, to counter, contest, and reject these and more modern, state-sanctioned atrocities. At the same time, Emerson was a foremost champion of the idea of "America." He ultimately understood America as a spirit, a potential, not as the machinery of the state. America, he believed, is found in its citizens.

Emerson's ideal citizen is a person who does not simply rely on what "experts" or politicians tell her or him. Rather, ideal citizens do their own investigation, develop their own opinions, and seek their own knowledge, among other ways, by talking to people from different backgrounds and with different experiences. Above all, Emerson urged people to trust themselves and not to relinquish their intellectual power to others, for to do so is to alienate a person from her- or himself. Rather, Emerson advocated a healthy skepticism of "certainties" and assumptions handed down from others so that a person can engage in a critical process of determining for her- or himself what is true and carving out her or his path. Emerson believed that within the limited framework of freedom in our lives, people can and must create their democratic individuality (West, 2004). He understood that to create and sustain a genuine democratic community, people must question prevailing dogmas, as well as their individual beliefs and biases. In summary, Emerson's primary concerns were that people must be courageous and possess dignity, productivity, creativity, and a keen knowledge of themselves and the society in which they live.

Dewey's Democracy as a Moral Problem

John Dewey, philosopher, educator and public speaker was, during the early part of the twentieth century, the most well-known U.S. philosopher who advanced pragmatism's position in philosophical discourse and among the educated public. Dewey was greatly inspired by Emerson's ideas and built on them with his own moral and intellectual vision of democracy. Although his star waned for many decades, he recently has been rediscovered, and today Dewey's appeal is considerable. As Morris and Shapiro (1993) explained:

> From the vantage point of the late twentieth century, when most of philosophy has become a highly technical specialty-subject with little obvious relevance to the social and political problems of our world, Dewey's sustained philosophical engagement with the social and political issues of his day stands as an attractive beacon. Dewey represents, perhaps, what social philosophy can hope to become. (p. xi)

Dewey has been credited with contributing greatly to contemporary discourses of democracy, particularly in the area of participatory and deliberative democracy (see Caspary, 2000). A cornerstone of Dewey's theory of democracy is a high level of participation by citizens in public deliberation and decision making. That is, citizens must engage in public deliberation in their local communities to influence broader political decision making. Deweyan democracy is a *decentered* deliberativism that does not assume that citizens will be expected to be statespeople. Rather, this form of democracy acknowledges the need for different spheres of democratic politics, including local forms of association in civil society to governance at state and national levels. Although the expectation is that the more local levels of association will be more directly democratic, Deweyan democracy is fully consistent with representative institutions at the levels of state and national governance. However, an important aspect of Deweyan democracy that must be underscored is that although there is a "division of epistemic labour between citizens, representatives and other holders of public office…what is denied is that these divisions represent differences of epistemic *kind*" (Talisse, 2005, p. 189). Although Dewey's vision called for elected representatives to help implement necessary public policies, he believed that these policies must be informed by knowledge that emerges through participatory deliberation, which begins in diverse local communities and the civil associations and schools that comprise them (Caspary, 2000; Talisse, 2005). His political philosophy stands in contrast to the "guardianship theory" of politics, heralded by Judge Richard Posner and others (see Talisse, 2005), which assumes that average people inherently are too irrational to engage responsibly in self-government. In the guardianship theory, governance must necessarily be concentrated in the hands of those who possess political wisdom—that is, those who "know" what is good, right, and just (Talisse, 2004).

As mentioned earlier, because "democratic ends require democratic methods for their realization" (Dewey, 1939/1993g, p. 205), people must be involved in the decisions that affect their lives. Dewey believed that inquiry, deliberation, consultation, persuasion, negotiation, and cooperation must be exercised in all arenas of social interaction, such as in the workplace and in schools, and should not be reserved for a special group of people, such as experts or political leaders.

He argued that public involvement in deliberation must extend to all social relationships and aspects of culture, including economics, politics, education, art, and religion (Caspary, 2000). This vision of democracy is both deep and far-reaching: Democratic methods must permeate *all* levels and domains of society, and the participation of all citizens is needed. The problem of the democratic society, in Dewey's view, is a moral one, dependent more on intelligence, education, communication, and participation than on the political machinery of a society. When people are knowledgeable about the implications and consequences of various beliefs, they are better equipped to participate in developing actions and resolutions to problems. *How* something gets done, therefore, follows from *what* should be done. What should be done is developed from the deliberation that ensues from a public with the capability and opportunity to participate in this deliberation (Dewey, 1927/1954).

Dewey understood that when great disparities of wealth exist among groups of people, equal participation in public deliberation is not possible. Concentrated wealth allows for the control and manipulation of public forums and mechanisms for public deliberation, such as the media, and determines what is and is not allowable for discussion (see Herman & Chomsky, 2002). The fact that the media, as of 2004, were controlled by only five corporations (Bagdikian, 2004) is a stark example of the way in which concentrated wealth limits the accessibility and visibility of diverse ideas necessary for democracy to thrive. With regard to the modern media, commercial and controlled as they are, we should keep Dewey (1941/1993f) in mind, writing as he was during the Second World War:

> The freedom which is the essence of democracy is above all the freedom to develop intelligence, intelligence consisting of judgment as to what facts are relevant to action and how they are relevant to things to be done, and a corresponding alertness in the quest for such facts. To what extent we are actually democratic will in the end be decided by the degree to which the existing totalitarian menace awakens us to deeper loyalty to intelligence, pure and undefiled, and to the intrinsic connection between it and free communication. (p. 208)

Civic engagement requires time, a minimum level of education, and material resources—all things that the poor often do not have in surplus due to their marginalized economic, educational, and social status. Fortunately, civic engagement from marginalized groups has occurred despite this fact and with great sacrifice and against seemingly insurmountable odds (the civil rights movement of the 1950s and 1960s is one example). From a Deweyan perspective, a fully developed participatory democracy cannot be actualized within a system that excludes effectively entire classes of people from civic engagement.

Similar to Emerson's interest in the character of *people* who comprise a democratic society versus the formal workings of the political system, Dewey stressed the *process* of democracy over any particular outcome. Dewey's

(1920/1950) axiom that "growth is the only moral end" emphasized that the most critical element to democracy is an inclusive, community-oriented process of inquiry, deliberation, and experimentation, not a search for timeless truths or general theories. This point does not suggest that some outcomes, such as those that strive to ensure that all people have the ability to meet their basic needs and opportunities for personal development and civic participation, are not more desirable and better for furthering a democratic society. However, Dewey rejected the use of scientific or ethical deliberation to create a new authority of thought that would become a new hegemonic force. As a pragmatist thinker, Dewey was staunchly antifoundationalist and stood against tendencies to systemize, create hierarchies, and obstruct human development. Dewey (1939/1993a) opposed quests of certainty and permanence because he recognized that

> all ends and values that are cut off from the ongoing process [of education and experience] become arrests, fixations. They strive to fixate what has been gained instead of using it to open the road and point the way to new and better experiences. (p. 244)

Such efforts to find certainty thwart the ability to remain open, poised, and responsive to address new situations and challenges. Dewey's emphasis on a democratic process positioned society to be flexible, perceptive, agile, and able to respond to emerging challenges of the times with creative acumen.

Inquiry and deliberation are the primary aspects of the Deweyan democratic process. Dewey's notion of inquiry is modeled after a humanistic version of the scientific process that combines imagination, thorough information gathering, reasoning and consideration of implications, and a historical sensitivity to other cultures and ways of life (Caspary, 2000). This process requires effective universal education for adults and children, which focuses on helping people to be effective inquirers and deliberators. For Dewey, education is the most significant process for any society because it helps a society to become a *community* and provides a way for people to develop a sense for being distinctive members of their community and the interrelatedness of all members of society. His view of education encompassed a pedagogy that included skills of critical inquiry, hands-on work, fostering creative problem-solving skills of students rather than providing answers, exploring one's thoughts and feelings, and being able to sustain deliberation without the security of a sense of certainty (Caspary, 2000).

In the word *deliberation*, the word *liberation* is found, and in Dewey's view, liberation is the self-realization of a person developed through the process of contributing to a common good. This democratic vision engages a dialectical relationship between the self and community, in which Dewey argued that people's self-realization could be achieved through the process of mutual inquiry, communication, and the moral development that accompanies such communion with others. The democratic process is one that both embraces and emerges from active dialogue among people with differing and diverse perspectives and values. To cooperate, as Dewey (1939/1993a) asserted,

> by giving differences a chance to show themselves because of the belief that the expression of difference is not only a right of the other persons but is a means of enriching one's own life experience, is inherent in the democratic personal way of life. (p. 244)

Dewey's vision of democracy is a "thick" one, as opposed to the "thin" ones that commonly are accepted in U.S. society. For Dewey, democracy is an expression of the commitment to utilize human creative potential to work toward a better future and to continuously improve the quality and experience of life for all members of society. It is an attitude and orientation toward fellow human beings that values the freedom of all people to develop their potential "in harmony" with the common good. Democracy, in this sense, is a process of claiming one's power, engaging in the project of self-creation, and participating in the continual formation of one's community. It is a constant state of creativity and transformation from old ideas and norms to new ones, rather than a set of social and political institutions or a specific set of values that, once created, need only be encapsulated and codified into law. In fact, such institutions are inherently conservative, having verified or mummified old ideas and values at the expense of the new.

The Deweyan concept of self-realization as emerging through a dialectical process of individual and communal inquiry complements Emerson's notion of the self-reliant individual and shows the ways that human beings' growth depends on communion (and communication) with others to be realized. Dewey's emphasis on knowledge as a communal process resulting in understandings that are always open to further revision rather than something permanent and ahistorical is a useful concept for moving beyond the limitations placed on human transformation that are perpetuated by foundationalist philosophy.

Rorty's Anti-Foundationalism

Richard Rorty's scholarship is an important addition to the vision of democratic society presented in this book thus far. Our use of Rorty's work builds on Emerson's emphasis on the self and Dewey's trust for a communal process of inquiry and deliberation, bringing Rorty's notion of *ironism* (discussed in Chapter 1) into the vision of creative democracy that we develop. As a reminder, Rorty's concept of ironism involves a recognition and acceptance of one's "final vocabulary," a self-awareness that

> the deepest convictions one holds are the result of past poetic and creative achievements. This goes along with the recognition that there never will be a final poem.

> There will always be space for self-creation, because no previous act of self-creation can be ratified by some nonhuman authority. (Rorty, 2006, p. 72)

Elsewhere, Rorty (1994) wrote:

> An ironist is someone who says that a liberal utopia isn't something that expresses the essence of human nature, the end of history, God's will, but is simply the best idea people have had about the object for which they work. Ironism, in this context, means something close to anti-foundationalism. (p. 115)

What counts for progress in society is the powerful effect of people's self-creation on others, its persuasive influence. Rorty called such people "strong poets." In an interview, Rorty (2006) explained why he picked that term:

> It seemed like a handy piece of terminology to use when emphasizing the fact that people like Plato and Galileo and Marx, people with great imaginations, people who altered the vocabularies with which we think about various matters, were no more offering conclusive arguments, or indeed anything much in the way of argument at all, for their views than poets. They just put their new visions on the table and made it possible for us to occupy a different perspective. So I adopted the term *strong poet* to denote anyone with a lot of imagination who has the courage to try to make everything in his or her field new, to change the way we look at things. (p. 122)

Rorty, a pragmatist intellectual, as were Emerson and Dewey, also is staunchly anti-foundational. He argued, along with Nietzsche, that the Western philosophical tradition of attempting to anchor human beliefs and practices onto transcendent and universal givens, such as God, Natural Law, Reason, or other fixed and immutable things, distracts us from working toward a more useful goal. Although this goal for Nietzsche was the creation of meaning through the self-overcoming of an *Übermensch*-type experience, for Rorty, it means creating new and better descriptions of ourselves and society that help to reduce suffering and increase human happiness. Rather than worrying about whether we are getting it "right," Rorty argued that it is more consequential to focus on whether there might be better descriptions of the world than the ones we currently hold.

In Rorty's (1999) view, all beliefs and practices grow out of human beings' experiences and the attempts to make sense of, and adjust to, the practical contingencies and conditions within which we live. Human values and standards of morality, and all moral and philosophical debates about what is right and wrong and good and bad, are created within the context of human understanding, which occurs within these historical contingencies and conditions (Bacon, 2005). From this perspective, it is not possible to defend one's belief without using justifications that are themselves bounded by historical contingencies. Any justification used to defend a belief (e.g., any criterion for judging what is good or bad) itself is a product of human thought and language emerging in the context of a certain place, time, and culture. There is no neutral language from which humans can develop criteria to judge various explanations and worldviews. Rorty would agree with Dewey's (1911/1993i) comment that "because observation has been socially trained, fixed by education, and because classifications and appraisals deposited in language have, from the very beginning, woven themselves into every perception and opinion, socially determined qualities are an inextricable part of any object" (p. 17). In other words, there is no timeless, ahistorical set of Truths to which one can appeal and, therefore, justifications for our beliefs, at some point, become circular. For example, if a Christian emphatically argues that a gay or lesbian experience is wrong because it is "sinful," he or she would be unable to justify this belief using neutral criteria to a non-Christian. The justification that "the Bible says so" is insufficient because it, too, is based on human understanding of the "word of God" and was written by human beings who existed during a particular place and time in history.

Similarly, if we were to argue that all humans have a "right" to clean water, adequate sanitation, health care, and the opportunity to earn a decent living, we cannot justify this on any grounds except that we believe that one human being is not inherently more deserving of basic life-sustaining necessities than any other, and that ensuring that everyone has basic needs met would produce a more creative, empowered, and healthier human society than the one that exists currently, and we would likely then have a better world in which to live. If we had to choose between the two worldviews, we would chose the latter, not because it was more in line with truth per se but because such a view exemplifies the type of world in which we would want to live. The fight is not over who is "right" but who has the moral authority to define, on the one hand, hate and prejudice, and, on the other, acceptance and compassion. That we value the latter over the former means nothing more than that we exemplify in person the citizens we want our neighbors to become. In other words, in constructing moral arguments about what is right and good, we depend on and use our historically contingent values and beliefs for justification (Bacon, 2005). Rorty (1989) called the set of beliefs that one holds that cannot escape justification by circular argument one's "final vocabulary." It is final in the sense that "those words are as far as he can go with language; beyond them there is only helpless passivity or a resort to force" (Rorty, 1989, p. 73).

Critics view Rorty's anti-foundationalism as a threat to human morality because they assume that if there are no commensurable Truths on which humans base their moral values and decisions, we will automatically dissolve into selfish nihilism and a Hobbesian "war of all against all." Not only is this an impoverished view of human moral capacity but it also is a misunderstanding to insist that such results are an inevitable outcome of anti-foundationalism. Rather, by repositioning values, beliefs, and moral standards in terms of vocabularies that we adapt based on historical contingencies instead of Truths, anti-foundationalism opens up a new realm of possibility for personal and social change. For example, if we examine our beliefs from the perspective that they are narratives or sets of meanings that we have adopted or accepted based on family traditions, culture, religion, or particular life experiences, it allows us to examine those beliefs, critique them, and perhaps see if there are other narratives that might be better. By "better," we mean that it either offers more hope, helps one to view people and situations differently than before, allows one to solve problems in new ways, or expands one's ability to get along with a wider set of people. In other words, a narrative, vocabulary, or folklore that, in Burke's (1973) words, functions as a better "equipment for living."[6]

Seeing our belief system as a final vocabulary instead of the "only right way" allows us to bracket that belief system and become more creative and open to other beliefs, values, and understandings. Rorty (1989), as we have seen, called this type of self-reflection "ironism." Such ironism, Rorty (2006) explained, "is just a sort of attitude, the way you feel about yourself, a form of life" (p. 44). Adopting an ironist practice and the associated ability to perceive one's beliefs as emerging from a particular set of historical circumstances rather than as Truth does not result in an *inability* to stand up for one's beliefs and moral standards. To the contrary, ironism calls on people to become more astute self-critics. It encourages us to revise and gain a heightened awareness of what we believe, and to accept or create the beliefs and values that seem most "right" to us given our best assessment of the alternatives. Thus, we are better equipped to become more active participants in our cultural, moral, and intellectual development, and able to take ownership of, and consequences for, our beliefs and actions. Ironism helps us to be the strong, creative people that Emerson envisioned rather than members of the "mob" who accept with blind faith the truths that are handed down from others, as Nietzsche feared.

In addition to fostering a more self-critical and culturally agile citizenry, ironism is a useful practice for working toward a socially just democracy. If we want to be more socially just, we need to relate to others who are very different from us and see that although differences exist between people, such differences become unimportant when "compared with similarities with respect to pain and humiliation" (Rorty, 1989, p. 192). Such realizations emerge from a capacity to experience and express compassion and solidarity, and an ironist awareness helps us to cultivate this capacity. As Rorty (2006) explained:

> What is important about a representative democratic government is that it gives the poor and weak a tool they can use against the rich and powerful, especially against the unconscious cruelty of the institutions that the powerful have imposed upon the weak. A democracy is distinguished not only by its forms of government, but also by the presence of institutions such as a free press, free universities, and an inde-

> pendent judiciary. These institutions help the nation come to grasp the existence of previously unrecognized forms of cruelty and suffering: the cruelty of whites against blacks, for example, or the suffering of gays. In a fully democratic society, unnecessary suffering would not exist. (p. 82)

Rorty, in this sense, helps us to see that we do not need dogmatism and universal transcendent Truths (which would never be agreed on, nor should they, for different belief systems contribute to the diversity on which all life flourishes) to be compassionate toward others and committed to improving social and economic conditions for all human beings.

Conclusion

Throughout this chapter, we argued that the writings of Friedrich Nietzsche, Ralph Waldo Emerson, John Dewey, and Richard Rorty underpin our notion of a creative democracy, a state of mind and a cultural way of being that emphasizes the potentiality and humanity of people above blind allegiance to religious, legal, or political dogma. All four thinkers exemplify our assumption that what matters is not what has been done in the past but what can be done in the future—a future limited only by our collective yearnings and imaginations and our faith in each other.

Notes

1. We recognize that this topology has become very convoluted in the two centuries since it first appeared in French politics during their revolutionary period (for a history of this concept, see Eatwell, 1989).

2. It is difficult to read Nietzsche and not concur with Goldman; Nietzsche is the singlemost inspiring writer we have ever read. Nietzsche's resemblance with pragmatism was recognized as early as 1911 (Rorty, 2007, p. 27; see also Danto, 2005).

3. Compare, for example, the discontent in the United States by citizens over the current war in Iraq, which is now in its fifth year, with the U.S. invasion of Grenada and the overthrow of its leftist government in 1983, and the U.S. invasion of Panama in 1989, in which its President General Manuel Antonio Noriega was seized and brought to the United States for trial and imprisoned, as well as earlier "success" stories, such as the U.S.-backed coup that destroyed Chile's social democracy in 1973 and killed its popular President Salvador Allende, all of which were completed "successfully" in a matter of weeks.

4. In commuting the 30-month prison sentence of his friend I. Lewis Libby Jr., President Bush announced that the prison term was "too severe" and that Libby and his family had already suffered enough (Liptak, 2007). Although this action showed that Bush does have feelings, it did not take into account that the policy of the Justice Department is, and has been, to be increasingly strict and harsh toward people convicted of crimes, with

more than 2 million people incarcerated in the United States, the vast majority of them poor and members of minority groups (Bureau of Justice Statistics, 2003).

5. Sontag (1969, 1966/2002) said much of the same during the Vietnam War. Although the world has changed tremendously since that time, the U.S. propensity to project hegemony worldwide has not. Others, of course, disagree with this analysis; for a traditional normative narrative of the United States as a benign victim of other people's cowardly acts, see Hanson (2002).

6. For Burke, literature, widely defined, functions generally to help people form attitudes to navigate situations that recur across time. Such discourse is a strategy, the result of names (or definitions) that allow us to understand and to control.

CHAPTER 7

Alienation and Power

As we have been suggesting throughout this book, the dominant understandings of democracy and communication—those created and reproduced through conventional and normative politics and disciplinary academic practices—hinder or minimize opportunities for individuals to be more critically aware of the forces that influence and shape their lives, and to become more engaged in creating a society that is inclusive, fair, and socially just (Rodriguez, 2001; Swartz, 2005). We also recognize, following Rorty (1989), that there are no metaphysical foundations, ahistorical or non-contextual certainties, on which to situate our commitment to social justice and progressive scholarship and, in fact, that none are necessary. We believe it is enough to argue for our beliefs and to enact them with our lives (including writing, and teaching), and to invite others to join us. We strive to model the vision we write about, to exemplify the ethos of engaged scholarly, supra-disciplinary and progressive critique. Academic or disciplinary objections to the contrary we consider to be short-sighted, dogmatic, and counterproductive (Swartz, 1997a, 1997b, 2005). We engage scholarship on *our* terms on behalf of the causes we support; any other stance would be dishonest to this intellectual project.

Through the communicative process, we have argued, individuals continually develop themselves and their communities (Rodriguez, 2001, 2006; Swartz, 1999b, 2005). Language is a significant element in the way we shape our understandings of reality; as humans change the way they talk about things, their beliefs, attitudes, and actions also change (Burke, 1984b; Postman, 1992). Such "redescription," noted Rorty (2007, pp. 53–54) in one of his final publications, "is an important task—by changing the ways we use words, we construct new intellectual worlds," new possibilities for being and for experiencing life. In this light, critical intellectuals, both inside and outside of academia, "read books in order to enlarge their sense of what is possible and important—either for themselves as individuals or for their society" (Rorty, 1999b, p. 127). Such people, public intellectuals in the most general sense, teach (formally or informally), not to communicate knowledge in a foundational sense, but to "stir people up" (Rorty, 1999b, p. 126). They (and we) read books "in the hope of becoming a different sort of person" (Rorty, 1999b, p. 126), one less burdened by the terms, conditions, and biases of the past. Thus, language in literature, art, and politics generally is an important resource of power for individuals and communities—power that can be used to institutionalize cruelty, poverty, hatred, and alienation or to emphasize human connectedness and facilitate redescription, transformation, and liberation.

The critical imagination and the politics of representation are particularly important to those in society who have been historically marginalized or oppressed (e.g., women, gays/lesbians, and African Americans), entombed by the reifications of hegemonic elites.[1] For these subaltern groups and their allies, the critical imagination serves the purpose of opening up alternative possibilities. The critical imagination enables marginalized others to form separate discursive spaces from the wider public, as well as to challenge unjust social hierarchies in the form of what we called in Chapter 1 "counterpublics." In one sense, counterpublics serve as a means for challenging the wider public arena and opening up the discursive space. Counterpublics can also be enclaved publics, however, that function as a space for "withdrawal and regroupment" (Fraser, 1996 p. 124) and are separate from and not dependent on the wider public. "Publics" are never fixed in a moment in time (Asen & Brouwer, 2001); rather, they are always changing and evolving, responding to the ways in which individuals imagine their identities and form collective representations. Imagination plays a significant role in the process of forming collective public identities because it is through communication that individuals are able to translate their experiences to others, recognize shared experiences, and imagine connections with others around particular themes and struggles. Imagination is what instantiates various publics at certain moments in time. Through the creative imagination, wider publics may imagine themselves in particular ways and also imagine and represent others in particular ways (Asen, 2002).

Interfering with the creation of a creative democracy, with its focus on social justice and inclusive community, is the condition of alienation so prevalent in the United States today—the experience of profound disconnection between people and their creativity and agency, a sense of impotence or lack of self-knowledge, and an unwillingness or incapacity to care about the suffering of others (Freire, 1970/2000; Fromm, 1992; Rodriguez, 2001; Swartz, 2005). Thus, we explore alienation as a pervasive, unfortunate, and unnecessary human condition in contemporary U.S. society that inhibits people from realizing the potential to develop their capacities and contribute to the overall well-being of others.[2]

Power, Alienation, and Communication

As suggested briefly in the introduction to this chapter, fundamental to understanding communication as epistemic and creative are notions of power and alienation. These concepts are central to the human experience and are resources (or hindrances) for individual, as well as social, edification and transformation. Humans are beings of rich and vibrant potential. Through a self-conscious awareness and cultivation of their power, people can identify, create, and seize opportunities to develop and realize this potential. At a societal level, power shapes norms, transforms society, and reproduces the social, economic, and political arrangements of the status quo (Swartz, 2005).

The term "power" often is used pejoratively, seen primarily as something that is "lorded over" others, used to impose or force one's will on others, and something that some people have and others do not. In this sense, power often is understood predominantly as *coercion*, in which people are subjected to others' power and are rendered defenseless and without choices for response or escape. From that perspective, people's worlds and options are closed when they are coerced; they are made to suffer. Feminist philosopher Marilyn Frye (1983) expressed this concept clearly:

> The experience of oppressed people is that the living of one's life is confined and shaped by forces and barriers which are not accidental or occasional and hence avoidable, but are systematically related to each other in such a way as to catch one between and among them and restrict or penalize motion in any direction. It is the experience of being caged in: all avenues, in every direction are blocked or booby trapped. (p. 4)

Frye's interpretation has important cultural resonance; slavery, racism, economic exploitation of the poor, the legal and social subordination of women, and the atrocities committed against Jews and minorities during Nazi Germany are well-known examples of power working in an overtly coercive and demeaning manner. Throughout history and up to the current time, power as coercion has been a recurring theme in human social life, resulting in a legacy of unspeakable horror. Such use of power is not to be underestimated and must be resisted, whenever possible.

Although coercion is one (significant) form of power and influence, power should not be understood only in this way and, more importantly, exertion of power *over* others should not be accepted as the "natural" mode of human relations (Rodriguez, 2001). Sadly, however, this repressive view of power often is the case, as Rodriguez (2001) has shown. In his research Rodriguez found that some level of coercion and the hierarchies it serves are assumed by people to be necessary for an orderly society; otherwise, it is believed, society would deteriorate into irrational chaos. The concentration of power within some groups is assumed to be necessary, and asymmetrical power relations are assumed to be a reflection of natural superiority/inferiority among members of a community. However, this view overlooks a more nuanced understanding of power. Against the normative ideology that claims hierarchy is a necessity for an orderly society, Rodriguez argued, hierarchy is an artifact of social devolution and the selfishness promoted through it impedes our potentiality and existential strivings—

strivings that are not limited to self-preservation instincts, such as securing food and shelter, but include the will toward creativity, community, and the development of people's mental, emotional, and spiritual capacities. An ideology that naturalizes hierarchy and competition does not explain these other human strivings and inhibits them from being actualized or perverts them. In contrast, Rodriguez emphasized cooperation and mutuality as modes of human relations that developed out of social evolution in human experience and that lead to a richer, more actualized and potentially healthier human experience (also see Kropotkin, 1902/1989). Viewing power as limited to coercion and power *over*, rather than power *to*, simplifies and limits understanding of power as a resource that is important for critical perception, self-actualization, and the building of creative and socially just communities.

The philosopher Michel Foucault changed the way that power is understood, showing the complexity and subtlety in the way that it manifests, perpetuates, and functions. As Foucault (1978) noted, what we are calling coercion or domination is not monolithic, not necessarily top down and uniform, not "that solid and global kind of domination that one person exercises over others, or one group over another, but the manifold forms of domination that can be exercised within society" (p. 96). Power, Foucault noted, is not "something that is acquired, sized, or shared, something that one holds on to or allows to slip way; power is exercised from innumerable points, in the interplay of nonegalitarian and mobile relations" (p. 94). Foucault added:

> The analysis [of power] should not attempt to consider power from its internal point of view and . . . should refrain from posing the labyrinthine and unanswerable question: "Who then has power and what has he in mind? What is the aim of someone who possesses power?" Instead, it is a case of studying power at the point where its intention, if it has one, is completely invested in its real and effective practices. (p. 97)

To determine these "real and effective practices," Foucault explored how rules of right become established by the relations of power through the production of discourses of truth. For Foucault (1995), "relations of power cannot be established, consolidated, or implemented without the production, accumulation, circulation and functioning of a discourse" (p. 443). He asserted that it is through the relations of power that discourses of truth are produced, which, in turn, determine the rules of right (i.e., what is allowable to do, think, and be, based on social and cultural norms). However, particular arrangements of the relations of power exist because people give credence to knowledge and practices that support those arrangements. In Foucauldian terms, power cannot be understood simply as something sovereign or centralized; rather, it is a resource drawn on and utilized by people and groups. Power is disciplinary; it functions through "natural" rules or norms—that is, it is found in the process of reification and normalization.[3]

For example, Ritzer's (2004) concept of "McDonaldization," in which the principles of the fast-food (or any corporatized) industry—such as efficiency, calculability, predictability, and control—have become interwoven into the broader mainstream U.S. society and culture is illustrative of the way that power, reification, and normalization function together. These principles, serving the corporate ends of ever-increasing profit and growth, can be seen not only in the wider food industry but also in the housing industry, where "McMansions" are built in suburban housing developments all over the country, in the automated customer service centers for virtually every large service provider, and in numerous other areas of social and cultural life in the United States and beyond.

The "McDonald's" ethos is so pervasive and extends to numerous mundane aspects of daily life (is "normal") because a majority of people accept it as inevitable or even as "progress." This ethos goes unquestioned, having become natural—a part of the "way things are." Bryman (1999) extended this idea to describe the way that the principles of Disney theme parks are dominating more sectors of U.S. society, as well as globally. The "dedifferentiation of consumption" (Bryman, p. 33) is one enactment of this ethos, in which previously separate aspects of consumer areas now are grouped together in "one-stop" developments where consumers can get all of their basic and entertainment needs met without ever having to leave the development. The casino/hotels in Las Vegas, Nevada, are a prime example of this development, as are large malls, such as the Mall of America in Bloomington, Minnesota, and Disney's planned community in Celebration, Florida. In each case, a fake and harmful ideal—the notion that we can define ourselves through consumption as well as consume our way to paradise—becomes material and corporate.

"Merchandising" is another aspect of Disneyization that has proliferated in recent years, in which companies sell products with copyrighted images and logos on them and consumers pay to be associated with some aspect of culture with which they want to identify (or be identified). Designer jeans, toys of characters from blockbuster films, and T-shirts with the names of well-known restaurants or bars are examples of this tendency to exploit, *ad nauseam*, the inanities of much popular and, unfortunately, political culture (see Dickinson, 2005). By consuming these products and the images they evoke, average citizens participate in reifying and reproducing these particular power relations; entrenched "dead speech," in White's (2006) terms, that destroys "the sense of self and the world upon which all meaningful speech ultimately depends" (p. 27). What is particularly troubling about Disney is that as the multinational media giant hides behind a cloak of sanguine innocence, it effectively seizes childrens' imagination and constructs messages for them that are not beneficial to how they conceptualize themselves, others, the world, or how they eventually think of their role as citizen. As Giroux (1999) noted, Disney is a "predatory corporation that views children's imaginations as simply another resource for amassing earnings" (p. 162). Value is sucked out of children in terms of profits and the children are left culturally immature in a hollowed-out democracy. In this way, Disney's merchandizing has set up particular power relations that serve the corporation's goals instead of the public's goals or the very real needs of children for culturally meaningful play and imagination. Parents, unfortunately, are often willing accomplices in this process, themselves influenced by the same systemic pressures to view the world through corporate-filtered lenses that confront their children. It is the parents, however, that serve as *reinforcements* of that world for their children. Giroux (1999) argued that this has incredible and overarching impact on our culture:

> As market culture permeates the social order, it threatens to cancel out the tension between market values and those values representative of civil society that cannot be measured in commercial terms but that are critical to democracy, values such as justice, freedom, equality, health, respect, and the rights of citizens as equal and free human beings. Without such values, students are relegated to the role of economic machines, and the growing disregard for public life is left unchecked. (p. 162)

No matter how "innocent" or "child friendly" Disney purports to be in terms of children's products and media, it is virtually impossible for this market-driven media conglomerate to address the values that are most significant for the future, such as a sense of justice, fairness, and health, and in some cases actively work against it (Dorfman, 1983; Dorfman & Mattelart, 1991). We all lose when our sense of ourselves and our social relationships and systems of power are informed by market-culture rather than one that is democratic and geared to human needs.

As this discussion illustrates, power and domination exist in the institutions, regulations, and social, political, and economic mechanisms that operate at all levels and in all domains of social life. All people participate in the relations of power, even if they are not aware of their participation; it is, simply, who they are as constructed, contested beings. This view is quite different from the traditional Marxist zero-sum conception of power, which sees power as being imposed from above onto others, or something that some groups have and others do not (Marx & Engels, 1848/1992). Understanding power as a *relation* (one that permeates and reaches into all areas of social life), not a static *thing*, underscores the idea that power constantly is being created, reproduced, and contested. All people participate in this process and contribute to shaping the relations of power, regardless of whether they are aware of this process. As Butin (2001, p.

169) noted, we "are all involved in accepting or resisting the normative constraints placed upon us"; none of us are "innocent," we are all complicit in the co-construction of the larger social reality, benefit selfishly from whatever small privilege we can claim, and are insensitive to the suffering of others. Individuals participate in reifying or resisting the norms and forms of domination that are produced through power. In this way, the choices that people make on a daily basis, in the seemingly mundane aspects of daily life, play a part in the relations of power in the construction and experience of everyday life.

"Alienation," a related concept to that of power, is a substantial barrier to understanding that all humans take part in the relations of power and, as such, engage every day in the reproduction of existing norms or the creation of new ones. *Alienation* can be understood as the condition that we experience when others determine who we will be, how we will think, and what we will do; an experience that we are unable to perceive fully (Swartz, 2005). When people are alienated, they have the sense that they cannot control their life and they lose the sense (if they ever had it) that they have the potential to change their environment. In such a condition, people are unable to recognize their creative potential and agency and cease to experience ownership over themselves, often leading to hopelessness, fatalism, or nihilism (Rodriguez, 2001).

Adopting a Foucauldian perspective on power can ameliorate such alienation by recognizing that one always possesses agency because one always is a participant in relations of power, and that resistance to the domination that one may experience, itself, is a powerful act. This view of power, therefore, potentially is liberating for people and can be used as a resource for cultivating one's sense of agency. This understanding also offers a way to be a more vigilant and perceptive cultural critic in a reinvigorated creative democracy, an individual who is able to identify keenly the limitations and consequences of various aspects of culture, to communicate this to others, and to plan strategic responses to them. With a Foucauldian perspective, in other words, one is better attuned to look beyond the obvious places where power functions, such as government or corporate institutions, and, instead, be aware of power in places considered to be the domain of the familiar, normal everyday life: places of employment, within the family, and physicians' office, as well as seemingly innocuous social traditions, such as religious or civic holidays, the foods we eat, habits of dress, and expressions of health and sexuality. Once we gain the vantage point that power is not necessarily a monolithic, centralized force, we can appreciate how it is netlike, circuitous, and pervasive, made by what Foucault (2006) called "discourses of truth" (p. 541). With this perspective, we become free to examine the ways we participate in reifying power relations and "truths" that may be at odds with our moral vision. People can resist and direct energy toward creating new communities and discourses to replace the dominant ones, as did Martin Luther King, Jr. and Mohandas Gandhi, to cite and discuss two well-known examples.[4]

Both King and Gandhi used power in the productive, neo-Foucauldian, and neo-pragmatic sense discussed here to bring about social change for ends productive of social inclusion. Neither individual had the force of an army or a gun behind him to advance his will (nor would either man have wanted this), and yet they both wielded great power and were highly consequential, having delivered redress and hope to millions of oppressed people around the world. King and Gandhi cultivated power through their approach to, and use of, communication as a means of battling widespread social and political alienation, to nurture community, social, and self-transformation. They were, in the vocabulary of this book, "strong poets" and heroic humanists.

Gandhi is known for his leadership of the Indian movement toward self-rule from British colonialism. The term *satyagraha*, which means "the force of truth" in Sanskrit, was coined by Gandhi to express the idea behind the new social movement that he was creating in India to challenge socially unjust and institutionalized relations, ranging from 200 years of British colonial rule to the brutal Indian caste system that systematically relegated large groups of people to the status of "untouchable." His philosophy, and the movement that it animated, has since provided an inspirational model to people all over the world engaged in efforts to further social justice, including King and the U.S. civil rights movement of the 1960s.

Satyagraha commonly is conflated in the West with civil disobedience or passive resistance. This interpretation, however, is incomplete (see Chaudhary & Starosta, 1992; Jesudasan, 1984). Although Gandhi did incorporate civil disobedience into his larger strategy for social change, this is only one aspect of the larger philosophy of *satyagraha* (Chaudhary & Starosta, 1992). *Satyagraha* is more accurately understood as a dialogic approach to social change. In this dialogic approach, change begins with the individual, and although it *may* result in acts of defiance, it does not begin there.

Gandhi's approach starts with verbal communication and moves to civil disobedience only in the case where all other communication attempts fail (see Bondurant, 1988). This approach makes sense when understood within the context of Gandhi's assumptions about humans, their relationship to one another, and the role of people in social transformation. Gandhi was committed to the idea that all humans have the potential for moral decision making and are capable of moral development, regardless of who they are or how much they have harmed others (Carlson, 1986; Chaudhary & Starosta, 1992). He also recognized that everyone has the potential to cause harm and, thus, boundaries between the self and others, or between "good" people and "evil" people, are blurred. *Satya-*

graha is enacted not only to "purify" the enemy of her or his erring ways (Carlson, 1986) but, equally, to purify the follower through rigorous self-discipline and self-reflection.

This purification can be seen as a confrontation of one's prejudices, biases, and values, or, in Rortian terms, one's final vocabulary. Purification also provides an opportunity for the people to examine their willingness to suffer for their commitment to justice at the hands of the enemy (Chaudhary & Starosta, 1992). Purification, therefore, is a significant aspect of Gandhi's philosophy. The person who is unwilling to suffer the consequences for her or his beliefs may turn to violence (Carlson, 1986; Chaudhary & Starosta, 1992; Jesudasan, 1984); however, and this is the key point, the willingness to bear *consequences* brings into harmony one's beliefs, words, and actions. The locus of social transformation for Gandhi is found in the individual in the context of the community and the choices that individuals make to recognize the worth and humanity of themselves and others.

Martin Luther King, Jr. also engaged the ethics of love for humankind and nonviolence to direct the U.S. civil rights movement during the mid to late 1950s and 1960s, ultimately resulting in the passage of the 1964 Civil Rights and 1965 Voting Rights acts. King's gospel expressed the idea of a more just nation, one that shed fully its brutally racist and selfish past. He articulated what he imagined in such a way that invited others, even those who did not initially support civil rights for the grandchildren and great grandchildren of this nation's former slaves, to see a nation that stood up for human rights and, at its core, honored the freedom and liberty of every one of its citizens. King, in essence, imagined a different possibility for the United States than the intolerant society in which he was raised, and he communicated expertly his alternative possibility to others so that they might imagine the same. As a leader in the civil rights movement, Martin Luther King was adept at weaving together and molding the imagination of his constituents. As Baker (1995) noted:

> The language and effectiveness of his [King's] civil rights leadership also point to a specific habit of mind. This habit of mind enabled him to convert the torturous, complex, heterogeneous lines and images of United States race relations into a strategically conceived and brilliantly articulated program of American social reform that led directly to a new and modern black publicity in America. The conceit is the linguistic correlative of a mind that imaginatively combines the most seemingly dissimilar things and orders of existence. (p. 23)

King was greatly inspired by Gandhi's philosophy of *satyagraha* and the idea that social change could be undertaken through nonviolent means, social resistance, and community building (see King, 1958/1986). Gandhi's method for social transformation was what allowed King, an ordained Baptist minister, to see how he could combine a principle of Christian pacifism with a strong and creative activism to affect social change in the areas of racial inequality, poverty, and, later, war (King, 1967/1989). King celebrated the worth of all human beings and fiercely opposed the institutionalized racism and poverty that plagued not only African Americans in the United States but people of all colors around the world. A recurring concept in his work was that of human connectedness and interdependence, with unity, worth, and dignity for all people being common themes. An "injustice anywhere," King (1963/1992) famously declared, "is a threat to justice everywhere" (p. 85). He reminded us that *everyone* is harmed when one human being suffers from deprivation and neglect; that none of us are above hurt and blame. King (1967) spoke to this idea of connection in almost every speech act he performed:

> In a real sense, all life is interrelated. The agony of the poor impoverishes the rich; the betterment of the poor enriches the rich. We are inevitably our brother's keeper because we are our brother's brother. Whatever affects one directly affects all indirectly. (p. 181)

Such an ethic inspires the creative utilization of power to advance this ethos of a wider human community. In King's civil rights model of activism, everyone possesses the potential and power to create positive change.

Examples that King talked about include speaking out against unjust normative ideologies, serving others in need, resisting unjust laws—such as the famous Montgomery bus boycott of 1955–1956 that helped to spark the civil rights movement (King, 1958/1986)—and building bridges with others different from oneself or one's group (Nojeim, 2004). King modeled for others his philosophy for social change by participating in direct acts of resistance to unjust laws and by serving others, as well as through public speaking and writing that criticized the institutionalization of racism and poverty and articulated a vision of a more humane society.

Although King was able to imagine a world different than what was offered to him, to embody it and to sacrifice his life for it, and although he communicated this message to millions of people, he could not—and did not—do this alone. Like Gandhi before him, King's "dream" was made up significantly by the workings of others—in this case, those men, women, and children who constituted the Black, progressive, and counterpublic critical imagination. As Baker (1995) noted:

> A different, sometimes invisible, black cultural work can be conceived as ceaselessly inventing its own modernity. In the concrete instance of southern Jim Crow legality, for example, it had to fashion a voice, songs, articulations, conversions of wish into politics. This creative agency enabled hundreds of thousands of black men, women and children to gain access to basic public accommodations. The black civil rights struggle, and particularly during the decade from 1955–1965, exempli-

> fies the active working of the imagination of a subaltern, black American counter-public. (p. 16)

The imaginative work of the Black masses and their allies is what provided the foundation for King's production of Black communicative power. The critical aspect of King's leadership is that he not only knew the significance of publicizing a Black and larger human rights consciousness but he knew how to perform it. With the help of King, nonviolent events such as sit-ins and marches were organized throughout the southern United States to protest segregation. His oratorical talent, religious sprit, and highly focused moral views of what constitutes a just America all contributed to the media's fascination with him. King's acute connection with the masses of Blacks and others solidified his following. His focus on gaining social, political, and economic justice for Blacks and poor people made the Black and progressive counterpublics a national scene for America during the 1950s and 1960s. Without the experience of the Black civil rights movement, it is difficult to imagine the progressive dynamism in politics and culture of the later 1960s.

Gandhi and King, in sum, both provide an alternative to the model of power as a negative social relationship embodied within coercion or competition. Their rhetorical approaches invited people to view power as a resource to be cultivated and used to further social justice ends. This power emerges from a profound sense of hope and is developed through self-awareness, a recognition that humans are inextricably connected to each other, and a realization that each person possesses agency and the potential to create change, regardless of her or his status in society or how that person may have acted in the past. In Rorty's (2006) words, "It is not a matter of finding something that is common to all, but of understanding that existing differences (among blacks and whites, heterosexual and homosexuals [for example]) are less important than we used to think" (p. 75). We are all, in fact, "featherless bipeds," and nothing but our language games—with rules that we write and act out—keeps us from experiencing a species-wide sense of solidarity. There is nothing dividing us that cannot be corrected by a healthy dose of the communicative imagination.

John Griffin, the White journalist who, with the help of a physician, darkened his skin and passed as a Black man for 6 weeks in the deep south, wrote about his experiences and provided a good example of how challenging the rules of the game changes one's perspective. As a result of his experience, which was highly traumatic for him, Griffin (2004) wrote:

> Humanity does not differ in any profound way; there are not essentially different species of human beings. If we could only put ourselves in the shoes of others to see how we would react, then we might become aware of the injustice of discrimination and the tragic inhumanity of every kind of prejudice. (p. 211)

Griffin went on to write that "the Us-and Them or I-and-Thou dichotomies do not exist. There is only one universal We—one human family united by the capacity to feel compassion and to demand equal justice for all" (p. 212). As Griffin concluded:

> The Other is simply Oneself in all the significant essentials. This alone is the key that can unlock the prison of culture. It will neutralize the poisons of the stereotype that allow men to go on benevolently justifying their abuses against humanity. (p. 212)

As suggested by Griffin, communication and power are woven together in that communication works in productive ways to generate knowledge and to produce and reproduce relations of power within which all people participate. When people are unaware of the ways that power works, they are more vulnerable to becoming alienated from themselves, as they are unable to consciously and intentionally direct and control their participation in such a system. Alienation results in people losing their agency, something that all people possess but atrophies without use. Human agency is a primary resource for making progressive social change, and is the "raw material," so to speak, for engaging in acts of resistance and creative action for social justice. Without such agency, we become beasts of burden, laboring under the conditions, terms, and visions of others.

Conclusion

In this chapter, we sketched a description of democracy in which the potential of people and not the machinery of a state political system provides the guiding force and direction of its future. This vision of democracy, what we call "creative democracy," is one in which diversity of ideas and meaningful participation of all groups in forming civic and political life is understood fundamentally as an essential aspect. This vision also is one in which pervasive, institutionalized inequality is considered unacceptable and in which all people have the means to provide for their basic needs and can engage in opportunities that develop their unique capacities and potential. This conception of democracy, inspired by the work of Dewey, Emerson, Foucault, Nietzsche, Rorty, and others ultimately is constituted in the character of its people—specifically, in lived practices. The responsibility for social change, then, rests in citizens' perceptions, attitudes, commitments, and behaviors, not in a faith in political institutions or in the benevolence of the power elite. As U.S. history has shown, "social and economic justice are not inevitable. Moral evolution is seldom driven by top-down initiative. When such evolution occurs, the driving force of change is usually the result of community vision and mass struggle" (Swartz, 2005, p. 122). The democratic principles of equality, liberty, and justice for all are not "givens" in Dewey's (1929/2005) sense but, rather, are "takens," ideas we extract from the world—and they must be contended for among competing visions in the ideological environments in which we exist. Actualizing these democratic principles, Dewey (1939/1993a) claimed, is, fundamentally, an intimate process:

> Democracy as a personal, an individual, way, of life involves nothing fundamentally new. But when applied it puts a new practical meaning in old ideas. Put into effect it signifies that powerful present enemies of democracy can be successfully met only by the creation of personal attitudes in individual human beings; that we must get over our tendency to think that its defense can be found in any external means whatever, whether military or civil, if they are separated from individual attitudes so deep-seated as to constitute personal character. (pp. 241–242)

As Dewey's passage makes clear, "society" is the manifestation of who we are collectively. Self and society are inextricably woven, for without others, the self has no meaning and is unable to develop; without individuals, there is no society. To change the way we do things as a society, we must change the way we do things as individuals. If we are to break free from the limitations of our current thinking that supports social injustice and hierarchy and move beyond the status quo, we must begin to talk, think, and act differently, as did C. P. Ellis. What we learn from Ellis is that transformation happens when we are willing to "step into another's shoes" and view reality from different points of view. Doing so requires a suspension of the belief systems we have come to accept and an ability to understand in a concrete, emotional, and cognitive manner the lives and values of others (Alexander, 1995). This is the communicative imagination in action: the ability to understand the ways in which the narratives and explanations for social issues are perspectival and to use communication to build community.

Notes

1. Throughout this chapter we are discussing language and the effect that language has on the construction of the self, but our approach to language is to see it as material. Our identities, while constituted by the language of identification, are also affected in traumatic ways by material conditions such as poverty and violence (Cloud, 1994; Swartz, 2005).

2. We consider alienation to be a negative thing, something to be avoided, something to struggle against. We recognize, however, that it is not an either/or binary, that one is either alienated or is not. We may be alienated in different ways and at different times. We also recognize that alienation can be generative, as in art and music, when distraught people produce beauty out of their private anguish.

3. Both Foucault and Rorty agreed that human knowledge claims and beliefs become "normal" or "real" only in the sense that they function within the constraints of a particular

culture. The conditions of "normality" are only as relevant to a culture as the conditional discourse that calls them into existence and endows them with significance. Rorty differed from Foucault on this point, however, in that he did not find it necessary to explore the micro-level conditions of desires to understand how people construct "normality." As Rorty (1979) explained, that which counts as normal solves "problems against the background of a consensus about what counts as a good explanation of the phenomena and about what it would take for a problem to be solved" (p. 320).

4. We note that the movements represented by both Gandhi and King were about much more than these two historical figures. While both men were remarkable, they stood on the shoulders of millions of people who suffered and labored for years to challenge unjust social relationships, as well as benefited from the historical *zeitgeist* of their times, the questioning of colonist and racist attitudes endemic in Western society.

Part Three

CHAPTER 8

Contrasting Platonic and Critical Models of Education

In the previous chapter, we described ways in which communication has the potential to edify, demystify, and provide opportunities for creating experiences for individuals to be better agents for social change in the troubled world we inherited. Communication and the critical imagination are particularly important for those communities, or counterpublics, that have experienced historical discrimination and recrimination, lack of opportunity and hope, or outright violence and oppression. Language enables people to establish important connections with others to begin to understand, rethink, challenge, and, ultimately, dismantle unjust social structures and power relationships. If nothing else, language, by connecting people to the experiences of others, provides inspiration for resistance and change. Communication, we have argued, makes us human and humanizing.

In this chapter, we explain how a critical education provides people with such transformative communication experiences, experiences that allow for, and encourage, a richer diversity compared to what we discussed in Chapter 1 as a limiting and socially detrimental "marketplace diversity." In Chapter 9, the next chapter, we discuss the value of critical pedagogy for transformative purposes, with specific attention given to service learning as a practical pedagogical practice for promoting edifying and progressive learning for college students. Such learning engenders a heightened awareness of the ways that social issues are constituted in multiple and interrelated structures and systems in the social, cultural, political, and economic landscapes, as well as a sense of hope and possibility for making useful and effective social change. Before we have that discussion, however, we first establish in this chapter the argument that central to pedagogy in a democratic society is a critical and self-reflective consciousness, one suspicious of received wisdom/authority and flexible in adapting to the contingencies of experience that affect all of our lives. We first contrast Platonic and critical models of education, emphasizing the benefits of critical and progressive approaches, and then elaborate on critical pedagogy in communication studies and offer an extended, specific example from our experience of working with one of our more recalcitrant students.

Platonic v. Critical Models of Education

The traditional Western model of education was developed from a Platonic model of knowledge, and continues to influence the normative pedagogy found in the U.S. educational system (Harkavy & Benson, 1998). As described in Chapter 3, the Platonic view approaches knowledge as something that is discovered in the ideal universe of permanent and fixed ideas (what Immanuel Kant called the "noumenal" world), a universe accessible by only those few individuals supposedly capable of transcending the limitations of the material world to enter the eternal world of ideas and who assume the "natural" superiority of the theoretical over that of the lived experience (Kant's phenomenal world). Such a stance assumes that communication is merely a mode of transmission and that "true" knowledge accurately represents nature and is free from human "subjectivity" and the corruptions of the passions, what Aristotle (1954) called the "defects of hearers" (p. 165). The implications of this philosophical perspective is that education, as a communicative process, becomes merely a handing down of "truths" to learners, as in the banking model of education critiqued so decisively by Brazilian educator Paulo Freire (1970/2000). The Platonic approach to education engenders an elitist "epistemarchy"—that is, a "rule by the Knowers" (Tallise, 2005), a self-elected aristocracy of knowledge professionals who discover and transmit Truth to the masses. An unfortunate, and serious, consequence of this educational approach is that students are hindered from engaging actively in the type of critical thinking and knowledge building that fosters growth, transformation, and new ways of seeing and being in the world. Rather than education being a process of the actualization of the capacity of people to be creative and critical and to create new knowledge that leads to social development, it is demoted to a process of sublimating one's intellectual, emotional and spiritual agency to doctrines of tradition, authority, and "epistemological totalitarianism" wherein cultural practices commodify a caste system "in which human beings are assigned different worth based upon their relative proximity to ahistorical assumptions of 'truth'" (Swartz, 1997, p. 3).

This approach to learning fosters the "banking model" of education (Freire, 1970/2000), in which knowledge is "transferred" from teacher to student, as though making a deposit in a banking account. In other words, instead "of communicating, the teacher issues communiqués and makes deposits which the students patiently receive, memorize, and repeat" (Freire, p. 58). Combined with the "market mentality" of neoliberalism and a conservative cultural ethos that, in recent years, has gained hegemony in U.S. society (Chomsky, 2004), the banking model threatens to turn formal education into a "prep school" for corporate America and a training ground for obedient citizens who fall in line and support, without questioning, the forces or privileges of the status quo (Wendt, 1994). In fact, the market mentality has become evident in higher education and is illustrated by the metaphor of the "student as consumer" (McMillan & Cheney, 1996). This metaphor encourages the practice of making disinterested students the arbitrators of the educational experience (e.g., "customers come first," "the customer is always right," and "customers are our bread and butter"), turning faculty into vendors or service providers. As McMillan and Cheney (1996) noted, "Keeping the educational process somewhat at arm's length, students may approach the university as they might a McDonald's drive through window: selecting an option with little thought to the process that created the Big Mac or the Quarter Pounder" (p. 5).

As the consumer metaphor suggests, the student "purchases" the knowledge of the educational establishment, illustrating the extent to which knowledge and learning have become commodified as goods for private consumption to further a person's place in the social and economic hierarchy rather than understood as a potentially transformative experience for human and social development. By privatizing the concept of education as a commodity to be sold and purchased, education as a social and public good loses significance as a public space for the development of civic relationships and responsibilities. In the banking concept of education, students receive, file, and store the deposits, but they do not meaningfully engage in their learning. Education becomes something done *to* them; it does not *concern* them—they feel like cogs in a vast impersonal machinery. An example of the above phenomenon is found in the didactic, standardized, test-taking orientation of public primary and secondary schools in this country. The focus on federally enforced standardized testing of math and reading de-emphasizes transformative learning and privileges mechanistic, a-contextual thinking (see the essays collected in Meier & Wood, 2004). The pressure on schools for their students to perform well on these standardized tests or else lose desperately needed funding creates a situation in which teaching focuses on "teaching to the test" rather than fostering critical-thinking skills, well-rounded competency, and creativity among students (Ricci, 2004). Civics, foreign languages, social studies, the arts, and even science have been severely limited to make room for standardized, test-focused instruction.[1] Student passion and creativity are sacrificed and the poetry and inspiration of learning is compromised or lost. Such conditions cannot be healthy for students or for society. As educator Wood (2004) noted, "I have searched in vain to find any study that says our children graduate as better employees, college students, or citizens as a result of taking more tests" (p. 35). Certainly, a solid foundation in basic skills of math and reading is absolutely necessary for a good education and a well-functioning citizenry (and institutional accountability is undoubtedly important), but there is no reason why this must occur at the expense of an edifying educational experience, one in which students contextualize and critique their worlds in socially meaningful and holistic terms.

In arguing for a critical education, we do not suggest that education for socialization is unimportant; to the contrary, socialization of young people is crucial for ensuring that common values are carried forth cross-generationaly so that there is some basis for functioning as a society of people who share a degree of common identity and moral/ethical worldview (Rorty, 1999b). Rorty (1999b) was entirely accurate when he stated that "even ardent radicals, for all their talk of 'education for freedom'...do not really want the high schools to produce, every year, a graduating class of amateur Zarathustras" (p. 117). What Rorty meant by this is that Nietzsche's Zarathustra, the protagonist of Nietzsche's book *Thus Spoke Zarathustra*, although utterly inspiring, liberating, and transformative as a counter-normative literary and philosophical figure, is not necessarily the person we would want our children to marry. Zarathustra's liberation, in many ways, is uncouth and antisocial.[2] Respect for others, basic standards of social behavior, and an understanding and appreciation of democratic principles are examples of some of the values that are important to impart through education (e.g., we want our children to politely wait their turn in line, eat with knives and forks, wash their hands after they use the toilet, and see themselves as valuable and supportive members of their communities). In this sense, socialization comes *before* individualization, as Rorty insisted. However, as students get older, such socialization must be balanced with criticism of that socialized identity. Education, then, becomes "a matter of inciting doubt and stimulating imagination, thereby challenging the prevailing consensus" (Rorty, 1999b, p. 118). In other words, for Rorty (1999b), and we agree, the

> point of non-vocational higher education is . . . to help students realize that they can reshape themselves—that they can rework the self-image foisted on them by their past, the self-image that makes them competent citizens, into a new self-image, one that they themselves helped to create. (p. 110)

Or, as Dewey (1916/1993j) reminded us "democracy has to be born anew every generation, and education is its midwife" (p. 122).

Although a "banking" model is useful for some purposes, such as passing on professional or technical skills and knowledge (what Rorty called "vocational education") that enable us to accomplish useful technical work in fields such as medicine and science, this aspect of learning alone is insufficient and can be counterproductive to creating a citizenry that is capable of, or even willing to, engage in moral public decision making and critically assess the moral consequences of various and contesting ideas. For example, in Nazi Germany (1931–1945), the regime utilized a highly skilled class of scientists and experts (some of the best in the world) who directed their knowledge to developing bureaucracies and technologies to torture and murder 6 million Jews, along with 6 million others, such as Poles, Gypsies, gays and lesbians, communists, socialists, labor organizers, and the mentally ill (Dwork & van Pelt, 2003). Clearly, professional or technical knowledge without equal knowledge in moral decision making is dangerous (Katz, 1992). Recognition of this danger is illustrated in the following note given each year to faculty by a school principal before the start of the fall semester:

> Dear Teacher: I am a survivor of a concentration camp. My eyes saw what no man should witness: Gas chambers built by *learned* engineers. Children poisoned by *educated* physicians. Infants killed by *trained* nurses. Women and babies shot and burned by *high school* and *college* graduates. So I am suspicious of education. My request is: Help your students to become human. Your efforts must never produce the learned monsters, skilled psychopaths, educated Eichmanns. Reading, writing, and arithmetic are important only if they serve to make our children more human. (cited in Shapiro, 1998, p. 55)

Against this idea of learning, mainstream pedagogy perpetuates the assumption that knowledge is not created but discovered, and that the existing social hierarchy (which privileges certain people based on class, gender, race, and sexual orientation, among other identities) is merely a reflection of the discovery of the correct understanding of the "natural order"—an assumption that reproduces the current relations of power and inhibits the human species from social, intellectual, and moral development.

Critical Education

In contrast to the "banking" or Platonic model of education as practiced traditionally, a critical education engages the learner in a cooperative process of knowledge creation based in real-world experiences, rather than simply ingesting and regurgitating abstract theories and facts. Instead of being a process of depositing or transferring information, education is viewed as a process of raising questions (or "problem posing") and imagining how things might be different and better than they are currently. Critical education is a process of inquiry in which existing assumptions, values, and beliefs are scrutinized, with the goal of intellectual and personal transformation, or "liberation" through dialogue and friendship (Dalton, 2003; Freire, 1970/2000). Such an education helps to overcome the personal alienation that is often fostered through the traditional model, and emphasizes the transformative potential of teaching and learning. Critical education is a way of transforming individuals, providing opportunities for them to become more empowered and perceptive of the influences that shape their thinking and how and what they are encouraged to think and feel. With this realization, students and teachers alike are better able to control the ways in which they think and challenge normative boundaries of truth (Swartz, 2005). This perspective views education as fundamentally about pushing beyond established boundaries of what is "knowable" and what is considered to be "knowledge." In other words, education can best serve human development when it encourages people to question the truths that are protected and reproduced through the myriad intersections of dominant norms, institutions, and discourses. Education also best serves society when it fosters creativity and encourages people to imagine and describe themselves and the world in terms that offer new ways of thinking and being. Critical pedagogy, in other words, is a tool for helping people to become agents for social change, against the norms that would prevent this from so being. In the words of McLaren (1995), such pedagogy "provides a starting point for linking knowledge to power and a commitment to developing forms of community life that take seriously the struggle for democracy and social justice" (p. 34).

A recent book by Fassett and Warren (2007) serves to ground our discussion of a critical education in the work of Paulo Freire, whose classic book *Pedagogy of the Oppressed*—published in 1970 amid the widespread struggles of peasants and workers throughout South and Central America against landed oligarchies and their murderous militias—has had a profound impact on educational theory throughout the humanities and social sciences, inspiring two generations of critical teachers and scholars. Central to Freire's writing is the importance of dialogue with students as co-learners/co-creators of knowledge, as opposed to students positioned as passive receptacles of an authoritative, elite, and hierarchical knowledge; concern for *praxis* and for social/political inclusion within larger communities dedicated to fairness and social justice; and for *conscientization*, the conscious power of one's agency to engage with and to influence one's social worlds. With such Freirean commitments in place, Fassett and Warren's book helps teachers to guide their students "to reflect and act upon the world in order to transform it, to make it a more just place for more people, to respond to our own collective pains and needs and desires" (p. 26).

Fassett and Warren (2007) supplemented the Freirean paradigm with the theories of Michel Foucault, Judith Butler, and Michel de Certeau, as well as with the homegrown communication education scholarship of Jo Sprague, Ronald Pelias, Thomas Nakayama, Robert Krizek, and others. Collectively, these scholars stand for the proposition that "doing critical communication pedagogy is about holding ourselves accountable for the ways we exist within the institutions that have shaped us" (Fassett & Warren, p. 89). When teachers enter a classroom, they bring with them a normative vision of the "good" and the "just" that they model for (or against) students. Their simple presence as the authority in the classroom alone, without more, can help or hinder students; without realizing it, teachers often embody and perpetuate the discursive forms and assumptions that they set out to confront with their teaching. As Fassett and Warren noted:

> Being a critical scholar is not about escaping, it is not about being or feeling better, and it is certainly not about doing easy research. Being a critical scholar is about always being accountable for not only what you intend but what kinds of effects you put in motion. It is about holding yourself responsible even when privilege tells you [that you] are not, about listening to others even through you feel you are entitled to speak. (p. 88)

Situating Fassett and Warren's (2007) notion of critical communication scholarship is a series of overlapping (and familiar for critical scholars) orientations that draw people together as critical educators. For instance, Fassett and Warren (p. 39) work from the axiom, as we have been discussing throughout this book, that "identity is constituted in communication"; that both teachers and students are molded by cultural and ideological forces. As Fassett and Warren wrote:

> Critical communication educators look to postmodern and Poststructural understandings of human identity, to senses of students and teachers as relational selves produced in collusion and collision, to theories and methodologies that help them account for identities as produced in cultural—and therefore inherently ideological—contexts. (p. 40)

Within the cacophony of these forces and desires that underlie self-perceptions, people's identities congeal, or perhaps splinter, and what they take to be their identities are the results of "performativity," their beings as enacted in discourse with one another. Throughout such performances, situated in the minutia of our lives, we become who we are, and we also become open (or not) to the constructions of others, to their performative identities. In this sense, human culture is dramatistic, poetic, joyful, and, above all, consequential.

Given that identity is relational, performative, emergent, and contextualized by ideology and the practices of others, the concept of power is understood as being "fluid and complex" (p. 41), something we all share to a degree and perhaps use inappropriately or with unintended consequences. Fassett and Warren (2007) remind us that a critical pedagogy must always be sensitive to our exercise of power and to the consequences of our actions. Likewise, Fassett and Warren direct us to focus on "concrete, mundane communication practices as constitutive of larger social and structural systems" (p. 43). The corollary to Fassett and Warren's point is that critical communication educators "embrace social, structural critique as it places concrete, mundane communication practices in a meaningful context" (Fassett & Warren, p. 45). In short, we must be mindful of the larger and smaller contexts in which teachers and students operate, in which they both perform.

Finally, Fassett and Warren (2007) highlight the importance of reflexivity, dialogue, and praxis in the educational process. This is most evident in their definition of *critical communication pedagogy* as "teaching and research addressed toward understanding how communication creates and may, therefore, challenge sociocultural oppressions—e.g., classism, racism, sexism, heterosexism, ableism, ageism, etc." (Fassett & Warren, p. 3). An important goal of their book is, thus, "to articulate a language of critique that accounts for how communication creates and makes possible our ability to see and respond" to social inequality (Fassett & Warren, p. 7). In this way, critical communication pedagogy is "explicitly reform oriented; researchers in this vein aim to change our world for the better" (Fasset & Warren, p. 52). Dialogue and language are seen as epistemic and generative in this process. Similar to Foucault's notion of power, which we discussed in Chapter 7, people create the world through discourse, and the results, in their positivity, become their lives. When pedagogy is approached from this critical perspective, the questions that emerge for classroom discussion become: Do we feel as if we live in the world of our making? Do we live the lives we want? How could our lives be different?

Fassett and Warren (2007) present their research through an autoethnographic methodology, which they described as a "reflexive accounting, one that asks us to slow down, to subject our experiences to critical examination, to expose life's mundane qualities for how they illustrate our participation in power" (p. 103). In the context of the classroom, the autoethnographic person struggles with her/his embodiment, authority, and disciplinary persona as that figure engages and interacts with non-disciplinary, intellectually novice students who, nevertheless, live and function in the larger world without often having to theorize or scrutinize their language or assumptions. Moreover, students may live on terms—although perhaps alien to teachers as disciplinary representatives (or captives, depending on one's perspective)—more successful or satisfying to themselves than the professional and philosophical terms teachers have to offer. In other words, critical communication pedagogy, in the sense evoked by Fassett and Warren, requires teachers to be open to students from *where they are*, and to realize that often they have a great deal to learn from them about their teaching strategies.

Fassett and Warren's (2007) book has helped to improve our critical pedagogy. We noticed this most clearly one semester in our Communication and Diversity in United States' History course, in which we contextualize and encourage students to probe and question their sense of self and community, helping students to explore important issues of diversity and community as they have been played out historically in the construction of U.S. culture. Using both primary source historical documents (such as videos, plays, legislative statutes and court decisions, old photographs, archival newspaper articles, personal letters from historical figures, advertisements, comics, and other cultural artifacts) and secondary source scholarly articles and chapters, students utilize historical, legal, critical, philosophical, sociological, and narrative approaches to study diversity and the conflict that often surrounds the quest for moral, social, and economic inclusion in this country. The overarching method of exploration in the course is what we have been calling the *communicative imagination*—our ability to name the constraints, as well as opportunities, placed on us by language so as to become morally intelligent agents in our relationships with others.

Topics in this course include an introduction to the communicative imagination, case studies of cultures in conflict, and the socialization process (how social movements, mass politics, and other cultural phenomena construct our cultural and individual identities). In so doing, students review notions of "otherness" and the fear that often surrounds such positioning, such as eugenics, scientific racism, and the manner by which diversity has been positioned in medical terms and controlled, and conflicts surrounding issues of class, race, gender, and sexual identity/orientation. In exploring these topics, students see how each of these categories and issues are constructed rhetorically and reinforced by normative communicative practices and habits. In engaging some of these practices, students begin to appreciate how individuals and groups in U.S. society can learn from the sacrifices of the past to construct a better future. Thus, upon completion of this course, students are expected to appreciate diversity and community in the United States as a site of struggle and potential for increased levels of justice, equality, and democracy.

Yet, as Fassett and Warren (2007) suggested, such an approach is not without challenges—not without students who see education as an *entrenchment*, and not as a *questioning* of their world. For example, we had to explain to a student that the term "White Power" or "White Pride" is a negative concept, not a symbol of social progress as is "Black Power/Pride" or "Chicano Power/Pride" (or "Gay Rights") because the "White Power/Pride" movement was a reaction (in fact, reactionary) to the claim for inclusion explicit in minority identity struggles. To this student, her whiteness was seen as a neutral, "given" identity, unfairly targeted by other racial and ethnic groups for past sins, crimes that do not in any sense concern her ("I never owned slaves," she remarked and also said, "I'm not responsible for how other countries treat their citizens"). Refusing to feel guilty or complicit for crimes/attitudes of the past (and perhaps blind to the continuing inequality of the present), she wanted to assert her whiteness on an equal basis with other competing (and perhaps threatening) groups in the racial/religious/cultural politics of contemporary culture. She wanted her whiteness to be taken on its "self-evident" and privileged terms.

Throughout the semester, this student expressed herself each class period with a vocabulary at odds with the course and the other students—for instance, she was vocally anti–gay rights, anti–affirmative action, anti–welfare state (i.e., anti-tax), an apologist for the Minutemen Project,[3] and committed fervently to what critical scholars call nationalistic or "normative Christianity" (see, e.g., Rockler, 2006). Not surprisingly, the other students were irritated by her views and, unfortunately, responded uncivilly. In turn, this student was clearly frustrated by what she perceived as a double standard in our society on the contentious issues of race and cultural politics. She felt "othered" by the class and was resentful.

Unlike the other students who made fun of her and treated her like a social pariah, we saw this woman's perspectives as productively challenging the assumptions of the course (and of the instructors), and we frequently defended or bolstered her views to help her feel less marginalized in class discussion. In an e-mail we wrote to her after a particularly tense class discussion, in which many of the other students "ganged up" on her, our commitment to this pedagogy crystallized:

> We would like to invite you again to drop by our office to chat about the course. You are doing great in the class (for the midterm evaluation that we turned in for you this week we assigned you an "A") and we appreciate you and your contributions. We sense, however, that you are a little frustrated in the course and we do recognize that some of the other students are not as polite to you as they should be in responding to your very conscientious and heartfelt positions on various topics. We hope that you continue to speak up in class and we promise to make more of an effort to help bolster your perspectives to help your classmates and ourselves better appreciate what you have to say.
>
> We are sincere in writing that we hope you would drop by our office sometime so that we can talk and we can better understand your perspectives. If you have any reading material that you would like us to read (articles, newspaper clippings, etc.) that would help us to understand better the issues from your point of view, we would be very happy to read them. Also, if you have some material that you think would be appropriate for the class to read, we would be happy to work those into the curriculum this semester and even in future semesters.
>
> In short, we want you to know that you are a welcomed and honored member of the class who asks important questions that challenge both ourselves and your classmates, and we think that is wonderful. This is *exactly* what we want our students to be able and willing to do.

Taking this stance allowed us to realize (over the course of the semester and with the help of Fassett and Warren's, 2007, book) that this student was allowing the language of other people to use her and manipulate her identity, rather than her being in control of her identity. Working with her, we realized that she meant well—she was not a racist, nor was she particularly intolerant or insensitive. Rather, she did not have the communication imagination necessary to reframe her identifications in different, more culturally sensitive and inclusive manners (e.g., to see herself as an "American" instead of as "White" or as a member of a specific religious community competing with others for influence in a world devoid of absolute theological truth).

Clearly, this student was culturally naïve (she was, after all, a young student from rural Colorado who attended Christian private schools prior to attending college). As a result, the scripts she evokes can be perceived as offensive to many people who focus on her unintended trigger vocabulary. Nevertheless, she started to appreciate that the language she used to describe her social world was not self-evident and natural (e.g., that her "whiteness" no longer embodies a privileged ontological meaning). She started to realize that her language choices positioned her in certain (negative) ways to others. Above all, she learned that language and communication exist in a historical context that situate her identity and the identities of others. Although she was not yet "there," in a multicultural sense, her progress, as measured by our interaction in class and in our discussion over her written work, exemplifies clearly what Fassett and Warren (2007) meant by critical communication pedagogy—a commitment to helping students where they are—along with ourselves—to be more self-aware of their abilities to author and take responsibility for their lives and for the world that they really do want to help create (for a more extended example of this pedagogy in action, see Lee, 2006).

This student, for her part, appreciated the effort we made to draw her into the substance of the course in a comfortable, nonjudgmental manner. In an e-mail she sent to us at the end of the semester, she wrote:

> I really, really enjoyed this class and I wish I would have opened up a little sooner, it just takes me awhile because I know that my opinions and point of view are far different than those of some of the other students but it was very refreshing to have you, the teacher, encourage me to speak out and feel comfortable with what I am thinking and what I believe.

This comment, more than any others we have received in our more than 10 years of teaching, made us feel satisfied with our pedagogy in ways that are too profound to express.

Conclusion

Throughout this chapter, we argued that a critical education provides individuals with transformative communication experiences, producing a richer diversity than what we discussed in Chapter 1 as a limiting and social detrimental "marketplace diversity." We argued that central to pedagogy in a democratic society is a critical and self-reflective consciousness. We first contrasted Platonic and critical models of education, emphasizing the benefits of critical and progressive approaches. We then outlined some of the traits of a critical communication pedagogy, using the work of Fassett and Warren (2007). We ended this chapter with our experience of working with a student who was herself critical of our critical pedagogy and at odds politically with the ethos of the course. By utilizing the perspectives of Fassett and Warren, we were able to reach out to her and to enfold her identity and concerns into the learning environment. In the next chapter (Chapter 9), we highlight the importance of service learning as a crucial component of the critical pedagogy that we endorse.

Notes

1. In a memorable scene from the film *Mr. Holland's Opus* (1995), the character played by Richard Dreyfuss, a high school music teacher who, for decades, clashed with the bureaucracy of the school over the value of his music program, is forced to retire when the school board decides to cut funding altogether for arts and music programs of the school. Appearing at a school board meeting to discuss this contentious issue, the teacher confronts the administration and says, in effect, "while you are busy teaching kids how to read and write, you are neglecting to give them anything to read or write about." This, we feel, is exemplary of the point we are making here.

2. Nietzsche's Zarathustra, a hermit, rejected companionship with people, and considered humanity to be "rabble." His rhetorical style was one of offense, dismissiveness, and insult. He came across as a ragged, dirty prophet of sorts and a difficult conversationalist. Nietzsche's Zarathustra's strength lies not in his interpersonal skills but in his rejection of received morality and his fashioning of a new one while, rough, is anti-nihilist and, in a broad sense, humanistic and kind.

3. The Minutemen Project was the brainchild of Jim Gilchrist, and commenced on October 1, 2004, to deter illegal immigration across the United States–Mexican border. This controversial group has been accused of being vigilantes and racists (SPLC Report, 2005).

CHAPTER 9

Service Learning

As we discussed in the previous chapter, a central requirement for an effectively functioning democracy in the progressive sense that we have evoked throughout this book is the participation of critically reflective and engaged citizens. At a minimum, a healthy society needs a *balance* between socialization and re-socialization, between its knowledge-gathering institutions and its commitment to edification. What is true for an academic discipline, in the sense evoked by Rorty (1996a) to follow, is also true for society in general if it wishes to avoid cultural and intellectual stasis—in other words, to remain *interesting*. In Rorty's (1996a) words, "A humanistic discipline is in good shape only when it produces both inspiring works and works that contextualize, and thereby deromanticize and debunk, those inspiring works" (p. A48).

We take Rorty's sentiment as representative of creative democracy and the role of education within such a society. It is through a critical pedagogical structure in schools and throughout public culture that such citizenship can be achieved. If schools would move away from their over-reliance on the banking model of education, which is evidenced by the inordinate amount of standardized testing at the expense of other creative learning processes, educators can focus activities and content on enabling students to reflect on their social relationships and the broader cultural environment. This type of critical education would better prepare students to be actively engaged in positive social reinvention and transformation.

A pertinent example of a critical pedagogy that provides an opportunity to confront both the limits of one's thought and socially produced and reproduced truths of society is "service learning." The growing literature on this pedagogical practice reveals a number of descriptions and frameworks for articulating the purpose and philosophical position of service learning. A general definition of *service learning* that derives from this literature is that it is an educational strategy that aims to engage learners actively through at least three key components: academic instruction, community service and critical reflection on the subject matter, and serving others (Artz, 2001; Butin, 2003; Varlotta, 1997). Moreover, there appears to be a general consensus on the criteria that enable service-learning practices to be considered legitimate, ethical, and useful (Butin, 2003): (a) *respect* (the service learning must respect the situations, perspectives, and ways of life of groups being served); (b) *reciprocity* (service learning should provide meaningful benefits not only to those providing the service but also to those being served); (c) *relevance* (the service must be relevant to the academic content, thus providing real-world experience of the issues being studied); and (d) *reflection* (an essential component to creating meaning and knowledge from the experience).

There are different, albeit overlapping, foci of service learning found in the literature. One common view of service learning emphasizes its value as a pedagogical tool for increasing academic achievement and helping students to gain further understanding of course content and other relevant subject mater. In this sense, service learning is a methodology for a richer and more world-relevant educational experience. Other descriptions focus on the potential of service learning to develop a sense of civic responsibility among students through serving communities in need, and still other descriptions identify the main goals of service learning as a personal growth opportunity for students in which they are challenged to examine their identities and life assumptions through engaging with the "other." The definition that we advocate, in conjunction with the arguments presented in this book, defines service learning as an educational experience that intends to foster an understanding of social justice, a fundamental appreciation for the interconnections between all people, and the need for healthy and sustainable communities to grow and thrive.

Service learning, understood as both a philosophy and a method of learning, has become implemented in schools and universities in recent years, providing a counterbalance to hierarchical, epistemarchist pedagogies that are typical throughout educational institutions in the United States. Service learning is a model of teaching/learning that connects theory, research, and action (i.e., *praxis*) through service work, reflection, and dialogue on systemic social issues such as poverty, health disparities, homelessness, and many others.

Theoretical Bases of Service Learning

The roots of service learning in modern history can been traced back to Francis Bacon (1561–1626), who argued that knowledge must be produced in connection with its use if it is to be beneficial. That is, the consequences of knowledge must be contended with, for it is in the process of being created that knowledge functions as a power for good rather than as a tool of oppression (Harkavy & Benson, 1998). Bacon rejected the ancient Greek aristocratic dualism of "superior" pure theory and "inferior" applied practice and, instead, emphasized that what is most useful in practice is most correct in theory and that the improvement of the human mind and the human condition is one and the same thing (see Harkavy & Benson, 1998). Bacon viewed the purpose of scientific inquiry and knowledge production to be for human problem solving.

In more modern times, the philosophical roots of service learning are commonly attributed to John Dewey and his advocacy of democratic education and theory of instrumental intelligence (see Harkavy & Benson, 1998; Rhoads, 2000). Dewey's perspectives were formed against the Platonic elitist theory of education discussed in Chapter 8, which claimed that learning occurred through rational theorizing alone, protected from the "corrupting" influences of materiality and subjectivity—what Dewey referred to as the "spectator theory of knowledge." Dewey is the theorist most well known for challenging this perspective and offering an alternative philosophy. His theory of instrumental intelligence is based on the perspective that knowledge is a social undertaking and focused on "intelligence," an ongoing process of "confronting problems and striving for resolutions that keep in touch with, and hence are responsive to, subsequent evidence and experience" (Talisse, 2005, p. 188). This emphasis on instrumental intelligence is the basis of the Deweyan "deliberative" or process-oriented democracy that views democracy as a "mode of collective problem-solving, that, like scientific inquiry, is fallibilist, experimentalist, and ongoing" (Talisse, 2005, p. 188). Knowledge, in the Deweyan perspective, thus, is redescribed as a process of "knowing" and occurs through solving problematic situations that emerge from the context of living.

Dewey's theory of instrumental intelligence asserts four main propositions: (a) reflective thought is an active response to the challenge of the environment, (b) everyone can contribute to knowledge, (c) people can best contribute when they participate in determining the purposes that guide their actions, and (d) the fundamental purpose of knowledge is to improve social well-being (Harkavy & Benson, 1998). An implication of Dewey's instrumental intelligence is that education should result in practical wisdom, created through a dialogic community process that is relevant to problems experienced in social life.

Dewey's theory spawned what was called the New Education movement. The New Education was Dewey's concept for a democratic education in which students help to shape their learning, assist in forming the curriculum, and reflect on its value. Central to this democratic pedagogy, the New Education emphasized the importance of connecting academic learning with application in problematic situations in communities. In this way, Dewey envisioned the community as a source of knowledge building, as well as a laboratory for the experimentation of potential solutions to problems. Schools and universities became not merely a place of knowledge transference but a site for modeling the democratic process that Dewey championed for society as a whole (see Talisse, 2005). Dewey's theory of instrumental intelligence and his New Education established the foundation for what is now commonly referred to as service learning.

The first notable creation of a service-learning model in an institution of higher education was at Columbia University in the early 1900s. The program was intended to link the university with New York City through combining theory with practice to address social issues in the city, and it did so successfully for a number of years (Harkavy & Benson, 1998). The program, unfortunately, was not long-lived due to changes in the university's leadership. During the 1960s, the concept of service learning was further shaped through the establishment of Volunteers in Service to America (VISTA) in 1965. VISTA was established during the civil rights era and the renewed vision among ordinary Americans for more equality across classes and groups of people. In 1965, the term "service learning" was first used to describe a project in East Tennessee, which linked Oak Ridge Associated Universities to local organizations in a collaborative effort to combine academic learning and practice in the communities. In 1968, the first national conference on service learning was held.

More recently, service learning gained widespread popularity in higher education with the establishment of Campus Compact in 1985, a nonprofit association dedicated to the promotion of service learning in colleges and universities. Founded by the presidents of Brown, Georgetown, and Stanford universities, Campus Compact was created in response to public criticism of a declining concern for social welfare and the public good among elite institutions of higher education, a turn that was furthered by the neoliberal ideology that gained ascendance during the Reagan years. Service learning through Campus Compact alone reportedly occurs in approximately 900 colleges and universities, and is now becoming accepted in some progressive and better funded primary and secondary public and private schools (Butin, 2003).

Social Justice–Oriented Service Learning

Service learning for social justice redirects the focus of service learning from charity to social change (see Tompkins, 2006), in that responsiveness to immediate needs is replaced by a multi-perspectival analysis of power and pervasive social inequality, identification of sources of power for changing social conditions, and engagement in social action that calls attention to injustice or helps to create more just conditions (Boyle-Baise & Langford, 2004). This approach to learning examines critically the ways in which social hierarchy functions and is normalized through relations of power that include laws, institutions, symbols, and everyday practices that mutually reinforce and reify each other. Central to social justice-focused service learning is an emphasis on the complex and multileveled nature of social problems, a touchstone that comes out of the recognition that historically and culturally simplistic interventions and inquiries into social issues have been unsuccessful (Swan, 2002). Besides examining the various levels at which inequality is produced and reproduced, a multi-perspectival approach also includes various knowledges or ways of seeing the issues under study. Local knowledge—knowledge that comes from those who are being "served"—typically is sought to help elucidate the issues from an "insider" perspective. The perspectives of those who are actively engaged in working to address the social issues are also collected, as well as academic writing that provides theoretical frameworks to guide analysis and discussion of the experience (Boyle-Baise & Langford, 2004; Butin, 2003; Swan, 2002). This knowledge and understanding is gained through dialogue both in the classroom setting and in the process of serving and/or collaborating with others who are adversely affected by normative power structures.

Social justice service learning, however, moves beyond the analysis of issues to identify agents, opportunities, and sites for social change. Mere examination of social problems without identifying potential avenues for change and acting upon that potential may engender hopelessness and despair (Boyle-Baise & Langeford, 2004). On the other hand, connecting awareness to actions in which everyday people can engage unlocks human potentiality for shaping one's life, community, and the norms that govern social life. As part of the learning process, students search for possibilities for resistance and change at the multiple levels at which power relations exist (e.g., intellectual, relational, institutional, and financial). Doing so enables students to better understand their agency and the fact that everyday behaviors, such as the way one talks about social problems, the businesses and organizations one supports, or the various choices one makes when interacting with others, can be sites of social change in addition to the broader, structural-level changes in laws or government. Identifying the arrays of potential opportunities and agents for change emphasizes the way in which social issues are socially constructed and reified and how everyone has the opportunity to participate in the shaping of this larger society by being conscientious actors in their local environment.

Critical education, and social justice service learning, in particular, involves a transformation of the self and becoming "different" than one was before the experience. The concept of the self takes on meaning and relevance only in the context of others (Mead, 1982). George Herbert Mead's (1982) social self theory illustrates this point. His theory describes the self as being comprised of two components: the "I," which represents the spontaneous and autonomous aspects of selfhood, and the "Me," the socialized part of the self, which is shaped by and, responds to, external and societal and environmental conditions and influences, such as social norms. It is the interaction of the two components that gives rise to a "self": It is impossible for the self to develop outside of social experience. Through critically examining the social world, one begins to understand the ways in which she or he has been made into a subject.

Through service learning experience, in particular, people are able to "cross borders," entering into the realities and understandings of others who have different cultural, social, and economic experiences than they do. Such border crossing "provides fruitful occasion to question the *sui generis* of such borders" (Butin, 2003, p. 1683) and they reveal the ways in which people participate in the sustaining of such borders. As Anzaldúa (1987) noted, "the Borderlands are physically present wherever two or more cultures edge each other, where people of different races occupy the same territory, where under, lower, middle and upper classes touch, where the space between two individuals shrinks with intimacy" (Preface, n.p.). Thus, in entering into the reality of others, people confront their beliefs, prejudices, narratives, and explanations for who they are and how the world is constructed, providing them with opportunities to revise these constructions.

Attitudes of entitlement or "natural" privilege are often challenged when the historical and cultural contingency of social borders and categories are understood and the recognition that others' realities are, or could be, a potential reality for oneself. Such edifying learning experiences can underscore an existential common denominator across human beings, regardless of the communities to which they belong—that all humans have the potential to experience, and wish to avoid, alienation and suffering. Through such encounters with others, service learning provides valuable opportunities for students to become conscious of, critically analyze, and reshape their "final vocabulary" in a reflection of their new understandings and experiences vis-à-vis others.

Finally, service learning is an important way to address the hopelessness and alienation that many people (especially young people) feel about their ability to affect social change, an alienation that is often compounded by traditional pedagogy that separates the realm of "knowledge" from that of lived experience. Through the service-learning experience and the identification of multiple sources of, and opportunities to, use power for compassionate, socially just ends, students come to recognize that possibilities for change always exist and that their social realities are not inevitable or fixed. The service-learning experience helps students to understand that the current social reality, instead, is a potential site of change and possibility.

A Social Justice–Oriented Service Learning Model

For service learning to be relevant and focused on issues involving social justice, it is important for schools to not only adopt such a learning philosophy but also to orient students and educate faculty to be prepared for a service-learning type of educational environment. One institution with which we have experience is exemplary in this regard. Regis University, which has campus locations in Colorado and Nevada, strives to integrate service learning and social justice into the mission of the institution.[1] Regis is a private Jesuit Catholic university founded in 1877 on the principle that students can receive an education that focuses on the development of social responsibility and service to others. It has many campus locations throughout two states to meet the needs of students, as well as an expanding distance-education program. Regis also boasts a nationally recognized adult-accelerated undergraduate program, the goal of which is to enable professionals, many of whom are already working in established careers, to further their education in an environment of like-minded peers, enhance their leadership potential, and engender in students a service and social justice sensibility. Although much of the social-justice philosophy at Regis is grounded in the Jesuit Catholic tradition (for an example of this tradition, see the *Faculty Resource Handbook*, and the university's web site: regis.edu), the school's service-learning model transcends religious affiliation and beliefs. In fact, the presence of religious diversity among faculty and students on campus, in addition to other aspects of cultural diversity, is one of the factors in which the university takes pride (*Faculty Resource Handbook*). There are no mandatory religious practices and instructors are not required to be Catholic or to orient their teaching to Catholic doctrine. Faculty members, however, are strongly encouraged to adopt a social justice orientation and, as much as possible, to align their class content accordingly. Instructors are often asked to consider and to articulate to their students how their course content can help students to further engage with the world around them and provide them with tools to positively address social problems. The following excerpt of the Regis mission statement reflects some of the components necessary for a social justice education:

> We seek to provide values-centered undergraduate and graduate education, as well as to strengthen our commitment to community service. We nurture the life of the mind and the pursuit of truth within an environment conducive to effective teaching, learning and personal development. Consistent with the Judeo-Christian principles, we apply knowledge to human needs and seek to preserve the best of the human heritage. We encourage the continual search for truth, values and a just existence. Throughout this process, we examine and attempt to answer the question: "How ought we to live?" . . . . [W]e encourage all members of the Regis community to learn proficiently, think logically and critically, identify and choose personal standards of values, and be socially responsible. We further encourage the development of the skills and leadership abilities necessary for distinguished professional work and contributions to the improvement and transformation of society. (regis.edu)

Empowered by this mission statement, faculty members are encouraged to develop assignments that require students to use the knowledge gleaned from each course in practical ways. In the adult-education program, called School for Professional Studies (or SPS), instructors are asked to avoid using standardized tests or other assignments that simply require a regurgitation of course content to demonstrate competency. Instead, competency is to be evaluated on the basis of a particular university-wide learning outcome module adapted to meet the mission of the university. The three areas in the module are *knowledge*, *ability*, and *commitment*. Students, of course, need to show that they have acquired the knowledge relevant to the discipline or content area that they study, but they are also expected to demonstrate knowledge of "diverse cultures, perspectives, and belief systems" and ought to be able to "think critically, communicate effectively, and use technology" (*Faculty Resource Handbook*). Students also must show commitment to "ethical and social responsibility, leadership and service to others, and learning as a lifelong endeavor" (*Faculty Resource Handbook*).

By emphasizing the critical-thinking and diversity components within a service-learning oriented education, instructors guide students into thinking beyond charity to the broader social constructs that create and perpetuate social inequities throughout society. Students, therefore, are encouraged to avoid thinking about their service to others as "charity work" that they perform without any careful thought or analysis of the social structures that threaten the well-being of particular groups of people. Whereas charity tends to emphasize the individual (for instance, how individuals end up in situations where they need the help, or charity, of others, as well as how a more privileged individual might help a less privileged one), a social-justice orientation to education centers around the collective and structural, how societal members co-construct particular systems that by the nature of their constructions disadvantage some and advantage and privilege others. Education focused on critical thinking and social justice, thus, enables students to examine political, cultural, and social institutions, and perhaps engenders a sense of both personal and social responsibility and commitment to others.

New faculty members joining the SPS program must undergo orientation, four hours of which is focused on background of the Jesuit social justice tradition in addition to a description of the service learning and social justice focus of the program. This orientation, as well as the relevant written materials, work to encourage faculty to think seriously about how they develop courses and how they provide a foundation for a critical education. In going through this program, and in our experience of teaching at Regis, we have found that students are very receptive to this foundation of social justice. In each of our communication classes, students are always asked to critically reflect on how they can incorporate the material they learned in the course to their life outside of the classroom and, specifically, how their understanding of communication can enable them to create the type of equitable, fair, and inclusive environment that they would like to see in the broader social world. Many students take the information back to their workplace and report on how they have positively influenced that environment; others reflect on the changes that they make in their personal life in terms of their relationships to others, the way they perceive themselves, and the way they engage as citizens as a result of their communication courses.

During the four-hour orientation, there are three key requests that are asked of instructors. The first request is that faculty members treat students as active collaborators in the learning process, which means encouraging students to ask questions of the content and making them responsible for actively engaging course concepts. Such practice satisfies two aspects of Dewey's theory of instrumental intelligence: not only can everyone contribute to knowledge but they contribute best when they can determine the guiding purpose of their actions (see Harkavy & Benson, 1998). Group discussion is encouraged more so than standard lecturing to privilege student interaction with one another and promote collaborative learning; it is through these class discussions that students contribute to knowledge construction, as well as identify ways in which they can make their education meaningful to their life and that of others. Students, therefore, are not to be thought of as empty vessels waiting passively to be filled with knowledge but, rather, as co-contributors to the educational process, people who are hungry for self and social discovery.

The second request is that instructors are asked to encourage students to use what they learn not only to benefit their life and career but also to benefit others and to enact social change. The question in the mission statement, "How ought we to live?" is one that is referenced quite often during faculty orientation and it is one that students are familiar with as well. Along with that question are other questions that focus attention on a just existence in an unjust society and the role of education in instigating a more just and equitable social structure. By posing the question, "How ought we to live?" in the context of an educational environment, instructors and students are invited to think about what society does *with* knowledge. Regardless of the topic area, whether it is economics, business, or communication, for example, students begin to understand that what they are learning should not be thought of as objective and separate pieces of knowledge alienated from real-world contexts. Rather, the information gleaned from any particular course of study can and ought to be used to understand the constructed nature of social inequity and aid in the quest to construct a more fair and just society.

The third request is for instructors to encourage and promote critical reflection with their students. Students need to be able to "examine underlying assumptions, consider alternatives, and develop a critically aware frame of mind" (*Faculty Resource Handbook*). Regis also emphasizes the need for "self-directed empowerment" where students engage in a "continual reinterpretation, renegotiation, and recreation of personal relationships, work lives, [and] social structures" (*Faculty Resource Handbook*). These guidelines for instructors reflect the core concepts of a critical education as theorized by Freire and Fasset and Warren (2007), discussed in Chapter 8. Students are treated as co-creators of knowledge, taught to be conscious of what and how they learn and to think further about the relationship between education and social transformation, and encouraged to think critically about what it means to live in a just society. They are inspired to imagine alternative possibilities of social interactions and social structure.

Regis University, in a sense, conceptualizes teachers as "transformative intellectuals" as described by Giroux (1993). Recognizing the transformative capacity of teachers means privileging the critical and constitutive nature of teachers' intellectual work over the traditional, instrumental view of knowledge "transmission." It means deemphasizing the banking model of education and emphasizing a critically engaged transformative one. Giroux argued how imperative it is for educators to "take active responsibility for raising serious questions about what they teach, how they are to teach, and what the larger goals are for which they are striving" (p. 275). Regis stresses the importance of teachers being conscientious about the ways in which they organize their classes because how a class is structured and how knowledge is conceptualized and discussed greatly influence learning experiences and outcomes. In a fundamental sense, Regis expects faculty to connect what students learn in the classroom to what students experience outside of the classroom. The university's goal is that students have been active and responsive enough in the classroom that they are able to see education as an important catalyst for positive social change. Furthermore, instructors are expected to help students to recognize and cultivate their agency in bringing about societal structural transformation. Regis emphasizes that *how* something is taught is often even more important than *what* is taught. As Giroux described it, political pedagogy recognizes the need to focus on the role of teaching methods in bringing about a particularly conscientious type of student:

> Making the political more pedagogical means utilizing forms of pedagogy that embody political interests that are emancipatory in nature: that is, using forms of pedagogy that treat students as critical agents; make knowledge problematic; utilize critical and affirming dialogue; and make the case for struggling for a qualitatively better world for all people. (p. 277)

If civic engagement is to be nurtured and supported, it is vital that classrooms are fundamentally democratic. The banking/transmission model of education actually works against civic democratic participation because it does not allow for critical interrogation, reflection, and creativity. Unfortunately, the current state of democratic participation in the United States is reflective of a transmission model of knowledge. Generally, people are more consumers than they are citizens, passively absorbing the messages received (mostly via popular media but also through social interaction that reinforces those mediated messages) about politics, policies, and civic participation. They then regurgitate that "knowledge" by voting how they have been told to vote, if they vote at all, or by transmitting those received messages to others—all with very little critical reflection or interrogation.

It is not that we are unimaginative or unintelligent as a citizenry. On the contrary, people have much more potential than they actually use in productive ways. Cultural critics frequently document how U.S. citizens are politically ignorant but extremely sophisticated when it comes to engaging sport or popular culture. To take one well-publicized example, a 2006 study by the McCormick Tribune Freedom Museum, revealed that only a quarter of the U.S. population could name a *single* of the five freedoms guaranteed in the First Amendment to the United States Constitution, whereas more than 50% could name at least two members of the fictional Simpsons cartoon family. In addition, one in five Americans believe that the "right to own a pet" is a First Amendment freedom ("Simpsons 'Trump' First Amendment," p. 2). On the other hand, as social critic Noam Chomsky (2002) observed, participants on radio call-in sports programs "have a tremendous amount of expertise, they have detailed knowledge of all kinds of things, they carry on these extremely complex discussions" (p. 99). The proliferation of fantasy sports leagues in recent years also attests to Chomsky's observation, in that large quantities of energy, enthusiasm, and intelligence are being wasted on frivolous cultural expression when the same intelligence and commitment could be directed toward trying to solve the many problems facing this nation. The question is not one of resources—intellectual or financial—it is a question of priority and commitment. It is, above all, a question of *interest*.

Sadly, people often act as consumers rather than citizens when they fail to fully think about and understand how certain policies and governmental action affect society as a whole, particularly those in society who have historically been underresourced or the victims of oppression. Citizenship and civic engagement necessitate conceptualizing the self as intricately interconnected with others, whereas a consumer mentality limits the focus to the independent and isolated self. This is exactly what Regis University strives to avoid: knowledge-as-commodity to be transmitted to the student-as-consumer who passively acquires information and, at the same time, inherently is disconnected from it. Political pedagogy theorized by Giroux (1993) requires that teachers establish a democratic classroom where students do not simply acquire knowledge but develop an understanding of the constructed nature of knowledge. In accomplishing this goal, teachers and students are able to understand that none of the unjust social structures are immutable, that they all have been constructed in complex ways that make them seem natural; because they have been constructed, however, they can also be deconstructed and reimagined in ways that are different and more just.

For students to develop an understanding of the constructed nature of knowledge and of the inequities in social systems, instructors must actively teach about citizenship and democracy, especially how to be a socially responsible citizen who is engaged critically within the democratic forum. Moodley and Adam (2004) argued that political literacy is a key element in teaching democracy:

> To support the appealing but abstract virtues of democracy, effective citizenship education would require concrete contextual analysis. Only by a critical exploration of how democracy functions in the everyday reality of the political community in which learners live—by comparing the ideals with the practice—can we hope to motivate students to narrow the gap and become active, engaged citizens. (p. 171)

In this sense, democracy and social justice need to be taken from the abstract and made more concrete for students. By critically examining and engaging with their communities and within their immediate environments, students begin to understand the relationship between themselves and society, in addition to understanding their responsibilities as citizens within a democratic country.

In examining Regis University's model of social justice and service learning, it is evident that there are four important factors that must be present for a school to function pragmatically as an institution that cultivates civic engagement and a commitment to equitable and just social transformation. The first factor is that a school or university must have as its fundamental goal a commitment to social justice. A prerequisite for this is that members of an institution must have a solid grasp on the prominent issues negatively affecting society, as well as an understanding of how inequitable social systems are constructed both concretely (e.g., in terms of laws, religious practices, public policies, and financial and educational institutions) and rhetorically (in terms of people's interactions and widely circulated messages and images). It is clear that Regis is committed to social justice considering all of the emphasis placed on it and the fact that it is written into the very mission and goals of the university and reinforced by significant resources (even here, however, we recognize that having such mission is no guarantee that it will be fully supported by the university, based on the experiences of the Communication Department at Loyola University Chicago, see Pearce, 2006). Once this commitment is established structurally within a school, it is then necessary to recruit faculty members who are focused on critical education and then nurture and support them in achieving it in the classroom. Regis does this by having even adjunct teaching candidates not only interview but also present a lecture presentation to a panel of other faculty members for evaluation before hiring. Once hired, new instructors must shadow veteran instructors for at least two classes to get a feel for the student population and the types of discussions that might occur during class sessions. Instructors can also utilize faculty and web-site resources, discussed below, to help with service-learning projects and other activities designed to interest students in social issues.

The third factor is that students must themselves be committed to the type of education they will receive in such an institution. Critical education requires a higher level of thought, commitment, and participation of students than does a banking model of education; consequently, students must be prepared to meet the demands of coursework that constantly challenge them to engage fully with material and to become socially responsible citizens. The students at Regis attend the university, in part, because the curriculum supports their social consciousness and their desire to contribute positively to society.

As outlined above, through an extensive faculty orientation process, as well as the distribution of detailed faculty handbooks, Regis University expends significant effort in cultivating a social justice mentality in its faculty. Similarly, students are also acculturated by attending informational sessions before they commit to enrolling and by constantly being exposed to the critical framework of education within courses and extracurricular activities. As important as the previous three factors are in achieving critical education or political pedagogy, they would not be effective if a program did not also provide concrete support and encouragement for faculty members and students seeking to make a positive impact on the world around them. Regis recognizes this and, therefore, provides extensive information for faculty, students, and others wanting to be able to apply their educational experiences to create a more just and humane world.

The Ignatian Collaborative for Service and Justice (the Collaborative) is a program at Regis University that provides faculty, students, and the community with practical resources for service and social justice action, the goal being to combine "engaged learning pedagogies to traditional coursework" (regis.edu). The vision for the program emphasizes the goal of service-oriented learning:

> Standing within the Catholic and Jesuit traditions, we strive not only to meet rigorous academic objectives, but also to challenge students to explore diverse perspectives, create meaningful relationships, develop a critical consciousness, and serve as

positive agents for social change for local and global justice. Students, faculty and community leaders participate in:

- Service-Learning
- Community-Based Learning
- Immersion Experiences
- Diversity Education
- Social Advocacy
- Justice Education
- Reflection Exercises
- Jesuit Traditions and Spirituality
- AmeriCorps
- Community-Based Work Study (regis.edu)

To meet these goals, the Collaborative provides instructors with "service-justice-ethics" course modules that are relevant to multiple disciplines. The Collaborative seeks to "tailor the curriculum to apply to all academic disciplines, providing instructors with consultation, training, mentorship, curricular tools, guided reflection, guest speakers and local immersion experiences" (regis.edu). With this wide variety of resources, instructors are able to integrate service learning into their curricular content regardless of the academic field and, therefore, are much more likely to meet university goals than if the school expected faculty to establish and promote critical education on their own. Students are given service resources in addition to a list of service-learning classes and scholarship information regarding Americorps, a network of programs at the local, state, and national level that collaborate in the effort of meeting the needs of the country in the areas of health, public safety, education, and the environment. Finally, the Collaborative enlists students, faculty, and staff to aid the greater Denver and Colorado community by partnering with nonprofit and start-up organizations, as well as government programs. Among other activities, Regis assists these organizations with health fairs, research, tutoring and mentoring, social advocacy, and immigrant and refugee services.

Regis University is exemplary of an institution grounded in critical pedagogy. Its institutional commitment to social justice, along with the faculty training and support, provide Regis students with a foundational skill-set of critical thinking, personal reflection, and civic engagement. Although Regis University's mission offers a solid start from which to conceptualize a political, critical pedagogy, it should not be considered a final model. To be relevant and current, any model of critical pedagogy must be able to flex and adapt to changing cultural, political, and social conditions. Although we might be able to theorize an answer to the question, "How ought we to live?" that basically involves a deep commitment to ending unjust social hierarchies, inequitable resource allocation, and systemic oppression, we must remain open to the fact that critical pedagogy requires constant reflection, interrogation, and recreation. Creative citizenship negates any type of final answer, for we must always strive to meet the real needs of individuals and groups in the moment.

Conclusion

In the two chapters on pedagogy, we discussed how schools are an important site of social transformation. Unfortunately, too many of our nation's schools treat students as consumers rather than as citizens. Information is essentially deposited and students are expected to regurgitate facts and figures without ever questioning the very nature of knowledge. Inequitable social structures go unexamined, and therefore unchallenged. By focusing on critical pedagogy, institutions of learning can also be institutions of positive social transformation. With a critical education, students learn to question received "truths" and develop the capacity to reimagine the social world in, hopefully, more equitable and just ways. Institutions, such as Regis University, that integrate social justice into their educational framework open up limitless possibilities for their students to better understand their world and their potential impact on it.

Note

1. Another widely accepted model is Santa Clara University located in Santa Clara, California. Established in 1851, the school has a rich history in the Jesuit tradition and educating students for a "life of service and leadership." As described in their mission statement, the university is dedicated to "educating students for competence, conscience, and compassion" and this is accomplished, in a manner similar to that of Regis University, through small class sizes and a curriculum focused on social justice values. http://www.scu.edu/about/history.cfm

CHAPTER 10

Final Remarks

Throughout this book, we have sketched a description of democracy and community that extends from the potentials that are already implicit in current society but which are frustrated and remain under-actualized. In our vision of an edifying society, we embrace the potential of people to better perfect their communities, and we remain suspicious of the machinery of the state political system to provide the guiding force and direction of our common future. This vision of democracy, what we, in a neo-pragmatic fashion, call "creative democracy," is one in which diversity of ideas and meaningful participation of all groups in forming civic and political life is understood fundamentally as an essential aspect. This vision also is one in which pervasive, institutionalized inequality is considered unacceptable and in which all people have the means to provide for their basic needs and are able to engage in opportunities that develop their unique capacities and potential.

This conception of democracy, broadly positioned in terms of Nussbaum's cosmopolitanism and inspired specifically by the work of Dewey, Emerson, Nietzsche, and Rorty, is ultimately constituted in the character of its people. The responsibility for social change, then, rests in citizens' perceptions, attitudes, and commitments, not in a faith in political institutions or in the benevolence of the power elite. As U.S. history has shown, "social and economic justice are not inevitable. Moral evolution is seldom driven by top-down initiative. When such evolution occurs, the driving force of change is usually the result of community vision and mass struggle" (Swartz, 2005, p. 122). The problem, however, is that people do not often struggle *en masse* and tend to accept the way things are as being inevitable.

At the center of creative democracy is a rejection of the guardianship theory of democracy and "epistemarchy," which claim that knowledge and what is "good," "right," and "just" are accessible only by certain groups and not others. As a society, we will make greater gains in social justice when such thinking is recognized and resisted, and when more people are able to perceive the ways that they can use their agency for creative influence in shaping their local environments. This vision requires a communication of hope and resistance to dominating and oppressive ideologies and practices. For example, the abolition of slavery, women's right to vote and own property, and the eight-hour workday were all achieved through sustained and committed *resistance* to the accepted Truths of their respective times—that of a "natural order," a hierarchy "written" by some transcendent Authority, in which, for instance, Whites are considered superior to Blacks, men are superior to women, and wealthy people are superior to the working class and the poor. These changes were also created through an alternative description of the way things can, and should, be. As Rorty (1993) noted, "The freer the imagination of the present the likelier it is that future social practices will be different from past practices" (p. 100).

The pragmatist/neo-pragmatist tradition emphasizes the potential for change through the pedagogical and the dialogical, which includes acts of resistance. This tradition assumes that disparities in resources, enormous polarizations in perceptions, or intense conflicts of interest can be overcome by means of education and communication (West, 1993). To engage in this creative work, people need opportunities for edifying education and communication that develops their communication imagination and heightens their critical perception. Critical education and service learning provide such opportunities. Given that formal education is an important public space for communication, such education could empower future generations to work toward and enact progressive social change.

REFERENCES

Alexander, T. M. (1995). John Dewey and the roots of democratic imagination. In L. Langsdorf & A. Smith (Eds.), *Recovering pragmatism's voice: The classical tradition, Rorty, and the philosophy of communication* (pp. 131–154). Albany: State University of New York Press.

Allen, A. (2001). Pornography and power. *Journal of Social Philosophy, 32*, 512–531.

Allen, B. J., Orbe, M. P., & Olivas, M. R. (1999). The complexity of our tears: Dis/enchantment and (in)difference in the academy. *Communication Theory, 9*, 402–429.

Allen, D. S. (2005). *Democracy, inc.: The press and law in the corporate rationalization of the public sphere*. Urbana: University of Illinois Press.

American Booksellers v. Hudnut, 771 F.2d 323 (1985).

Anderson, J. A. (1996). *Communication theory: Epistemological foundations.* New York: Guilford Press.

Anderson, J. A., & Baym, G. (2004). Philosophies and philosophic issues in communication, 1995–2004. *Journal of Communication, 54*, 589–615.

Andreas, J. (2004). *Addicted to war: Why the U.S. can't kick militarism* (3rd ed.). Culver City, CA: A.K. Press.

Anzaldúa, G. (1987). *Borderlands: The new mestiza = La frontera*. San Francisco: Spinsters /Aunte Lute Books.

Aristotle. (1954). *Rhetoric*. (W. R. Roberts, Trans.). New York: Random House.

Arnett, R. (1990). The practical philosophy of communication ethics and free speech as the foundation for speech communication. *Communication Quarterly*, *38*, 208–217.

Aronson, R. (1999). Hope after hope? *Social Research*, *66*, 471–494.

Artz, L. (2001). Critical ethnography for communication studies: Dialogue and social justice in service-learning. *Southern Communication Journal, 66*, 239–250.

Asen, R. (2002). Imagining the public sphere. *Philosophy and Rhetoric, 35*, 345–367.

Asen, R., & Brouwer, D. C. (2001). Introduction: Reconfigurations of the public sphere. In R. Asen and D. C. Brouwer (Eds.), *Counterpublics and the state* (pp. 1–34). Albany: State University of New York Press.

Bacon, M. (2005). A defense of liberal ironism. *Res Publica*, *11*, 403–423.

Bagdikian, B. H. (2004). *The new media monopoly*. Boston: Beacon Press.

Baker, H. A., Jr. (1995). Critical memory and the back public sphere. In The Black Public Sphere Collective (Eds.). *The black public sphere: A public culture book* (pp. 7–37). Chicago: University of Chicago Press.

Barsamian, D. (2001). *The decline and fall of public broadcasting*. Boston: South End Press.

Beaud, M. (2001). *History of capitalism, 1500–1980*. New York: Monthly Review Press.

Bender, T. (2006). The American way of empire. *World Policy Journal*, *23*, 45–61.

Bernstein, R. J. (1985). Dewey, democracy: The task ahead of us. In J. Rajchman and C. West (Eds.), *Post-analytic philosophy* (pp. 48–58). New York: Columbia University Press.

Best, S., & Kellner, D. (1991). *Postmodern theory: Critical interrogations*. New York: Guilford Press.

Biesecker, B. (1992). Michel Foucault and the question of rhetoric. *Philosophy and Rhetoric, 25*, 351–364.

Bitzer, L. (1968). The rhetorical situation. *Philosophy and Rhetoric*, *1*, 1–14.

Black, E. (1970). The second persona. *Quarterly Journal of Speech*, *56*, 109–119.

Blake, C. N. (2007, Spring). Pragmatist hope. *Dissent*, pp. 95–100.

Bloom, H. (1973). *The anxiety of influence: A theory of poetry*. New York: Oxford University Press.

Bondurant, J. V. (1988). *Conquest of violence: The Gandhian philosophy of conflict*. (New rev. ed.). Princeton, NJ: Princeton University Press.

Boyle-Baise, M., & Langford, J. (2004). There are children here: Service learning for social justice. *Equity and Excellence in Education, 37*, 55–66.

Bradbury, R. (1953). *Fahrenheit 451*. New York: Ballatine Books.

Brodsky, G. (1982). Rorty's interpretation of pragmatism. *Transactions of the Charles S. Peirce Society*, *18*, 311–337.

Brouwer, D. C., & Squires, C. R. (2003). Public intellectuals, public life, and the university. *Augmentation and Advocacy*, *39*, 201–213.

Brown, W. (2000). Nietzsche for politics. In A. D. Schrift (Ed.), *Why Nietzsche still?: Reflections on drama, culture, and politics* (pp. 205–223). Berkeley: University of California Press.

Bryman, A. (1999). The Disneyization of society. *Sociological Review*, *47*, 25–49.

Bureau of Justice Statistics (2003, April 6). Nation's prison and jail population exceeds 2 million inmates for first time. Retrieved September 24, 2007 from http:/usgovinfo.about.com/gi/dynamic/offsite.htm?zi=1/XJ&sdn=usgovinfo&cdn=newsisues&tm=28&gps=247_804_1020_599&f=00&tt=2&bt=0&bts=1&zu=http%3A//www.ojp.usdoj.gov/bjs/abstract/pjim02.htm

Burke, K. (1966). *Language as symbolic action: Essays on life, language and method.* Berkeley: University of California Press.

Burke, K. (1969). *A grammar of motives*. Berkeley: University of California Press. (Original work published 1945)

Burke, K. (1973). *The philosophy of literary form: Studies in symbolic action*. Berkeley: University of California Press.

Burke, K. (1984a). *Attitudes towards history*. Berkeley: University of California Press. (Original work published 1935)

Burke, K. (1984b). *Permanence and change: An anatomy of purpose*. Berkeley, CA: University of California Press. (Original work published 1935)

Bush, G. W. (2001a, November 10). *President Bush speaks to United Nations*. Retrieved September 10, 2007, from http://www.whitehouse.gov/news/releases/2001/11/20011110-3.html

Bush, G. W. (2001b, September 11). *Statement by the president in his address to the nation.* Retrieved August 18, 2006, from http://www.whitehouse.gov/news/releases/2001/09/20010911-16.html

Bush, G. W. (2002, February 4). *President calls for $48 Billion dollar increase in defense spending*. Retrieved September 10, 2007, from http://www.whitehouse.gov/news/releases/ 2002/02/20020204-1.html

Bush, G. W. (2006a, April 18). *President Bush nominates Rob Portman as OMB director and Susan Schwab for USTR*. Retrieved May 15, 2006, from http://www.whitehouse.gov/news/releases/2006/04/ 20060418-1.html

Bush, G. W. (2006b, April 10). *Remarks by President Bush on the global war on terror*. Retrieved May 15, 2006, from http://www.state.gov/r/pa/ei/wh/rem/64287.htm

Bush, G. W. (2007, Jan. 19). *National sanctity of human life day.* Retrieved June 23, 2007, from http://www.whitehouse.gov/news/releases/2007/01/print/20070119. html

Butin, D. (2001). If this is resistance I would hate to see domination: Retrieving Foucault's notion of resistance within educational research. *Educational Studies*, *32*, 157–176.

Butin, D. (2003). Of what use is it? Multiple conceptualizations of service learning within education. *Teachers College Record, 105*, 1674–1692.

Caballero, B. (2007). The global epidemic of obesity: An overview. *Epidemiologic Reviews*, *29*, 1–5.

Carlson, A. C. (1986). Gandhi and the comic frame: "*Ad bellum purificandum*." *Quarterly Journal of Speech*, *72*, 446–456.

Caspary, W. R. (2000). *Dewey on democracy*. Ithaca, NY: Cornell University Press.

Chaudhary, A. G., & Starosta, W. J. (1992). Gandhi's salt march: A case study of Satyagraha with rhetorical implications. *World Communication*, *21*, 1–13.

Cheung, C-Y. (2001). *Lu Xun: The Chinese gentle Nietzsche*. New York: Peter Lang.

Chomsky, N. (2002). *Understanding power: The indispensable Chomsky*. (P. R. Mitchell and J. Schoeffel, Eds.). New York: New Press.

Chomsky, N. (2004). *Hegemony or survival: America's quest for global dominance*. New York: Henry Holt.

Christensen, L. (2006, Fall). *Reading injustice, celebrating solidarity*. Retrieved September 10, 2007, from http://www.rethinkingschools.org/archive/21_01/hurr211.shtml. Rethinkingschools.org

Cloud, D. (1994). The materiality of discourse as oxymoron: A challenge to critical rhetoric. *Western Journal of Communication*, *58*, 141–163.

CNN.com. (2001, December 7). *Ashcroft: Critics of new terror measures undermine effort*. Retrieved September 10, 2007, from http://archives.cnn.com/2001/US/12/06/inv.ashcroft.hearing/

CNN.com. (2003, Oct. 17). *Rumsfeld defends general who commented on war and Satan*. http://www.cnn.com/2003/US/10/16/rumsfeld.boykin.ap/

CNN.com. (2007, September 14). CNN World Weekly. General David H. Petraeus. http://www.cnn.com/2007/WORLD/americas/09/13/ww.petraeus.profile/index.html?iref=newssearch

Conquergood, D. (1995). Between rigor and relevance: Rethinking applied communication. In K. N. Cissna (Ed.), *Applied communication in the 21st century* (pp. 79–96). Mahwah, NJ: Lawrence Erlbaum.

Cook, J. A., Jr. (1994, March). Thurgood Marshall and Clarence Thomas: A glance at their philosophies. *Michigan Bar Journal*, *73*, 298–303.

Coopman, T. M. (2007). Spectrum wars: Bridging factionalism in the fight for free radio. In L. R. Frey & K. M. Carragee (Eds.), *Communication activism* 2 vol. (pp. 223–254). Cresskill, NJ: Hampton Press.

Dalton, M. (2003). Media studies and emancipatory praxis: An autoethnographic essay of critical pedagogy. *Journal of Film and Video, 55* (2–3), 88–97.

Danto, A. (2005). *Nietzsche as philosopher*. (Exp. ed.). New York: Columbia University Press.

Davidson, O. G. (1996). *The best of enemies: Race and redemption in the new South*. New York: Scribner.

Deetz, S. (1992). *Democracy in an age of corporate colonization*: *Developments in communication and the politics of everyday life*. Albany: State University of New York Press.

de Moraes, L. (2005, September 3). Kanye West's torrent of criticism, live on NBC. *Washingtonpost.com*. http://www.washingtonpost.com/wp-dyn/content/article/2005/09/03/AR2005090300165.html

Dewey, J. (1954). *The public and its problems*. Athens: Ohio University Press. (Original work published 1927)

Dewey, J. (1978). Reconstruction in philosophy. In J. A. Boydstron, (Ed.), *The middle works of John Dewey* (Vol. 12). Carbondale: Southern Illinois University Press. (Original work published 1920)

Dewey, J. (1993a). Creative democracy: The task before us. In D. Morris & I. Shapiro (Eds.), *John Dewey: The political writings* (pp. 240–245). Indianapolis, IN: Hackett. (Original work published 1939)

Dewey, J. (1993b). Democracy and human nature. In D. Morris and I. Shapiro (Eds.), *John Dewey: The political writings* (pp. 219–229). Indianapolis, IN: Hackett. (Original work published 1939)

Dewey, J. (1993c). Renascent liberalism. In D. Morris and I. Shapiro (Eds.), *John Dewey: The political writings* (pp. 142–152). Indianapolis, IN: Hackett Publishing Company. (Original work published 1935)

Dewey, J. (1993d). John Dewey responds. In D. Morris & I. Shapiro (Eds.), *John Dewey: The political writings* (pp. 246–248). Indianapolis, IN: Hackett Publishing Company. (Original work published 1950)

Dewey, J. (1993e). The economic basis of the new society. In D. Morris and I. Shapiro (Eds.), *John Dewey: The political writings* (pp. 169–172). Indianapolis, IN: Hackett Publishing Company. (Original work published 1939)

Dewey, J. (1993f). The basic values and loyalties of democracy. In D. Morris and I. Shapiro (Eds.), *John Dewey: The political writings* (pp. 207–209). Indianapolis, IN: Hackett Publishing Company. (Original work published 1941)

Dewey, J. (1993g). Democratic ends need democratic methods for their realization. In D. Morris and I. Shapiro (Eds.), *John Dewey: The political writings* (pp. 205–206). Indianapolis, IN: Hackett Publishing Company. (Original work published 1939)

Dewey, J. (1993h). The need for a recovery of philosophy. In D. Morris and I. Shapiro (Eds.), *John Dewey: The political writings* (pp. 1–10). Indianapolis, IN: Hackett Publishing Company. (Original work published 1917)

Dewey, J. (1993i). The problem of truth. In D. Morris and I. Shapiro (Eds.), *John Dewey: The political writings* (pp. 10–19). Indianapolis, IN: Hackett Publishing Company. (Original work published 1911)

Dewey, J. (1993j). The need of an industrial education in an industrial democracy. In D. Morris and I. Shapiro (Eds.), *John Dewey: The political writings* (pp. 121–124). Indianapolis, IN: Hackett Publishing Company. (Original work published 1916)

Dewey, J. (1999). *Liberalism and social action*. Amherst, NY: Prometheus Books. (Original work published 1935)

Dewey, J. (2005). *The quest for certainty*. New York: G. P. Putnam. (Original work published 1929)

Dickinson, G. (2005). Selling democracy: Consumer culture and citizenship in the wake of September 11. *Southern Communication Journal*, *70*, 271–284.

Dillon, M., & Garland, L. (2000). *Ancient Greece: Social & historical documents from archaic times to the death of Socrates*. New York: Routledge.

Dorfman, A. (1983). *The empire's old clothes*. New York: Penguin.

Dorfman, A., & Mattelart, A. (1991). *How to read Donald Duck: Imperialist ideology in the Disney comic* (3rd ed.). New York: International General. (original work published in 1971)

Dwork, D., & van Pelt, R. J. (2003). *Holocaust: A history*. New York: W. W. Norton.

Dyson, M. E. (2001). *I may not get there with you: The true Martin Luther King, Jr.* New York: Free Press.

Dyson, M. E. (2006). *Come hell or high water: Hurricane Katrina and the color of disaster.* New York: Basic Civitas

Eatwell, R. (1989). The rise of "left-right" terminology: The confusions of social science. In R. Eatwell & N. O'Sullivan (Eds.), *The nature of the right: European and American politics and political thought since 1789* (pp. 32–46). London: Pinter.

Emerson, R. W. (1983). Self reliance. In J. Porte (Ed.), *Essays: First series, essays and lectures* (pp. 260–275). New York: Library of America. (Original work published 1841)

Emerson, R. W. (2003). *Nature and selected essays* (L. Ziff, Ed.). New York: Penguin. (Original work published in 1841)

Engen, D. E. (2000). The communicative imagination and its cultivation. *Communication Quarterly, 50*, 41–57.

Englund, T. (2000). Rethinking democracy and education: Towards an education of deliberative citizens. *Journal of Curriculum Studies, 32*, 305–313.

Faculty Resource Handbook, Regis University, School for Professional Studies, Undergraduate Program, at http://academic.regis.edu/ghodne/handbook/SectionA/index.htm

Fassett, D. L., & Warren, J. T. (2007). *Critical communication pedagogy.* Thousand Oaks, CA: Sage.

Faux, J. (2004, April 25). Losing ground. *The American Prospect.* Retrieved September 10, 007, from http://www.prospect.org/cs/articles?articleId=7639

Fish, S. (2002, Summer). Can postmodernists condemn terrorism? Don't blame relativism. *Responsive Community*, pp. 27–31.

Fitzgerald, M. (2004, November/December). Militarism: A way of life. *The Humanist*, pp. 26–31.

Foucault, M. (1970). *The order of things: An archaeology of the human sciences.* New York: Vintage Books.

Foucault, M. (1972). *The archaeology of knowledge* (A. M. Sheridan Smith, Trans.). New York: Pantheon Books.

Foucault, M. (1977). *Language, counter-memory, practice: Selected essays and interviews* (D. F. Bouchard & S. Simon, Trans.). Ithaca, NY: Cornell University Press.

Foucault, M. (1978). *The history of sexuality* (R. Hurley, Trans.). New York: Pantheon Books.

Foucault, M. (1983). Preface. In G. Deleuze and F. Guattari, *Anti-Oedipus: Capitalism and schizophrenia* (pp. xi–xiv; R. Hurley, J. M. Seem, & H. R. Lane, Trans.). Minneapolis: University of Minnesota Press.

Foucault, M. (1984a). Nietzsche, genealogy, history. In P. Rabinow (Ed.), *The Foucault reader* (pp. 76–100). New York: Pantheon Books.

Foucault, M. (1984b). What is enlightenment? In P. Rabinow (Ed.), *The Foucault reader* (pp. 32–50). New York: Pantheon Books.

Foucault, M. (1995). Power/knowledge. In J. P. Sterba (Ed.), *Social and political philosophy: Classical Western texts in feminist and multicultural perspectives* (pp. 443–452). Belmont, CA: Wadsworth Publishing.

Foucault, M. (2006). Power, right, truth. In R. E. Goodin and P. Pettit (Eds.), *Contemporary political philosophy: An anthology* (2nd ed., pp. 541–548). Malden, MA: Blackwell Publishing.

Fraser, N. (1996). Rethinking the public sphere: A contribution to the critique of actually existing democracy. In C. Calhoun (Ed.), *Habermas and the public sphere* (pp. 109–142). Cambridge, MA: MIT Press.

Fraser, S., (Ed.). (1995). *The bell curve wars: Race, intelligence, and the future of America*. New York: Basic Books.

Frazer, M. L. (2006). The compassion of Zarathustra: Nietzsche on sympathy and strength. *Review of Politics, 68*, 49–78.

Freire, P. (2000). *Pedagogy of the oppressed* (M. B. Ramos, Trans.). New York: Continuum. (Original work published 1970)

Frey, L. (2006). Across the great divides: From nonpartisan criticism to partisan criticism to applied communication activism for promoting social change and social justice. In O. Swartz (Ed.), *Social Justice and Communication Scholarship* (pp. 35–51). Mahwah, NJ: Lawrence Erlbaum Associates.

Frey, L. R., Pearce, W. B., Pollock, M. A., Artz, L., & Murphy, B. A. (1996). Looking for justice in all the wrong places: On a communication approach to social justice. *Communication Studies, 47*, 110–127.

Frey, L. R., & Carragee, K. M. (Eds.) (2007a). *Communication activism* (2 Vols.). Cresskill, NJ: Hampton Press.

Frey, L. R., & Carragee, K. M. (2007b). Communication activism as engaged scholarship. In L. R. Frey & K. M. Carragee (Eds.), *Communication activism* (2 Vols., pp. 1–64). Cresskill, NJ: Hampton Press.

Frey, L. R., & Underwood, E. D. (2007). Communication and community: Clarifying the connection across the communication community. *Communication Yearbook, 31*, 370–418.

Fromm, E. (1992). Marx's concept of man. In E. Fromm (Ed.), *Marx's concept of man* (pp. 1–89). New York: Continuum. (Original work published 1961)

Frye, M. (1983). *The politics of reality: Essays in feminist theory*. Trumansburg, NY: Crossing Press.

Garrison, J. (1993). A strong poet's perspective on Richard Rorty. *Studies in Philosophy and Education, 12*, 213–221.

Garvey, T. G. (2000). *The Emerson dilemma: Essays on Emerson and social reform*. Athens: University of Georgia Press.

Geertz, C. (1973). *The interpretation of cultures: Selected essays*. New York: Basic Books.

Ghosh, J. (2002, May 25–June 7). Consumerism as patriotism. *Frontline,* 19 (11). Retrieved September 10, 2007, from http://www.hinduonnet.com/fline/fl1911/ 19111130.htm

Giroux, H. A. (1993). Teachers as transformative intellectuals. In H. S. Shapiro and D. E. Purpel (Eds.), *Critical social issues in American education: Toward the 21st century* (pp. 272–277). New York: Longman.

Giroux, H. A. (1999). *The mouse that roared: Disney and the end of innocence*. Lanham, MD: Rowman & Littlefield.

Giroux, H. A. (2006, March/April). The politics of lying: The assault on meaning in Bush's America. *Tikkun*, pp. 36–37; 65–66.

Giroux, H. A., & Giroux, S. S. (2004). *Take back higher education: Race, youth, and the crisis of democracy in the post-civil rights era.* New York: Palgrave McMillan.

Global unease with major world powers (2007, June 27). *The Pew Global Attitudes Project.* Retrieved September 10, 2007, from http://pewglobal.org/ reports/pdf/256.pdf

Goldman, E. (1969). *Anarchism and other essays*. New York: Dover. (Originally published 1917)

Goldman, E. (1970). *Living my life* (Vol.1). New York: Dover. (Originally published 1931)

Goodheart, E. (1997). *The reign of ideology*. New York: Columbia University Press.

Gould, S. J. (1994). Curveball. *The New Yorker, 70*, p. 139.

Gray, F. D. (2002). *The Tuskegee syphilis study: The real story and beyond.* Montgomery, AL: NewSouth Books.
Greenspan, A. (2007). *The age of turbulence: Adventures in a new world.* New York: Penguin Books.
Griffin, J. H. (2004). *Black like me: The definitive Griffin estate edition, corrected from original manuscripts.* San Antonio, TX: Wings Press.
Guerrero, A. (2002). *Silence at Boalt Hall: The dismantling of affirmative action.* Berkeley: University of California Press.
Habermas, J. (1985). *The theory of communicative action.* (2 Vols.; T. McCarthy, Trans.). New York: Beacon Press.
Hadler, N. M. (1999). Laboring for longevity. *Journal of Occupational and Environmental Medicine, 41*, 617–620.
Haney-Lopez, I. F. (1998). *White by law: The legal construction of race.* New York: New York University Press.
Hansen, M. H. (1991). *The Athenian democracy in the age of Demosthenes: Structure, principles, and ideology* (J. A. Crook, Trans.). Cambridge, MA: Basil Blackwell.
Hanson, V. D. (2002). *An autumn of war: What America learned from September 11 and the war on terrorism.* New York: Anchor Books.
Harkavy, I., & Benson, L. (1998, Spring). De-Platonizing and democratizing education as the bases of service learning. *New Directions for Teaching and Learning, 73*, 11–20.
Hatab, L. J. (1995). *A Nietzschean defense of democracy: An experiment in postmodern politics.* Chicago: Open Court.
Hauser, G. (1999). *Vernacular voices: The rhetoric of publics and public spheres.* Columbia: University of South Carolina Press.
Herbert, B. (2007, August 14). 100,000 gone since 2001. *The New York Times.* Retrieved September 10, 2007, from http://select.nytimes.com/2007/08/14/ opinion/14herbert.html
Herman, E. S., & Chomsky, N. (2002). *Manufacturing consent: The political economy of the mass media.* 2nd ed. New York: Pantheon Books. (Original work published 1988)
Herrnstein, R. J., & Murray, C. (1994). *The bell curve: Intelligence and class structure in American life.* New York: Free Press.
Hollihan, T. A. (1994). Evidencing moral claims: The activist rhetorical critic's first task. *Western Journal of Communication, 58*, 229–234.
hooks, b. (1991). Theory as liberatory practice. *Yale Journal of Law and Feminism, 4,* 1–12.
hooks, b. (2000). *Where we stand: Class matters.* New York, Routledge.
hooks, b. (2003). *Teaching community: A pedagogy of hope.* New York: Routledge.
Hunter, J. D. (1991). *Culture wars: The struggle to define America.* New York: Basic Books.
Huxley, A. (1998). *Brave new world.* New York: Perennial Classics. (Original work published 1932)
Irons, P. (1999). *A people's history of the Supreme Court: The men and women whose cases and decisions have shaped our constitution.* New York: Viking.
James, W. (1965). *Pragmatism.* New York: Meridian Books. (Original work published 1907)
Jesudasan, I. (1984). *A Gandhian theology of liberation.* Maryknoll, NY: Orbis Books.
Johnson, A. (2000, Summer). The politics of Richard Rorty. *New Politics, 8*, 103–121.
Judis, J. B. (2005, Fall). The author of liberty: Religion and U.S. foreign policy. *Dissent*, pp. 54–61.
Kairys, D. (1993). *With liberty and justice for some: A critique of the conservative Supreme Court.* New York: New Press.
Karnow, S. (1997). *Vietnam: A history* (2nd Rev. ed). New York: Penguin Books.

Katz, S. B. (1992) The ethic of expediency: Classical rhetoric, technology, and the Holocaust. *College English, 54*, 255–275.

Kaufmann, C. (2004). Threat inflation and the failure of the marketplace of ideas: The selling of the Iraq war. *International Security, 29*, 5–48.

Kaufmann, W. (1974). *Nietzsche: Philosopher, psychologist, antichrist* (4th ed.). Princeton, NJ: Princeton University Press.

Kavanagh, J. H. (1995). Ideology. In F. Lentricchia and T. McLaughlin (Eds.), *Critical terms for literary study* (2nd ed., pp. 306–320). Chicago: University of Chicago Press.

Kellner, D. (2003). Cultural studies, multiculturalism, and media culture. In G. Dines & J. M. Humez (Eds.), *Gender, race, and class in media: A text-reader* (2nd ed., pp. 1–9). Thousand Oaks, CA: Sage.

Kent, G. (2002). Food trade and food rights. *UN Chronicle, 1,* 27–29.

Kersten, A. (1986). Philosophical foundations for the construction of critical knowledge. In M. McLaughlin (Ed.), *Communication Yearbook* (Vol. 9, pp. 756–774). Beverly Hills, CA: Sage.

King, M. L., Jr. (1967). *Where do we go from here? Chaos or community*? New York: Harper & Row.

King, M. L., Jr. (1986). *Stride toward freedom*. New York: Harper and Row. (Original work published 1958)

King, M. L., Jr. (1989). *The trumpet of conscience*. New York: HarperCollins. (Original work published 1967)

King, M. L., Jr. (1992). Letter from a Birmingham jail. In J. W. Washington (Ed.), *I have a dream: Writings and speeches that changed the world* (pp. 83–100). San Francisco: HarperSanFrancisco. (Original work published 1963)

Kinzer, S. (2006). *Overthrow: America's century of regime change from Hawaii to Iraq*. New York: Times Books/Henry Holt.

Kivel, P. (2004). *You call this a democracy?: Who benefits, who pays and who really decides*? New York: Apex Press.

Koopman, C. (2006). Pragmatism as a philosophy of hope: Emerson, James, Dewey, Rorty. *Journal of Speculative Philosophy*, *20*, 106–116.

Kropotkin, P. (1989). *Mutual aid: A factor of evolution*. New York: Black Rose Press. (Original work published 1902)

Kuhn, T. (1996). *The structure of scientific revolutions* (3rd ed.). Chicago: University of Chicago Press. (Original work published 1962)

Lee, W. (2006). The desire to know and to love is never too small: My musings on teaching and social justice. In O. Swartz (Ed.), *Social justice and communication scholarship* (pp.193–214). Mahwah, NJ: Lawrence Erlbaum.

Lee, W. and Wander, P. (1998). On discursive amnesia: Reinventing the possibilities for democracy through discursive amnesty. In M. Salvador & P. M. Sias (Eds.), *The public voice in a democracy at risk* (pp. 151–172). Westport, CT: Praeger.

Lefort, C. (1988). *Democracy and political theory* (D. Macey, Trans.). Minneapolis: University of Minnesota Press.

Liptak, A. (2007, July 4). Bush rationale on Libby stirs legal debate. *The New York Times*. Retrieved September 10, 2007, from http://www.nytimes.com/2007/07/04/washington/04commute.html?ei=5070&em=&en=099e5073200596c9&ex=1183694400&pagewanted=print

Llosa, A. V. (2005, July 11). The killing machine from *The Motorcycle Diaries* to the ubiquitous T-shirts bearing his image, Che Guevara has gone from communist icon to capitalist brand. But few of his contemporary admirers know the historical truth about the man they invoke. An unsparing re-examination of one of the West's most persistent heroes. *The New Republic*, p. 25.

Loewen, J. W. (2000). *Lies across America: What our historic sites get wrong.* New York: Simon & Schuster.

Loewen, J. W. (2005). *Lies my teacher told me: Everything your history textbook got wrong.* New York: New Press.

Longford, G. (2001). "Sensitive killers, cruel aesthetes, and pitiless poets": Foucault, Rorty, and the ethics of self-fashioning. *Polity, 33,* 569–592.

Lummis, D. C. (1996). *Radical democracy.* Ithaca, NY: Cornell University Press.

MacKinnon, C. A. (1993). *Only words.* Cambridge, MA: Harvard University Press.

Manicas, P. T. (1982). John Dewey: Anarchism and the political state. *Transactions of the Charles S. Peirce Society*, *18*, 133–158.

Margolis, J. (2002). Dewey's and Rorty's opposed pragmatisms. *Transactions of the Charles S. Peirce Society*, *38*, 117–135.

Marshall, A. (2003, Spring). Guerrilla marketing. *Men's Fashions of the Times*, pp. 52–54.

Marx, K. (1963). *The eighteenth Brumaire of Louis Bonaparte.* New York: International Publishers. (Original work published in 1852)

Marx, K., & Engels, F. (1992). *The communist manifesto.* New York: Oxford University Press. (Original work published 1848)

McChesney, R. W. (2004). *The problem of the media: U. S. communication politics in the 21st century.* New York: Monthly Review Press.

McDermott, J. J. (1989). The pragmatists. In G. F. McLean (Ed.), *Reading philosophy for the 21st' century* (pp. 245–263). Lanham, MD: University Press of America.

McGee, M. C. (1980). The "ideograph": A link between rhetoric and ideology. *Quarterly Journal of Speech*, *66*, 1–16.

McKerrow, R. (1989) Critical rhetoric: Theory and praxis. *Communication Monographs*, *56*, 92–111.

McLaren, P. (1995). *Critical pedagogy and predatory culture: Oppositional politics in a postmodern era.* New York: Routledge.

McMillan, J., & Cheney, G. (1996). The student as consumer: The implications and limitations of a metaphor. *Communication Education*, *45*, 1–15.

Mead, G. H. (1982). *The individual and the social self: Unpublished work of George Herbert Mead* (D. L. Miller, Ed.). Chicago: University of Chicago Press. (Original work published 1914)

Meier, D., & Wood, G. (Eds.). (2004). *Many children left behind: How the No Child Left Behind Act is damaging our children and our schools.* Boston: Beacon Press.

Merida, K., and Fletcher, M. (2007). *Supreme discomfort: The divided soul of Clarence Thomas.* New York: Doubleday.

Mills, C. W. (1958). The structure of power in American society. *British Journal of Sociology*, *9*, 29–41.

Mills, C. W. (1963). *Power, politics, and people: The collected essays of C. Wright Mills* (I. L. Horowitz, Ed.). New York: Ballatine Books.

Moodley, K., & Adam, H. (2004). Citizenship education and political literacy in South Africa. In J. A Banks (Ed.), *Diversity and citizenship education: Global perspectives* (pp. 159–184). San Francisco: Jossey-Bass.

Morris, D., & Shapiro, I. (1993). Editors' introduction. In D. Morris & I. Shapiro (Eds.), *The Political Writings* (pp. ix–xix). Indianapolis, IN: Hackett.

Moskos, C. (2002). Reviving the citizen-soldier. *The Public Interest, 147*, 76–85.

Mousseau, F., & Mittal, A. (2006, March–April). Food sovereignty: Ending world hunger in our time. *The Humanist*, pp. 24–26.

Mr. Holland's Opus [film] (1995). Directed by Stephen R. Herek.

Murphy, J. M. (2003). "Our Mission and our moment": George W. Bush and September 11th *Rhetoric & Public Affairs, 6*, 607–632.

Murphy, R. (2006). *East Asia: A new history* (4th ed.). New York: Pearson Longman.

N. A. A. C. P. v. Alabama, 357 U.S. 449 (1958).

Nietzsche, F. (1967a). *Ecce homo* (W. Kaufmann, Trans.). New York: Vintage Books. (Original work published 1887)

Nietzsche, F. (1967b). *On the genealogy of morals* (W. Kaufmann and R. J. Hollingdale, Trans.). New York: Vintage Books. (Original work published 1908)

Nietzsche, F. (1968). *The will to power*. (W. Kaufmann & R. J. Hollingdale, Trans, W. Kaufman, Ed.). London: Weidenfeld & Nicolson. (Original work published 1901)

Nietzsche, F. (1976). *The portable Nietzsche* (W. Kaufmann, Trans.). New York: Penguin Books. (Original work published 1954)

Nietzsche, F. (1996). *Human, all to human* (R. J. Hollingdale, Trans.). New York: Cambridge University Press. (Original work published 1878)

Nojeim, M. J. (2004). *Gandhi and King: The power of nonviolent resistance*. Westport, CT: Praeger.

Northrup, N. (2004, December 6). Bracing for reversal of Roe. *New Jersey Law Journal*, p. 943.

Nussbaum, M. (1994). Patriotism and cosmopolitanism. In J. Cohen (Ed.), *For love of country: Debating the limits of patriotism* (pp. 2–17). Boston: Beacon Press.

Nussbaum, M. (1997). *Cultivating humanity: A classical defense of reform in liberal education*. Cambridge, MA: Harvard University Press.

Okrent, D. (2004, May 30). Weapons of mass destruction? Or mass distraction? *The New York Times*. Retrieved December 26, 2006, from http://query.nytimes.com/gst/fullpage.html?res=9C06E7DC1E3EF933A05756C0A9629C8B63

O'Leary, C., & Platt, T. (2001). Pledging allegiance: The revival of prescriptive patriotism. *Social Justice, 28*, 41–44.

Orwell, G. (2003). *Animal farm and 1984*. New York: Harcourt. (Original works published in 1945 and 1948, respectively)

Oxfam International. (2006, September). *In the Public Interest: health, education, and water and sanitation for all*. Retrieved September 19, 2006 from http://www.oxfam.org/en/policy/briefingpapers/bp_public_internest

Parenti, M. (1993). *Inventing reality: The politics of news media* (2nd ed.). New York: St. Martin's Press.

Parenti, M. (2007). *Democracy for the few* (8th ed.). Belmont, CA: Wadsworth.

Pearce, W. B. (2006). Reflections on a project to promote social justice in communication education and research. In O. Swartz (Ed.), *Social Justice and Communication Scholarship* (pp. 215–238). Mahwah, NJ: Lawrence Erlbaum.

Pericles. (1995). Funeral oration. In J. J. Murphy & R. A. Katula (Eds.), *A synoptic history of classical rhetoric* 2nd ed. (pp. 217–221). Davis, CA: Hermagoras Press.

Postman, N. (1992). *Conscientious objections: Stirring up trouble about language, technology and education*. New York: Vintage Books.

Postman, N. (2005). *Amusing ourselves to death: Public discourse in the age of show business*. New York: Penguin Books. (Originally published 1988)

Pratkanis, A. R., & Aronson, E. (2001). *Age of propaganda: Everyday use and abuse of persuasion* (Rev. ed.). New York: W. H. Freeman.

R.A.V. v. City of Saint Paul, 505 U.S. 377 (1992).

Revkin, A. (2007, April 1). Poor nations to bear brunt as world warms. *The New York Times*. Retrieved September 10, 2007, from http://www.nytimes. com/2007/04/01/science/earth/01climate.html?ei=5088&en=6c687d64add0b7ba&ex=1333080000&partner=rssnyt&emc=rss&pagewanted=print

Rhoads, R. A. (2000). Democratic citizenship and service learning: Advancing the caring self. In M. B. Magolda (Ed.), *Teaching to promote intellectual and personal maturity: Incorporating students' worldviews and identities into the learning process* (pp. 27–44). San Francisco: Jossey-Bass.

Ricci, C. (2004). The case against standardized testing and the call for the revitalization of democracy. *Review of Education, Pedagogy and Cultural Studies*, *26*, 339–361.

Rieff, D. (1998). Therapy or democracy? The culture wars twenty years on. *World Policy Journal*, *15*, 66–77.

Ritzer, G. (2004). *The McDonaldization of society* (Rev. new century ed.). Thousand Oaks, CA: Pine Forge Press.

Rockler, N. R. (2006). *Friends,* Judaism, and the holiday armadillo: Mapping a rhetoric of postidentity politics. *Communication Theory*, *16*, 453–473.

Rodriguez, A. (2001). *On matters of liberation (I): The case against hierarchy*. Cresskill, NJ: Hampton Press.

Rodriguez, A. (2002). Culture to culturing: Re–imaging our understanding of intercultural relations. *Journal of Intercultural Communication, 5,* Article 4. Retrieved September 10, 2007 from http://vpa.syr.edu/crs/FacultyProfile/FacultyProfile/CultureToCulturlishedPaper.pdf

Rodriguez, A. (2006). Social justice and the challenge for communication studies. In O. Swartz (Ed.), *Social Justice and Communication Scholarship* (pp. 21–34). Mahwah, NJ: Lawrence Erlbaum.

Rorty, R. (1979). *Philosophy and the mirror of nature*. Princeton, NJ: Princeton University Press.

Rorty, R. (1989). *Contingency, irony and solidarity*. New York: Cambridge University Press.

Rorty, R. (1993, Spring). Feminism, ideology, and deconstruction: A pragmatist view. *Hypatia*, 8, 96–103.

Rorty, R. (1994). After philosophy, democracy. In G. Borradori (Ed.). *The American Philosopher: Conversations with Quine, Davidson, Putnam, Nozick, Danto, Rorty, Cabell, MacIntrye, and Kuhn* (pp. 103–117; R. Crocitto, Trans.). Chicago: University of Chicago Press.

Rorty, R. (1996a, February 8). The necessity of inspired reading. *The Chronicle of Higher Education*. Retrieved September 10, 2007, from http://chronicle.com/subscribe/login?url=/che-data/articles.dir/ar42.dir/issue-22.dir/22a04801.htm

Rorty, R. (1996b). Who are we? Moral universalism and economic triage. *Diogenes, 44,* 5–15.

Rorty, R. (1998a). Pragmatism as romantic polytheism. In M. Dickstein (Ed.), *The revival of pragmatism: New essays an social thought, law, and culture* (pp. 21–36). Durham, NC: Duke University Press.

Rorty, R. (1998b). Pragmatism of Richard Rorty: Without illusion, but with conviction. [Interview] *Kritika & Kontext* pp. 3–4, 11–17.

Rorty, R. (1998c). *Truth and progress*. New York: Cambridge University Press.

Rorty, R. (1999a). Failed prophecies, glorious hopes. *Constellations, 6,* 216–221.

Rorty, R. (1999b). *Philosophy and social hope*. New York: Penguin Books.
Rorty, R. (2000). The moral purposes of the university: An exchange. *The Hedgehog Review, 2,* 106–120.
Rorty, R. (2003, Fall). Humiliation or solidarity? *Dissent*, pp. 23–26.
Rorty, R. (2006). *Take care of freedom and truth will take care of itself: Interviews with Richard Rorty* (E. Mendieta, Ed.). Stanford, CA: Stanford University Press.
Rorty, R., & Engel P. (2007). *What's the use of truth?* (P. Savidan, Ed.; W. McCuaig, Trans.). New York: Columbia University Press.
Donald H. Rumsfeld, August 29, 2006 Address at the 88th Annual American Legion National Convention. Retrieved from http://www.defenselink.mil/Speeches/Speech.aspx?SpeechID=1033
Russell, B. (1993). *Skeptical essays*. London: Routledge. (Originally published 1928)
Saletan, W. (2006, March 5). Life after Roe. *The Washington Post*, p. B01.
Sartre, J-P. (1989). *No exit, and three other plays*. New York: Vintage International. (Originally published in 1944)
Schauer, S. (1982). *Free speech: A philosophical inquiry*. New York: Cambridge University Press.
Schiappa, E. (2003). *Defining reality: Definitions and the politics of meaning*. Carbondale: Southern Illinois University Press.
Schlesinger, Jr., A. (2003, January 7). What ever happened to protest? *Newsweek*, Retrieved September 10, 2007, from http://www.msnbc.com/news /843843.asp?cb=-719123265
Schrag, C. O. (1999). Praxis. In R. Audi (Ed.), *The Cambridge dictionary of philosophy*. 2nd ed. (2nd ed., p. 731). New York: Cambridge University Press.
Scott, R. L. (1967). On viewing rhetoric as epistemic. *Central States Speech Journal, 18*, 9–17.
Shapiro, H. S. (1998). Clinton and education: Policies without meaning. In H. S. Shapiro and D. E. Purpel (Eds.), *Critical social issues in American education: Transformation in a postmodern world* (2nd ed., pp. 45–55). Mahwah, NJ: Lawrence Erlbaum.
Sheehan, C. (2006). *Peace mom: A mother's journey through heartache to activism*. New York: Atria Books.
Shiffrin, S. H. (1999). *Dissent, injustice, and the meanings of America*. Princeton, NJ: Princeton University Press.
Shiva, V. (1997). *Biopiracy: The plunder of nature and knowledge*. Boston: South End Press.
Shotter, J. (1993). *Conversational realities: Constructing life through language*. Thousand Oaks, CA: Sage.
Simons, T. and O'Connell, M. (2003, Feb.). *Married-Couple and Unmarried-Partner Households: 2000*. U.S. Department of Commerce. Retrieved from http://www.census.gov/prod/2003pubs/censr-5.pdf
Simpsons "trump" First Amendment. (2006, March 1). *BBC News*. Retrieved, July 1, 2007, from http://news.bbc.co.uk/1/hi/world/americas/4761294.stm
Singer, I. B. (1973). *The fools of Chelm and their history* (I. B. Singer & E. Shub, Trans.). New York: Farrar, Straus and Giroux.
Singer, P. (2002). *One world: The ethics of globalization*. New Haven, CT: Yale University Press.
Sklar, H. (2003, May). Imagine a country: Life in the new millennium. *Z Magazine, 16*. Retrieved September 10, 2007 from http://zmagsite.zmag.org/May2003/sklarprint0503.html
Smiley, T. (2006). *The covenant with black America*. Chicago: Third World Press.

Smith, C. R., and Hunsaker, D. M. (2004). *The four freedoms of the first amendment.* Long Grove, IL: Waveland Press.

Snow, E. (1994). *Red star over China.* New York: Grove Press. (Original work published 1938)

Solomon, M. (1985). The rhetoric of dehumanization: An analysis of medical reports of the Tuskegee Syphilis Project. *Western Journal of Speech Communication, 49*, 233–247.

Sontag, S. (1969). *Styles of political will.* New York: Farrar, Straus and Giroux.

Sontag, S. (2002). What's happening in America? In A. Charters (Ed.), *The portable sixties reader* (pp. 120–124). New York: Penguin. (Originally published 1966)

Sontag, S. (2003). Reflections on September 11th. In M. L. Silfy and C. Cerf (Eds.), *The Iraqi war reader: History, documents, opinions* (pp. 215–216). New York: Simon & Shuster.

Southern Poverty Law Center. (2005, June). *Racists join Minuteman project.* Retrieved September 10, 2007 from http://www.splcenter.org/center/splcrepor t/article.jsp?aid=150

Squires, C. (2001). The black press and the state: Attracting unwanted attention. In R. Asen & D. C. Brouwer (Eds.), *Counterpublics and the state* (pp. 111–136). Albany: State University of New York Press.

St. John, J., & Shepherd, G. J. (2004). Transcending tolerance: Pragmatism, social capital, and community in communication. In P. J. Kalbfleisch (Ed.), *Communication Yearbook* (Vol. 28, pp. 167–187). Mahwah, NJ: Lawrence Erlbaum.

Staubhaar, J., and LaRose, R. (2002). *Media now: Communications media in the information age* (3rd ed.). Belmont, CA: Wadsworth/Thomson Learning.

Stopbigmedia.com rallies public opposition to media concentration. (2006, June 21). *Stopbigmedia.com.* Retrieved September 10, 2007, from http://www.stopbigmedia.com/-press1

Stromburg, R. N. (1996). *Democracy: A short, analytical history.* Armonk, NY: M. E. Sharpe.

Subrer, J. P. (1994). Kant, Levinas, and the thought of the other. *Philosophy Today, 38,* 294–316.

Swan, S. (2002). Rhetoric, service and social justice. *Written Communication, 19*, 76–108.

Swartz, O. (1996a). On power: A discussion of Richard Rorty and Michel Foucault. *World Communication, 25*, 13–20.

Swartz, O. (1996b). Praxis. In T. Enos (Ed.), *Encyclopedia of rhetoric and composition: Communication from ancient times to the information age* (p. 553). New York: Garland.

Swartz, O. (1997a). *Conducting socially responsible research: Critical theory, neo-pragmatism and rhetorical inquiry.* Thousand Oaks, CA: Sage.

Swartz, O. (1997b). Disciplining the "other": Engaging Blair, Brown, and Baxter. *Southern Communication Journal, 62*, 253–256.

Swartz, O. (1999a). *Socialism and communication: Reflections on language and left politics.* Brookfield, VT: Ashgate Publishing Company.

Swartz, O. (1999b). *The view from* On the Road*: The rhetorical vision of Jack Kerouac.* Carbondale: Southern Illinois University Press.

Swartz, O. (2001). *Persuasion as a critical activity.* Dubuque, IA: Kendall/Hunt Publishing.

Swartz, O. (2004a). Normative morality and the U.S. Constitution. *Nature, Society, Thought, 17*, 283–305.

Swartz, O. (2004b). Toward a critique of normative justice: Human rights and the rule of law. *Socialism and Democracy, 18*, 185–209.

Swartz, O. (2005). *In defense of partisan criticism: Communication studies, law & social analysis.* New York: Peter Lang.

Swartz, O. (2006). Reflections of a social justice scholar. In O. Swartz (Ed.), *Social Justice and Communication Scholarship* (pp. 1–19). Mahwah, NJ: Lawrence Erlbaum.

Talisse, R. B. (2004). Dewey's defense of democracy: We must commit to intelligent inquiry. *Free Inquiry, 24,* 35–37.

Talisse, R. B. (2005). Deliberative democracy defended: A response to Posner's political realism. *Res Publica, 11,* 185–199.

Terchek, R. J., & Conte, T. C., (Eds.) (2001). *Theories of democracy: A reader.* Lanham, MD: Rowman & Littlefield.

Terkel, S. (1980). *American Dreams: Lost and found.* New York: Pantheon Books.

Tompkins, P. K. (2006). Communication, charity, social justice, and the abolition of homelessness. In O. Swartz (Ed.), *Social justice and communication scholarship* (pp. 53–75). Mahwah, NJ: Lawrence Erlbaum.

Uchitelle, L. (2007, July 15). The richest of the rich, proud of a new gilded age. *The New York Times.* Retrieved September 10, 2007, from http://www.nytimes.com/2007/07/15/business/15gilded.html?hp

Varlotta, L. (1997). Confronting consensus: Investigating the philosophies that have informed service-learning's communities. *Educational Theory, 47,* 453–476.

Vickery, M. (1984). *Cambodia: 1975–1982.* Boston: South End Press.

Wander, P. (1983). The ideological turn in modern criticism. *Central States Speech Journal, 34,* 1–18.

Wander, P. (1990). The politics of despair. *Communication, 11,* 277–290.

Wander, P., & Jenkins, S. (1972). Rhetoric, society, and the critical response. *Quarterly Journal of Speech, 58,* 441–450.

Weil, S. (1977). *The Simone Weil reader* (G. A. Panichas, Ed.). New York: McKay.

Wendt, R. (1994). Learning to "walk the talk": A critical tale of the micropolitics at a total quality university. *Management Communication Quarterly, 8,* 5–46.

West, C. (1989). *The American evasion of philosophy: A genealogy of pragmatism.* Madison: University of Wisconsin Press.

West, C. (1993). *Keeping faith: Philosophy and race in America.* New York: Routledge.

West, C. (2002). An interview with Cornel West. *Tikkun, 17,* 12–14; 28.

West, C. (2004). *Democracy matters: Winning the fight against imperialism.* New York: Penguin Press.

White, J. B. (2006). *Living speech: Resisting the empire of force.* Princeton, NJ: Princeton University Press.

Williams, J. (1998). *Thurgood Marshall: American revolutionary.* New York: Time Books.

Wilshire, B. (1997). Pragmatism, neopragmatism, and phenomenology: The Richard Rorty phenomenon. *Human Studies, 20,* 95–108.

Wood, G. (2004). A view from the field: NCLB's effects on classrooms and schools. In D. Meir & G. Wood (Eds.), *Many children left behind: How the No Child Left Behind Act is damaging our children and out schools* (pp. 33–50). Boston: Beacon Press.

World Health Organization (2007). *Principles for evaluating health risks in children associated with exposure to chemicals.* Retrieved on September 10, 2007, from http://whqlibdoc.who.int/publications/2006/924157237X_eng.pdf

Wroclavsky, E. (2005, Aug. 30). Guevara kin revolt against marketers: Family launches lawsuit in effort to curb exploitative images. *National Post* (Canada), A15.

Xun, L. (1985). *Selected works* (Vol. 1) Beijing, China: Foreign Languages Press.

Zinn, H. (1990). *The politics of history: With a new introduction* (2nd ed.). Urbana: University of Illinois Press.

Zinn, H. (2002a). *Disobedience and democracy: Nine fallacies on law and order.* Boston: South End Press. (Original work published 1968)

Zinn, H. (2002b). Without history. *Tikkun, 17,* 30–32.
Zinn, H. (2005). *A people's history of the United States*. New York: Harper Perennial. (Original work published 1980)

INDEX

A

Aaronson, R., 66, 71
Activism
  against corporate media, 36–38
  of C. P. Ellis, 52–53
  of Ghandi, 114–15
  of Martin Luther King, 115–17
  of Simone Weil, 56
  social justice and, 28
Adam, H., 146
Alienation
  communication and, 32–33
  power and, 113–14
  service learning and, 140
Allen, B. J., 60
the American Dream, 19
Animal Farm (Orwell), 37, 42
anti-foundationalism
  neo-pragmatism and, 68, 75
  Rorty's, 101–5
Anzaldúa, G., 139–40
Aristotelian concepts, 63–64, 124
Asen, R., 55
Ashcroft, John, 25, 27
Athens, democracy in, 11–12
Atwater, Ann, 53

B

Bacon, Francis, 136
Baker, H. A., Jr.
  on civil rights, 115, 116–17
  critical memory and, 38
  on racial segregation, 78–79
banking model of education
  egotism of, 84
  over-reliance on, 135
  Platonic and, 124–26
  v. democratic participation, 145
  See also education
basic human needs, 14
Beatty, Captain, 32
The Bell Curve (Herrnstein and Murray), 64
Bender, T., 26
Bernstein, Richard, 26–27
Biesecker, Barbara, 3
Bill of Rights, 19
Black community
  communicative power and, 33, 46, 52–53
  critical scholarship and, 64–65
  social reform by, 115–17
  U.S. Supreme Court and, 16–17
  See also racism
Bloom, H., 57
Boykin, William (Lt. Gen.), 25–26
Bradbury, Ray, 31–32
Brave New World (Huxley), 31–32
Bryman, A., 111
Burke, Kenneth
  anti-foundationalism and, 104
  creative democracy and, 14, 29
  perspectivalism and, 84
  on symbolic communication, 48, 54, 67
  tragic-frame approach and, 66
Bush, George H.W. (President), 17
Bush, George W. (President)
  9/11 event and, 49–51, 92, 94
  disastrous effects of, 19, 27, 45
  manipulation by, 10–11, 94
  silencing dissent, 25
Butler, Judith, 128

C

Campus Compact, 138
charity, 142
Chavez, Caesar, 21
Chelm, history of, 1–2
Cheney, Dick, 27
Cheney, G., 125
Chomsky, Noam, 21, 145
citizenship
  critical education and, 135
  definition of, 43
  entertainment model of, 29–34

service learning and, 145–46
thick description of, 77
civil disobedience
Ghandi and, 114–15
need for, 33–34
social justice and, 27
civil rights
human rights and, 15
Martin Luther King and, 114–17
Supreme Court and, 17–18
class identity, 20
classless society, 19–20, 77
coercion, 109–10
Columbia University, 138
commercialism, of diversity, 18–19, 22–23
commodity, education as, 125, 145–46
communication
creativity and, 4
as critical pedagogy, 130
democracy and, 12
Dewey's views on, 98–101
edifying, 40
as epistemic, 46–53
Ghandi and, 114–15
importance of, 2–3, 43–45
liberating effects of, 52–53
power and, 117–18
Regis University and, 143–49
social justice and, 27–29, 32–33
Communication and Diversity in United States' History course, 130–33
communicative imagination
in action, 81, 117–19
creative democracy and, 54–57
in history course, 130–33
community
cosmopolitanism and, 86
deliberative democracy and, 100–101
transformative force of, 78–79
in U.S. history, 130–31
conscientization, 128
constitutive perspective, 46–53
consumerism
citizenship and, 145–46
cultural diversity and, 18
in education, 124–25
McDonaldization/Disneyization and, 111–12
pornography and, 46–47
corporate media. *See* media
cosmopolitanism, 85–87
counterpublics, 34, 108, 116–17
critical communication pedagogy, 130
critical education
importance of, 127–33, 135
service learning and. *See* service learning
critical imagination
counterpublic, 108, 116–17
importance of, 123
social justice and, 35–40
critical memory, 38
critical paradigm, 63–68, 127–33
criticism, importance of, 24–29

D

dead speech, 56–57, 111
de Certeau, Michel, 128
Declaration of Independence, 11
deliberative democracy, 98–101
democracy
in 5th century Athens, 11–12
communication and, 27–29, 43–45, 54–57
cosmopolitanism and, 85–87
as a creative process, 12–13, 14
definition of, 11
Dewey's views, 97–101
Emerson's views, 96–97
guardianship theory of, 44–45, 98, 150
perspectivalism and, 79, 80–84
positive goals of, 13–14, 20–21
Rorty's views, 101–5
social justice and, 24–25, 27
street, 33–34, 36
Supreme Court and, 17–18
thick/thin descriptions of, 77–78
Dewey, John
commitment to democracy, 29, 76, 93
creative democracy and, 2–3, 13–14, 19

critical democracy and, 24–27
deliberative democracy and, 97–101, 119
dogmatic thinking and, 85
guardianship theory and, 44, 98
instrumental intelligence and, 137
perspectivalism and, 80–81, 86
pragmatism and, 68
dialogical scholarship, 60–63, 84
See also education; scholarship
direct democracy, 11
discrimination
communicative imagination and, 117–18
language and, 46–47
weightism as, 4
See also racism
discursive amnesia, 36–37, 38
Disneyization, 111–12
dissent
against corporate media, 36–38
guardianship theory and, 44
need for, 27, 28–29, 34
silencing of, 25–26
diversity
of appearance, 16–17
inclusion and, 11
market driven, 16–20
overview, 4, 10
Regis University and, 142
in the United States, 15–16
in U.S. history, 130–31
Dobson, James, 47
dogmatic thinking, 52, 85, 90, 107
Dyson, M. E., 65

E

edifying communication, 40
See also communication
education
banking model of, 84, 124–26, 135, 145
as commodity, 145–46
critical, 127–33, 135
as critical communication, 130
deliberative democracy and, 99–101
Platonic model, 124–27
service learning in. *See* service learning
See also scholarship
electronic entertainment, 30–31
Ellis, C. P., 52–53, 81, 119
Emerson, Ralph Waldo, 96–97
empire of force, 56
Engen, D. E., 54, 55
Englund, T., 70
entertainment model, of citizenship, 29–34
Epidemiologic Reviews, 4
epistemic perspective, 46–53
exclusionary practices
moral issue of, 34, 37
in the United States, 9
v. solidarity, 2

F

Faculty Resource Handbook (Regis University), 141–42, 144
Fahrenheit 451 (Bradbury), 31–32
Falwell, Jerry, 47
Fassett, D. L., 128–29
Federal Communications Commission (FCC), 36
final vocabulary, 103–4, 115
First Amendment, 33, 35
Fish, S., 51–52
Foucault, Michel
critical imagination and, 40, 67
perspective on power, 110, 113–14
writings of, 21
foundationalist critical theory, 66–67, 69–70
Freire, Paulo, 124, 128
Frey, L. R., 28, 60, 62
Frye, Marilyn, 109

G

Galileo, 102
gay community issues, 15, 19, 83, 103, 108, 131
Geertz, Clifford, 78
Ghandi, Mohandas, 114
Giroux, H. A., 112, 144, 146

GLBT (gay, lesbian, bisexual and transgender) community, 47
    See also gay community issues
Goldman, Emma, 90–91
Goodheart, E., 69
Gould, S. J., 64
Griffin, John, 117–18
guardianship theory, of democracy, 44–45, 98, 150
Guevara, Che, 18

H

Hadler, N. M., 76–77
Hatab, L. J., 80, 91
Heller, Jean, 61
Herrnstein, Richard, 64
hierarchy, social
    foundationalist thinking and, 85–86, 100, 109–10
    language and, 2, 46–47
    objective scholarship and, 60–61
    service learning and, 138, 148
    v. democracy, 12, 30–31, 77
hope, and critical imagination, 39–40
Hurricane Katrina, 64
Hussein, Saddam, 92
Huxley, Aldous, 31–32

I

Ignatian Collaborative for Service and Justice, 147–48
imagination
    communicative, 54–57
    critical. *See* critical imagination
    narrative, 55
inclusion, 11–12, 13
inquiry, 98–101
intelligence
    instrumental, 137
    moral, 55
Iraq war, 59
    American response to, 93, 105
    communication regarding, 49–50
    defense of, 45
    dissent towards, 25–26
ironism, 101–4

J

James, William, 68

K

Kant, Immanuel, 124
Kaufmann, C., 10–11
King, Martin Luther, Jr.
    creative democracy and, 17, 21
    impact of, 42, 114–17
Kinzer, Stephen, 50
Kivel, Paul, 30
Krizek, Robert, 128
Ku Klux Klan, 52–53

L

language
    creative aspect of, 48–49
    as epistemic, 46–53
    as living/dead speech, 56–57
    power of, 44, 107–8
    See also communication
Lee, W., 37
Lefort, Claude, 91
liberation, 52
living speech, 56–57
Loyola University, 147

M

MacKinnon, Catherine, 46–47, 58
marketplace diversity
    the American Dream and, 19–20
    Che Guevara and, 18
    commercialism and, 18–19
    Supreme Court and, 16–18
markets
    diversity and. *See* marketplace diversity
    education and, 124–25
    as non-beneficent, 22, 111–12
Marshall, Alexandra, 18
Marshall, Thurgood, 16–18
Marx, Karl, 12, 21, 102
Marxism, 66, 76–77, 112
McCormick Tribune Freedom Museum study, 145

McDermott, J. J., 84
McDonaldization, 111
McLaren, P., 128
McMillan, J., 125
Mead, George Herbert, 139
media
 power of, 35–38
 wealth and, 99
memory, critical, 38
Mendela, Nelson, 21
Men's Fashions of the Times, 18
merchandising, 111–12
Mills, C. W., 12, 44–45, 62
Minutemen Project, 132, 134
Montgomery bus boycott, 116
Moodley, K., 146
moral intelligence, 55
morality
 critical imagination and, 38–39
 Rorty's views on, 102–5
 in scholarship, 60–64
Morris, D., 98
Murray, Charles, 64
Myers, Michael, 65

N

NAACP, *v. Alabama*, 33
Nakayama, Thomas, 128
narrative imagination, 55
nationalist identification, 94–95
neo-pragmatism
 King and Ghandi and, 114
 perspectivalism and, 80, 82
 reflexive critical scholarship and, 68–70
 Rorty and, 62
New Education movement, 137
New York Times, 13
Nietzsche, Friedrich Wilhelm
 inspiration of, 37, 90–92
 nationalist attitudes and, 94
 perspectivalism and, 76, 80, 81–82
 politics of, 21, 89–90
 quasi pragmatism of, 83
 Zarathustra and, 126
9/11 event, 49–51, 92
1984 (Orwell), 31–32
No Exit, 3
nonviolence, 114–17
normality, 119–20
Nussbaum, M., 55, 86–87, 150

O

Oak Ridge Associated Universities, 138
Obama, Barack (President), 65
objective scholarship, 60–63
Olivas, M. R., 60
Orbe, M. P., 60
The Order of Things, 40
Orwell, George, 31–32, 37

P

paradigm
 critical, 63–68, 127–33
 definition of, 62
participatory democracy, 98–101
 See also democracy
pedagogy. *See* education
Pedagogy of the Oppressed (Freire), 128
Peirce, Charles, 68
Pelias, Ronald, 128
Pericles, 12
perspectivalism, 79, 80–84
Pew Global Attitudes Project, 95
Plato, 44, 102
Platonic model, of education, 124–27
pornography
 discriminatory language and, 46–47
 as power, 58
Posner, Richard (Judge), 98
Postman, N., 29–30, 31–32
Powell, Michael, 36
power
 alienation and, 113–14
 coercion and, 109–10
 communication and, 117–18
 as fluid and complex, 129–30
 Foucault's views on, 110–11
 Gandhi and Martin Luther King and, 114–17
 of language, 107–8
 of McDonaldization/Disneyization, 111–12

as participatory, 112–13
pornography as, 58
service learning study of, 139
struggle against, 35–37
pragmatism, 68–69
praxis
definition of, 63
struggle against, 35–37, 128
Proclamation of National Sanctity of Human Life Day, 94
progressiveness, 20–21
public amnesia, 36–37, 38
public discourse, 45–46
purification, and *satyagraha*, 115

R

racism
community and, 78–79
critical scholarship and, 64–66
discriminatory language and, 46
Ku Klux Klan and, 52–53
See also Black community
reflexive critical scholarship, 67–70
See also scholarship
Regis University, as a social justice-oriented learning model, 141–49
representative democracy, 11
See also democracy
research
critical scholarship and, 130, 136
as a moral activity, 60–63, 71
social justice, 27–28
Rice, Condoleezza, 27
Rieff, D., 16, 18
Ritzer, G., 111
Robinson, Pat, 47
Rodriguez, Amardo
communication and, 43, 44
hierarchy and, 85–86, 109–10
liberation and, 52
reification and, 4, 14
Roosevelt, Franklin Delano, 23
Rorty, Richard
anti-foundationalism of, 101–5
classless society and, 76–77
community and, 14, 78
education and, 47–48, 126, 135
living speech and, 57, 107
morality and, 19–21
pragmatism and, 68–69, 71, 83
solidarity and, 2–3, 117
Truth and, 82
rule by the Knowers, 124
Rumsfeld, Donald, 25–26, 27, 45
Russell, Bertrand, 82

S

Santa Clara University, 149
Santayana, George, 29
Sartre, Jean Paul, 3
satyagraha, 114–15
Schlesinger, Arthur, Jr., 93
scholarship
communication, 28
corporate media, 35–36
critical paradigm form of, 63–68, 127–33
dialogical approach to, 60–63, 84
social justice, 24
School for Professional Studies, 142–44
self-realization, 100–101
self-reliance, 96–97
service learning
overview, 135–36
social-justice model, 140–49
social-justice oriented, 138–40
theoretical bases of, 136–38
Shapiro, I., 98
Sheehan, Cindy, 27
Shepherd, G. J., 14, 27
Shiva, V., 48–49
social hierarchy. *See* hierarchy, social
social justice
communication and, 27–29
critical imagination and, 35–40
democracy and, 24–25, 27
Paul Kivel and, 30
scholarship, 24
service learning focus, 138–40
service learning model, 140–49
social self theory, 139–40
solidarity, 2–3
Solomon, M., 61
Sontag, S., 51–52

speech, dead/living, 56–57, 111
    See also communication; language
Sprague, Jo, 128
Squires, C., 33
St. John, J., 14, 27
street democracy, 33–34, 36
    See also democracy
strong poets, 102, 114
student as consumer, 124–25
Suber, Jere Paul, 2
symbols
    communication and, 3, 48, 50
    communicative imagination and, 54–55
    democracy and, 14
    human use of, 67

T

terministic screens, 48–49
terrorism, 51–52
thick descriptions
    of democracy, 78
    Dewey and, 101
thin descriptions, 78, 79
Thomas, Clarence, 16–17
tragic-frame approach, 66–67
Truth(s)
    education and, 124
    neo-pragmatism and, 82–83
    resistance to, 150–51
    Rorty's views on, 103–5
    transformative communication and, 85
Tuskegee syphilis study, 60–61

U

United States
    9/11 event and, 49–52
    diversity and community in, 15–16, 130–33
    harm to other nations, 26, 50, 95, 105
    McDonaldization/Disneyization in, 111–12
    nationalist attitudes, 92–94
    political ignorance in, 145
U.S. Supreme Court
    creative democracy and, 17–18
    Franklin D. Roosevelt and, 23
utopianism, 75–76

V

Volunteers in Service to America (VISTA), 138

W

Wander, P., 37
Warren, J. T., 128–29
weightism, 4
Weil, Simone, 56
West, Cornel, 68–69, 75–76
West, Kanye, 64–65
White, James Boyd, 55–56, 57
White Power/Pride, 131
Wood, G., 124–25

X

Xun, Lu, 39–40

Z

Zarathustra, 126, 134
Zinn, Howard
    civil disobedience and, 33–34
    critical memory and, 38
    moral objectivity and, 61–62
    utopianism and, 76